Britain divided

The growth of social exclusion in the 1980s and 1990s

Edited by Alan Walker and Carol Walker

CPAG Ltd, 1-5 Bath Street, London EC1V 9PY

CPAG promotes action for the relief, directly or indirectly, of poverty among children and families with children. We work to ensure that those on low incomes get their full entitlements to welfare benefits. In our campaigning and information work we seek to improve benefits and policies for low-income families, in order to eradicate the injustice of poverty. If you are not already supporting us, please consider making a donation or ask for details of our membership schemes and publications.

Poverty Publication 96

Published by CPAG Ltd
1-5 Bath Street, London EC1V 9PY

© CPAG Ltd 1997

ISBN 0 946744 91 2

Cover illustration by Fiona White and design by Devious Designs 0114 275 5634
Typeset by Nancy White 0171 607 4510
Printed by Progressive Printing UK Ltd 01702 520050

CONTENTS

ABBREVIATIONS

AEN	additional education needs
CB	child benefit
CIPFA	Chartered Institute of Public Finance Accountants
CSA	Child Support Agency
CTC	City Technology College
DE	Department of Employment
DfEE	Department for Education and Employment
DH	Department of Health
DRV	dietary reference value
DSS	Department of Social Security
GM	grant maintained
HBAI	Households Below Average Income
HEA	Health Education Authority
HMSO	Her Majesty's Stationery Office
HRT	habitual residence test
ICB	incapacity benefit
IS	income support
JSA	jobseeker's allowance
LEA	local education authority
LETS	local exchange trading schemes
LFS	Labour Force Survey
LMS	local management of schools
LS	longitudinal study
NACAB	National Association of Citizens' Advice Bureaux
OECD	Organisation for Economic Cooperation and Development
SERPS	state earnings-related pension scheme
SMR	standardised mortality ratio
UB	unemployment benefit
YT	Youth Training

FOREWORD

This book is the latest in a long standing tradition of CPAG pre-election publications to review trends in poverty and inequality during the period of office of the outgoing Government, to assess the link between these and Government policy and to make the case for action. This time we go back to 1979 – because the ends have remained the same even where the means to achieve them have altered. Policy changes have generally occurred only when the chosen direction has so unequivocally hit the buffers (as with home ownership) that there has been no alternative but to switch tack. Throughout all four Conservative administrations, however, there has been remarkable continuity in both the broad sweep of policies pursued and in the underlying assumptions.

The editors describe the evidence amassed in this volume as 'a huge indictment of the disastrous record of four Conservative governments towards Britain's most vulnerable and insecure citizens' (see Chapter 18). By the same stroke, however, it exposes the modest nature of Labour's counter proposals. If, as charged in Chapter 1, current-day inequality is the outcome of a purposefully pursued strategy, it is unlikely to be resolved merely as a spin off from other policies, as Labour appears to hope – relying on the provision of education, training and child care. Meanwhile the Conservatives have made clear their wish to continue full pelt down the free market road. There is no evidence that either of the two main parties is committed to addressing poverty and inequality at a structural level.

Over the last 18 years much political energy has been devoted to denying the existence of poverty – most recently Peter Lilley refused to draw up a national poverty eradication programme – despite the Government committing itself to doing so at the 1995 World Summit on Social Development. According to Lilley, such a programme was unnecessary as the UK already had social protection systems in place. Attitudes towards inequality have been more ambiguous. By some it has been regarded as a positive virtue – an engine of enterprise, providing incentives for all (see Chapter 1). But, without hope, there is no incentive.

As a society, we have become used to operating at the level of perception rather than fact, to responding to the sensationalist sound-bite rather than more sober in depth research. We live in an era where political change is as likely (some would say more likely) to be achieved by people living up trees or down tunnels as by heavyweight authoritative tomes. Perhaps this is symptomatic of distrust, not only of politicians and journalists, but of the so-called 'facts' they purvey.

In *Britain Divided* the reality gap between perception and fact is revealed. John Hills blows a hole in the myth of any economic imperative for lower taxation and public spending. Even the British public in repeated opinion surveys have shown themselves amenable to the idea of paying more tax for better services (what they may well be less keen on is paying more for less and worse). There is no 'demographic timebomb' of an ageing population. Welfare spending has remained a relatively constant 25 per cent of gross domestic product (GDP) over the last 20 years. Means-testing does not result in better targeting, or even in savings in the longer term. Although the official unemployment rate has been falling, it remains almost twice as high as the rate in April 1979: 24 per cent of the male working-age population was 'non-employed' in 1996. The School Milk Campaign estimates that up to two million British children suffer from poverty-related malnutrition.

Furthermore, there is mounting evidence that inequality is harmful and not just to the individuals who find themselves on the wrong end of the growing divide. The OECD has emphasised the long term economic damage of the Government's approach (see Chapter 1) and there is mounting evidence that rising inequality is associated with increases in the crime rate and ill health. Curiously, while redistribution has become a politically taboo subject, there has clearly been a very great deal of it – from poor to rich.

Another feature of the last 18 years has been the extent to which debates have been bogged down in discussions of definitions. If you reject all measures of poverty, routinely fail to monitor the effect of your own policies, stop collecting some statistics altogether (eg, the General Household Survey), or frequently change the basis for them – as has happened to unemployment statistics, it becomes easier to deny problems and/or disown responsibility for them, should they nevertheless be shown to exist. New benefits with new names have been introduced when, in fact, they were largely cuts to old ones. Interestingly, there is some evidence of 'renaming' when it comes to solutions proposed – somehow suggesting that people make compulsory payments for pensions, etc. into arms-length semi-privatised institutions is quite different to proposing an increase in tax; Peter Townsend refers to the regulation of privatised utilities as public administration by the back door.

Whether we like it or not, we have a free market economy and it is unlikely to go away. We face an increasingly complex arena containing quangos, Next Steps Agencies, privatised utilities, the voluntary sector, local authorities and employers in which it is not always possible to make simplistic distinctions between the private and public spheres. There has been, however, an overwhelming drive for privatisation and deregulation which appears to have been ideologically rather than rationally driven (see Chapter 13) – but if the over-riding objective were to get more money into Treasury coffers now (getting the most from sell-offs being only a secondary consideration) perhaps no further rationale is required. An alternative rationale might have been to consider what would best reduce poverty and inequality, or how to ensure the security of all, and particularly those at greatest risk, or, who or what is in the best position to identify and meet need. Either way, the unpalatable fact remains, as John Hills points out, that whether provision is public or private, whether through paying contributions for state benefits or premiums for private insurance cover, redistribution over the lifecycle is still necessary if we are to avoid poverty in old age, for example.

The other key event in the lifecycle (inexcusably) associated with the risk of poverty is the arrival of children. Under the regime of the 'Party of the Family', the traditional family has for many ceased to be an economically effective unit, although the risk of poverty for lone parents remains far higher than for couples with children. Certainly there is an overwhelming body of evidence to show that households with children tend to be less well off than those without. For families with children, the problems have been particularly acute with nearly a third of all children living in poverty according to the latest figures.

Children bear the brunt of poverty, fall foul of our cultural short-termism and are accorded few rights. Yet, this societal abuse of our young gets little attention. The only way it seems possible to get today's adults to react at all is through impressing on them the risk that today's children may, in turn, wreak their revenge on us in our old age. Even the most politically correct lobbyists are prone to equating investment in children with investment in the future, as if they were a commodity.

The policies proposed by politicians and the media are superficial, while the problems of poverty and inequality are entrenched, profound and complex. The focus remains on the individual, despite the fact that the causes are overwhelmingly structural. Sound-bites are short and political promises too often short-lived, while the solution to poverty and inequality requires sustained commitment over the long term. Let us hope that, whatever the outcome, the forthcoming election constitutes a watershed: a time for a new and urgent commitment to the reduction of poverty and inequality and to putting children and their future first in the list of government priorities. Again, whatever the outcome, CPAG will continue to fight for an end to the scandal of child poverty.

Sally Witcher
Director

PREFACE

The sudden realisation that it is nearly 10 years since the publication of *The Growing Divide* prompted us to put together this new edition. As in 1987, CPAG's staff and friends responded wonderfully to our requests for contributions. The fact that virtually everyone we approached agreed at once to contribute is a testimony to the strength of their commitment to the cause of fighting poverty and social exclusion. All of the authors produced their chapters within an extremely tight schedule and the quality of this work is a tribute to their expertise. David Bull and Sally Witcher read and commented helpfully on the manuscript. As Chair of CPAG's publications committee, Peter Golding was characteristically supportive. Deborah Lyttelton provided help and support as well as overseeing the production of the book, Pascale Vassie edited the manuscript, Alison Walker helped with the proof reading and last, but not least, Marg Walker prepared the manuscript with her usual efficiency and calmness under pressure. We are extremely grateful to all of those who contributed in different ways to the production of this pamphlet.

Audrey Harvey, a founder member of CPAG in 1965, and the first head of the Citizens' Rights Office, sadly died in April 1997. Hilary Arnott, who made a later contribution to the work of CPAG and major contribution to *The Growing Divide*, died tragically in December 1994. Both were tireless campaigners on behalf of the poor and excluded. This book is dedicated to their work and their memory.

Alan Walker   Sheffield
Carol Walker   March 1997

ABOUT THE CONTRIBUTORS

Fran Bennett is currently self-employed, working on social policy issues, especially social security and poverty. She is a former director of CPAG.

Michaela Benzeval is a Fellow in Health Policy Analysis at the King's Fund Policy Institute.

Alice Bloch is Senior Lecturer in Social Policy Research in the Department of Sociology, University of East London.

Paul Convery is Director of the Unemployment Unit.

Norman Ginsburg is Professor of Social Policy in the Department of Policy Studies, Politics and Social Research, University of North London.

Lisa Harker was Research and Information Officer with the Child Poverty Action Group until April 1997. She now works for the BBC.

John Hills is Reader in Economics and Social Policy at the London School of Economics.

Marilyn Howard is a social security researcher.

Tim Lang is Professor of Food Policy and Director of the Centre for Food Policy, Thames Valley University.

Jane Millar is Professor of Social Policy at the University of Bath.

Catherine O'Donnell is Senior Research Officer with the Low Pay Unit.

Carey Oppenheim is Senior Lecturer in Social Policy, at South Bank University.

David Piachaud is Professor of Social Policy at the London School of Economics.

Helga Pile is Senior Research Officer with the Low Pay Unit.

George Smith is currently University Research Lecturer at the Department of Applied Social Studies and Social Research, University of Oxford. He was, from 1984 to 1996, research consultant to HMI and subsequently to OFSTED, London.

Teresa Smith is a University Lecturer in Applied Social Studies at the Department of Applied Social Studies and Social Research,

University of Oxford.

Elaine Kempson is Programme Director of the Family Finances Group, Policy Studies Institute.

Peter Townsend is Emeritus Professor of Social Policy at the University of Bristol.

Alan Walker is Professor of Social Policy at the University of Sheffield.

Carol Walker is Principal Lecturer in Social Policy at Sheffield Hallam University.

Robert Walker is Professor of Social Policy Research at the Centre for Research in Social Policy, Loughborough University.

Gemma Wright is a Research Assistant at the Department of Applied Social Studies, University of Oxford.

Introduction: the strategy of inequality

Alan Walker

CPAG has a 27 year old tradition of publishing a pre-election examination of the records of governments – Labour and Conservative alike – with regard to the poor. 1997 is no exception although, in this case, rather than looking at the impact of one administration, the 1992–97 Major government, we have widened the focus to cover all four Conservative governments since 1979. The reasons for doing so are, first, that there is a remarkable continuity between the Thatcher and Major governments in both the broad sweep of the policies pursued and, especially, in the assumptions underlying them. Secondly, the huge rise in social exclusion and poverty represents a continuous thread stretching back over 18 years, such that it is difficult to isolate the impact of one particular administration.

The fact is that many thousands of poor families can trace the start of their misfortune back to the recession of the early 1980s, a recession that was deepened and prolonged by government policies, and subsequent changes of administration have not improved their position but, rather, have been responsible for worsening it. As this book shows, poverty and social exclusion have increased remorselessly over the last 18 years and not one of the four Conservative governments has had an explicit policy to combat them. At the other end of the income spectrum, many of those who were favoured in the 1980s and who benefited from policies such as tax cuts and privatisation, are still living off the proceeds. Thus, although there is significant movement in and out of poverty (see Jarvis and Jenkins, 1995, and Chapter 4), blame for the current high levels of poverty and social exclusion and the huge social division between rich and poor, cannot be laid at the door of one particular Conservative government, they are all culpable. Income inequality appears to have peaked in the early 1990s but it remains high compared with other European countries and the big increase in the 1980s has not been reversed.

Previous CPAG pre-election publications have examined the track record of individual Conservative governments: *Thatcherism and the Poor* (Bull and Wilding, 1983), *The Growing Divide* (Walker and Walker, 1987) and *Windows of Opportunity: Public Policy and the Poor* (Becker, 1991). Of course for the past 18 years there have only been Conservative governments. Just in case we should be accused of political bias, back in the 1960s and 1970s, when Labour was last in power, CPAG published pre-election pamphlets critical of its record (CPAG, 1970; Field, 1978). (Indeed some people accused CPAG of contributing to the Labour election defeat in 1970.) Nor do we want to suggest that the problems of poverty and social exclusion were invented by Mrs Thatcher in 1979. Government longevity can create the illusion that it is responsible for everything that befalls a nation, good and bad. However, as we have noted, CPAG has an honourable record of criticising previous Labour Governments for failing to combat poverty, particularly among families with children (see also Townsend and Bosanquet, 1972; Bosanquet and Townsend, 1980). Our indictments of the Thatcher and Major governments, over the last 18 years, are that they have jointly been responsible for the biggest increases in poverty and social exclusion since the Second World War and that they have purposely pursued policies which widened social divisions in British society, particularly between rich and poor. The problems of poverty and social exclusion did not begin in 1979 but, since then, they have grown at an unprecedented rate to a point where they seriously disfigure Britain and undermine its claim to be a civilised society. Furthermore, as Will Hutton (1995) and others have shown, these social divisions have become so wide that they are damaging the country's economic performance.

This book is also intended to update and build on the analysis in *The Growing Divide*. That was the first publication to expose the extent of the new social divisions that had been generated by the first phase of Thatcherism and to comprehensively document the interrelated forms of social exclusion that were then emerging. It obviously struck a chord with the public, at least the concerned sections of it, because it became CPAG's best selling pamphlet and has been translated into Japanese (and published with a picture of Margaret Thatcher on the cover!). Subsequently others have confirmed the central thesis of *The Growing Divide* that government policies have been responsible for increasing social divisions and social exclusion (see for example Hutton, 1995; Hills, 1995).

Looking back over nearly 20 years two things are striking. First, there is the sheer scale of the growth of poverty and social exclusion (examined in detail in Chapter 2). According to the Government's own favoured definition of low incomes (below 50 per cent of average income) the numbers living in poverty grew from 5 million in 1979 to just under 14 million in 1993/94 (from 9 per cent of the population to 25 per cent). The rise in poverty among children was even more dramatic – from 1.4 million (10 per cent of all children) in 1979 to 4.2 million (32 per cent) in 1993/94 (DSS, 1996).

Secondly, there is the remarkable fact that British society has 'accepted' this widespread impoverishment and the sometimes grotesque inequalities that have become so commonplace. Although 'acceptance' in this case is signalled solely by the Government's repeated re-election rather than in any evidence of a positive preference for greater poverty and inequality *per se*. Indeed, as John Hills reports in Chapter 15, over the course of the 1980s surveys have shown the British public expressing a rising preference for increased taxation and more spending on health, education and social benefits – from 32 per cent in 1983 to 61 per cent in 1995 (Jowell *et al*, 1996, p187).

Why the Government was re-elected in the face of this mounting rejection of its social priorities is a question that is beyond the scope of this book to answer thoroughly. But part of the explanation lies in the greater salience at elections of economic policy compared with social policy and self-interest as opposed to community interest. There are also the different priorities accorded by the public to different items of social spending: with health being placed much higher than social security and, within the latter, the level of support for extra spending on pensions is more than double that for unemployment benefit and more than five times that for benefits for lone parents (Jowell *et al*, 1996, p199). Thus there is no straightforward basis for a united anti-poverty voting coalition. Then there is the media.

For much of the past 18 years the Government has been assisted by a largely uncritical and in some cases credulous media. There are a few honourable exceptions but, for the most part, there has been acceptance of the policies and their adverse social consequences, including the lie that there was no alternative, and a failure to challenge the Government's attempts to obscure the impact of its policies and stifle public debate – whether it be the discontinuation of the annual publication of poverty statistics, the switch from a benefit-related measure of poverty to an average income one, the restriction of access to official data on the relationship between social class and health, or the 30 or so changes in the calculation and presentation of the unemployment count since 1979. It is true that for a short while after the main alteration (downwards) in the way of counting unemployment, news bulletins used the description 'unemployed and claiming benefit' but this was soon truncated to fall in line with the Government's intention behind the revision. (Also some researchers too readily accepted the redefinition of 'long-term unemployed' from six months to 12 months.) A typical case of the 'reading the Government's press release syndrome' that gripped the media in the 1980s was the then BBC's economic correspondent on the 6 o'clock news, 11 April 1988, referring to the publication of the low income statistics: 3 million are 'better off' and 3.5 million are 'doing less well'! Towards the end of the 1992–97 Major Government, some commentators became critical of certain policies and some pundits even joined the Opposition, but they did not do so until the New Labour project looked likely to succeed.

THE STRATEGY OF INEQUALITY

As we have noted, poverty and inequality did not arrive on the scene with the election of Margaret Thatcher in 1979. However, up to 1979, there was a broad political consensus that one important function of government was to try to combat poverty and to reduce, rather than increase, social and economic inequalities. It is not possible to identify a concerted anti-poverty strategy on the part of any government since the 1945–50 Labour administration, nor are there individual measures which made dramatic inroads into the deep-seated inequalities that have characterised post-war Britain – though the 1975 Social Security Act, backed by an all-party consensus, which created the state earnings related pension (SERP) did offer the prospect of a substantial reduction in poverty among older people as it matured later in this decade (until, that is, it was both cut in half and undermined by the 1986 Social Security Act). Furthermore, it is difficult to imagine the 1977/79 consolidation of tax and family allowances into child benefit taking place under either the Thatcher or Major governments. But the main point is that, prior to 1979, the political consensus favoured reducing poverty and inequality. Although the pace of change was painfully slow, inequalities in wealth had been narrowing over the post-war period.

A new era began in 1979. A government was elected, the leadership of which was driven by a radical political philosophy. The New Right or neo-liberal doctrine, quickly labelled Thatcherism, valued freedom from taxation and high public spending on welfare above the need for large sections of the population to be freed from poverty and social exclusion. Indeed, the level of state intervention necessary to tackle poverty was viewed as economically harmful, although, paradoxically, increased expenditure on other programmes such as law and order and defence was not regarded in the same threatening light.

Rather than seeing inequality as potentially damaging to the social fabric, the Thatcher governments saw it as an engine of enterprise, providing incentives for those at the bottom as well as those at the top. Rather than reflecting the Butskellite consensus on the key role of the state in welfare, the Thatcher governments concentrated on reducing it, at least its role as a direct *provider* of benefits and services. (Its scope for manoeuvre was limited severely in the early 1980s by the impact of its own economic policies, particularly the rise in unemployment.) In rejecting the post-war Butskellite legacy, the new Conservative administration distanced itself from the 'one-nation' Conservatives, such as Macmillan and Heath, whose policies were blamed for contributing to Britain's lack of enterprise. Therefore 1979 represented a watershed in British social policy: the replacement of a weak and highly circumscribed consensus on the case for combating poverty – which at least kept this issue on the political agenda, however low down its position – with a proactive 'strategy of inequality' (Walker, 1990).

Thus it was that Britain, in the 1980s, was used in effect as a testing ground for an, at best, unproven economic and social ideology (though, of course, the free market economic policies were seen to fail abjectly in the 1930s recession). The Government's neo-liberal inspired approach towards the welfare state has consisted of five interwoven strands which, with varying degrees of emphasis, have been continuous over the last 18 years. First, cutting social expenditure; second, state-subsidised privatisation or the extension of market principles within the welfare state; third, replacing universal benefits and services with selective, means-tested – in the Conservative euphemism, 'targeted' – ones; fourth, reducing taxation to provide incentives and encourage the growth of alternative forms of private and voluntary welfare; and fifth, centralisation of resource control and decentralisation of operational responsibility. Three key assumptions underpinned this approach to social policy and the welfare state.

First of all there was the assertion that the welfare state creates dependency and that this dependency is morally debilitating. This view was expressed most forthrightly by John Moore MP (1987) when he was Secretary of State for Social Services but he was merely echoing the views of his party leader, which she set out as early as 1968 at the Conservative party's annual conference. Then Margaret Thatcher voiced scepticism about the welfare state and its tendency to undermine 'desirable' social values such as self-discipline, hard work and personal responsibility (Wapshott and Brock, 1983). The intellectual roots of this philosophy stretch back even further, via Hayek and Victorian morality, to Adam Smith.

Secondly, there was the belief that any form of welfare provision – family, self-help, NGOs, but especially that of the market – is superior to welfare from the state. This reflects the classic *laissez-faire* aversion to the public sector as well as the flawed theory of consumer sovereignty. The resulting policy prescription was to roll back state frontiers in welfare and to encourage other forms of provision, especially private ones, to fill the gap.

Thirdly, there was the pre-eminence of the enterprise culture, based on the twin assumptions that such enterprise would be boosted by increasing financial incentives for those at the top of the income distribution (and conversely that the taxation necessary to fund social welfare stifles such initiative) and that the fruits of this entre-preneurial activity would 'trickle down' to benefit the rest of society. This view was set out with haunting clarity by Lord Young (1985, p2) when he was Secretary of State for Industry:

> successful enterprise does bring material reward in society. General standards of living rose steadily and substantially through most of the Victorian era … So in looking at the generation of Victorian entrepreneurs and the result of their achievements, we need not feel guilty that their success was at the expense of the poor.

Thus the strategy of inequality achieved some legitimacy, at least in the eyes of its proponents, because it was expected to add to the common good. Were they justified in their confidently expressed assumption? The overwhelming weight of evidence, summarised in this volume, proves that the assumption was wrong. The picture is not simply one of increasing social divisions underpinned by a widening gap between rich and poor but also, crucially, rather than floating up with the rising tide of economic growth, the real incomes of the poorest have actually been sinking since 1979. According to the Government's own statistics, between 1979 and 1993/94 the real incomes (after housing costs) of the bottom tenth of the income distribution fell by 13 per cent, while those of the top tenth rose by 65 per cent (see Chapter 2 for further evidence of the absence of 'trickle down'). Both Conservative Prime Ministers and the governments they have led since 1979 share responsibility for this pauperisation and the misery it entails.

As well as this moral (self) justification for the strategy of inequality it seems that Thatcher's assertion that 'there is no alternative' carried influence with some commentators. It may well be that her strictures resonated with the increasing currency of the globalisation thesis and the mistaken opinion of some of its adherents that, because of the constraints of global competition, all governments are following a similar path. This is a view encouraged by ministers in both the Thatcher and Major governments claiming that their policies were being emulated throughout Europe and the World. In fact, as Walker shows in Chapter 4, Britain's high levels of poverty and social exclusion stick out like a sore thumb in Europe. Moreover, Britain stands out in the OECD as having one of the sharpest rises in inequality between 1977 and 1991 (Atkinson *et al*, 1996). In truth, many of Britain's European partners must have looked on in amazement both at the extreme nature of the experiment that has been conducted on the British public over the last 18 years and its failure to generate public outrage and opposition.

SOCIAL EXCLUSION

The academic and policy debate has moved on over the past 10 years and, largely due to the influence of the European Union, the term 'social exclusion' is beginning to replace that of 'poverty'. While we regard this Europeanisation of the poverty debate as a wholly welcome development, we still think that there is merit in retaining the term 'poverty' and distinguishing it from 'social exclusion'. In practice, the rigid distinction sometimes drawn between these two concepts is misleading, at least, that is, if a relative definition of poverty is employed. For example, according to Townsend (1979, p31):

> Individuals, families and groups in the population can be said to be in poverty when they lack the resources to obtain the types of diet, participate in the activities which are customary, or are at least widely encouraged or approved, in the societies to which they belong.

Although the reduction of this broad concept of participation down to an income poverty line has been criticised (Ringen, 1988; Berghman, 1995), it is not very different from the following definition of social exclusion, especially when one takes into account Townsend's wide ranging notion of 'resources'.

> Social exclusion is a broader concept than poverty, encompassing not only low material means but the inability to participate effectively in economic, social, political, and cultural life, and, in some characterisations, alienation and distance from the mainstream society. (Duffy, 1995)

Nonetheless, as Room (1995) has argued, the two concepts differ in their intellectual and cultural heritages, with poverty being rooted in the liberal tradition of Anglo-Saxon societies while social exclusion reflects the conservative and social democratic legacies of continental countries. Thus in this volume we have retained the distinction: regarding *poverty* as a lack of the material resources, especially income, necessary to participate in British society and *social exclusion* as a more comprehensive formulation which refers to the dynamic process of being shut out, fully or partially, from any of the social, economic, political and cultural systems which determine the social integration of a person in society. Social exclusion may, therefore, be seen as the denial (or non-realisation) of the civil, political and social rights of citizenship (Marshall, 1950; Room *et al*, 1991). This comprehensive focus is reflected in the scope of this volume as well as the more familiar analyses of poverty.

THEME AND PLAN OF THE BOOK

Like *The Growing Divide*, this book focuses on the defining theme of both the Thatcher and Major premierships: the increasingly divided nature of British society and, in particular, the chasm that has been created between rich and poor. The expert contributors document the processes that have led to widening social divisions in Britain, especially the massive increase in poverty and social exclusion since 1979, as well as reporting on the main dimensions of that poverty and social exclusion.

Despite Thatcher's promise to bring 'harmony' and 'hope' and Major's apparent commitment to the creation of a classless society, their governments will be forever tainted by the biggest rise in poverty and social exclusion since the 1930s. Countless official and independent reports have documented this remorseless trend over the last 18 years, including *Social Trends*, the Scarman Report, the Church of England's *Faith in the City*, the Joseph Rowntree Foundation Inquiry into Income and Wealth, the Social Justice Commission and numerous CPAG and National Association of Citizens Advice Bureaux (NACAB) reports. This volume is but the latest, though most comprehensive, contribution. At the same time it has become apparent, mainly through the work of organisations like CPAG, NACAB, the Disability Alliance, the Family Welfare Association and ATD Fourth World, that, at the sharp end, those bearing the largest burden of the government's strategy are the very poorest.

There is disturbing evidence of desperate poverty on a scale not witnessed in Britain since the 1930s. Furthermore, because the largest group in poverty comprises families with children and children are, therefore, disproportionately exposed to poverty, two generations are being blighted at the same time. For example, as discussed in Chapter 11, Britain is seeing the return of diseases associated with poverty and malnutrition, such as rickets and tuberculosis, which most health experts had hoped were banished for ever. The School Milk Campaign estimates that up to two million British children are suffering from poverty related malnutrition. Three in every four children in care come from families living on income support. As many as 2,000 children die in infancy in England and Wales because they are unlucky enough to be born into a poor family rather than a better-off one.[1] Income support pays £10.55 per family, plus between £16.45 and £28.85 per child, depending on their ages; yet one estimate puts the average cost of a child in

---

1. That is, the 'excess' mortality calculated by applying the infant mortality rate of the richest households to those of the poorest. Overall, death rates are four times higher in poor areas compared with rich ones (Wilkinson, 1996).

Britain in the region of £52 per week (Berthoud and Ford, 1996). At the other end of the income scale, the top 1 per cent have benefited from more than £900 per week in tax cuts alone since 1978/79.

This book is being published to coincide with the 1997 General Election as a conscious attempt to remind politicians and the public that combating poverty and social exclusion should be a primary goal of any government in a civilised society (and it is an indication of this country's inurement to poverty that such efforts have to be made to get it back on to the policy agenda). This examination of the past and current records of Conservative governments since 1979 serves as a warning to the next government. Not only has the strategy of inequality failed even indirectly to improve the prospects of the poorest but, in making comfortable Britain even more comfortable, it has widened social divisions to such an extent that they threaten economic performance. Again it is indicative of the extent to which successive Conservative governments have captured the policy agenda and focused it more and more narrowly on economic efficiency that we have to present a case against poverty and social exclusion in economic terms.

There never was a sound economic case behind the strategy of inequality, only ideological dogma and self interest. Reducing taxes on the rich does not result in an increase in entrepreneurial activity, though it does make a lot of people even richer. But what has become clear only recently is that the strategy has actually damaged Britain's economic performance. It is a *narrowing* of income differentials that is associated with faster economic growth, not the reverse (Wilkinson, 1996). Even the OECD has highlighted the 'worrying inequalities' present in some of its members, notably Britain and the US, and noted that the growing divide between workers has not been matched by any increase in upward mobility. Moreover, the OECD (Atkinson, 1996) has emphasised the long-term economic damage of the government's strategy:

> economic inequality in general hampers education and training reform ... high income inequality can act to constrain pupil achievements in the lower tail of the distribution ... continued increases in educational participation and attainment may be difficult to achieve so long as inequality is high and/or rising.

Of course, economic or income inequality also damages the social fabric of society, especially social cohesion. For example, rising inequality is associated with increases in crime and death rates from heart disease (Wilkinson, 1996).

The experience of the last 18 years demonstrates that a narrow focus on economic efficiency and economic growth will not solve social problems such as poverty and social exclusion but, rather, will make them worse. Instead, what is required is a balanced approach which assesses policy proposals on the basis of their economic and social consequences for the whole population. The overall goal should be to improve the quality of life of all citizens and the starting point must be combating both the poverty that afflicts the most vulnerable and the different forms of social exclusion that affect a much wider range of British citizens.

The book is divided into three sections. The first considers the various processes that have increased social divisions and social exclusion over the past 18 years. In Chapter 2, Carey Oppenheim outlines the huge growth in poverty and inequality and analyses their main causes. She also looks at the impact of poverty on those most directly affected. In Chapter 3, Helga Pile and Catherine O'Donnell examine the roles of changes in earnings, wealth and taxation in creating a more sharply divided society. Chapter 4, by Robert Walker, places Britain in the context of its European partners and shows that Britain has the highest rate of poverty in the EU (measured in terms of income) and the highest incidence of low pay. He also examines two indicators of social exclusion: social assistance and homelessness. Chapter 5 focuses on the unprecedented rise of means-testing in Britain since 1979. David Piachaud argues that the Government has purposely 'targeted' the most vulnerable and politically expendable in its desire to cut public expenditure and has failed to tackle the major disincentives associated with means-tests. Finally in this section, Marilyn Howard summarises some of the main changes that have been made to the social security system since 1979, changes which were at the heart of the social and economic strategy pursued by successive Conservative governments and which bear a heavy responsibility for the increases in poverty and social exclusion.

The second section of the book covers the main dimensions of poverty and social exclusion, reflecting the more comprehensive approach discussed earlier. Jane Millar, in Chapter 7, emphasises that it is women who are both at the highest risk of poverty and who are likely to experience it for longest. But she also shows that men too have been the victims of government policy, losing rights to various benefits such as unemployment benefit. Chapter 8, by Alice Bloch, examines why it is that people from Black and ethnic minority communities are more likely to experience poverty and social exclusion than their white counterparts. Chapter 9 focuses on the issue that is, apparently, at the top of the political agenda, education. George Smith and his colleagues show that, whatever the future promises, educational opportunities and results have become more unequal since 1979 and that the marketisation of education has provided choice for the few rather than guaranteeing access to good quality education for all. Norman Ginsburg deals with housing in Chapter 10. He shows that housing needs have been increased and housing inequalities accentuated over the past 18 years and that housing policies have made a direct contribution to the growing divide between rich and poor. Chapter 11, by Michaela Benzeval, examines the increase in health inequalities in Britain since 1979 and the failure of successive Conservative governments to provide an adequate response. This chapter also includes an extensive agenda for action which emphasises the importance of tackling family poverty in any strategy to reduce health inequalities. Unemployment is a major cause of poverty and social exclusion and, in Chapter 12, Paul Convery documents the return of mass unemployment, its causes and economic costs. The privatisation of utilities played a central role in the programmes of each of the Conservative governments of the 1980s and 1990s and, in Chapter 13, Elaine Kempson outlines the cumulative impact on low income households. The final contribution in this section is by Tim Lang who examines the relationship between food poverty and health and shows how changes in food retailing have created new mechanisms of social exclusion.

The third section of this book represents a four-pronged conclusion. First of all, in Chapter 15, John Hills demolishes the lie that Britain cannot afford a welfare state. In Chapter 16, Lisa Harker outlines an approach to preventing poverty among families with children. In Chapter 17, Peter Townsend challenges both Conservative and Labour parties to show how it is possible to combat poverty without redistribution. He presents a powerful argument against privatisation. In the final chapter, we pull together some of the main threads from previous chapters and call on the nation to make poverty a priority **now**. The Appendix, by Fran Bennett, contains a detailed catalogue of the main policy changes affecting poor families from June 1979 up to August 1996.

REFERENCES

Atkinson, A B, Rainwater, L and Smeeding, T (1996), *Income Distribution in OECD Countries*, Paris, OECD.

Atkinson, A B (1996), 'Drawing the line', *Guardian*, 6 November 1996.

Becker, S (1991) (ed.) *Windows of Opportunity – Public Policy and the Poor*, CPAG.

Berghman, J (1995) 'Social Exclusion in Europe: Policy Context and Analytical Framework' in G. Room (ed.) pp10-28.

Berthoud, R and Ford, R (1996) *Relative Needs*, PSI.

Bosanquet, N and Townsend, P (1980) (eds) *Labour and Equality*, Heinemann.

Bull, D and Wilding, P (1983) (eds) *Thatcherism and the Poor*, CPAG.

CPAG (1970) *Poverty and the Labour Government*, CPAG.

DSS (1996) *Households below Average Income, a statistical analysis 1979–1993/4*, HMSO.

Duffy, K (1995) *Social Exclusion and Human Dignity in Europe*, Council of Europe.

Field, F (1978) *Children Worse Off Under Labour?*, CPAG.

Hills, J (1995) *Joseph Rowntree Foundation Inquiry into Income and Wealth*, Volume 2, Joseph Rowntree Foundation.

Hutton, W (1995) *The State We're In*, Jonathan Cape.

Jarvis, S and Jenkins, S P (1995) *Do the Poor Stay Poor?*, ESRC Research Centre on Micro-Social Change, University of Essex.

Jowell, R, Curtice, J, Park, A, Brook, L and Thomson, K (1996) (eds) *British Social Attitudes – the 13th Report*, Dartmouth.

Marshall, T H (1950) *Citizenship and Social Class*, CUP.

Moore, J (1987) Speech to Conservative Constituency Parties, 26 September.

Ringen, S (1988) 'Direct and indirect measures of poverty', *Journal of Social Policy*, vol 17, pt 3, pp351-65.

Room, G (1995) (ed.) *Beyond the Threshold*, The Policy Press.

Room, G et al (1991) *National Policies to Combat Social Exclusion*, European Commission, Brussels.

Townsend, P (1979) *Poverty in the United Kingdom*, Penguin Books.

Townsend, P and Bosanquet, N (1972) (eds) *Labour and Inequality*, Fabian Society.

Walker, A (1990) 'The strategy of inequality: poverty and income distribution in Britain 1979-89' in Taylor, I (ed) *The Social Effects of Free Market Policies*, Harvester-Wheatsheaf, pp29-48.

Walker, A and Walker, C (1987) (eds) *The Growing Divide – A Social Audit 1979-1987*, CPAG.

Wapshott, N and Brock, G (1983) *Thatcher*, Macdonald & Co.

Wilkinson, R (1996) *Unhealthy Societies: The Afflictions of Inequality*, Routledge.

Young, Lord D (1985) Speech at St Lawrence Jewry, 6 November.

Section One

CREATING POVERTY AND SOCIAL EXCLUSION

2 The growth of poverty and inequality

Carey Oppenheim

INTRODUCTION

Looking back over our shoulders at the last 18 years, we see two sets of contrasting images flash by. There are the enduring symbols of poverty and inequality: silent shipyards, empty shopping malls boosted momentarily for Christmas, the wasted youth of homeless young people, isolated outer estates, valley upon valley without working mines, boarded up windows of crime-ridden inner city estates, vandalised playgrounds, schools in jeopardy, the reappearance of tuberculosis.

But alongside there are also the kernels of possibility and regeneration (less amenable to pen-portraits as they are more tentative): jobs creation for the long-term unemployed to meet new needs using benefit and European money, local exchange trading schemes (LETS) where people exchange their skills – plumbing for baby-sitting – in a non-cash economy, partnerships between Kids Club Networks and TECs to foster after-school care, jobs, training and voluntary experience, family and school reading schemes where both children and parents make leaps in their literacy. Such initiatives have sprung up in defiance of their environment searching for their own solutions.

To tell the story of what has happened since the late 1970s involves contradictory elements: on the one hand the UK has experienced an almost unparalleled rise in inequality in the industrialised world (with the exception of New Zealand) and on the other there are pockets of hope as individuals, communities, voluntary organisations, local government and businesses carve out new solutions. This chapter looks at the context and evidence of the changes in poverty and inequality, the impact of these divisions and the way ahead.

THE IDEOLOGICAL AND ECONOMIC CONTEXT

While there are ideological differences between the Thatcher and Major governments, with the latter softening some of the harsher edges of the neo-liberal agenda, it is possible to pull out three key elements of a Conservative approach to poverty and inequality. First, the Government defined its role as providing a minimum for those in poverty rather than tackling the broader questions of social injustice. Instead, the market was to cater for rising living standards (Hoover and Plant, 1989). The 'trickle-down' theory assumed that the growing economy would automatically provide improved living standards for those at the bottom. Second, the Government, in various guises, has attempted to deny the existence of poverty. John Moore's *End of the Line for Poverty* speech in 1989 when he was Secretary of State (which argued that absolute poverty no longer existed and relative poverty was a misnomer for inequality) was perhaps the most dramatic intervention (Moore, 1989). More recently, the response of the current Secretary of State, Peter Lilley MP, to the Joseph Rowntree Foundation Report's analysis of the sharp rise in inequality over the 1980s, was to 'shoot the messenger' questioning the political neutrality of its author (Hills, 1995). The latest instance of denial is the refusal to comply with the UN Social Summit's requirement to set out a national strategy to tackle poverty. Lilley argued that the social conditions in the UK did not warrant such a strategy. Third, there has been a strong emphasis on personal responsibility for poverty, heavily influenced by the work of writers like Charles Murray, an American political scientist, whose views were widely promoted by the Institute for Economic Affairs (Murray 1984, 1990, 1994, 1996) and the *Sunday Times*. Murray argued that a growing underclass, characterised by its behaviour – high levels of illegitimacy, crime and labour market drop-out – was threatening the social fabric. At its most reductionist, the New Right redefined poverty as 'dependency' which was seen as a behavioural problem caused by the welfare state itself. These ideas have shaped the contours of a debate in which individual explanations of poverty have had much greater prominence than in any other post-war period.

Alongside the ideological sea-change, the UK has been buffeted by major economic upheavals, exacerbated by the Government's fierce adherence to narrow monetary targets and to deregulation. There have been two recessions in the space of a decade, unemployment reaching over three million in 1986 and again in 1991. The shape of the labour market has been radically altered, with the persistent rise of economic inactivity or the hidden unemployment which is much less responsive to economic growth than official unemployment, the continued decline in male full-time work and rise in female part-time work among couples, the growth of jobless households and the greatly widening gap between low paid and the high paid. Paradoxically, we have witnessed a dramatic sharpening of inequalities alongside the persistent denial of any government responsibility for the problem.

THE EVIDENCE

Presenting the evidence about poverty and inequality is not a straight-forward exercise. UK governments of all political persuasions have resolutely refused to tread the difficult path of adopting an official definition of poverty. Much of the debate about poverty has focused unhealthily on how we define and measure it with accusations and counter-accusations of statistical manipulation on all sides. Certainly, in the 1980s, the refusal to use the term 'poverty' in official documents, combined with secrecy, created a widespread distrust of official data. Latterly, there has been greater co-operation and openness between government and outside bodies over low income statistics. There is a great deal of material on the subject – here some key figures are drawn from the latest official source of data, Households Below Average Incomes (HBAI) 1993/94 (DSS, 1996). Table 2.1 shows how poverty (defined as 50 per cent of average income after housing costs) grew rapidly over the 1980s, rising from 5 million (9 per cent of the population) to just over 14 million in 1992/93 (25 per cent) and then dropping back slightly to 13.7 million in 1993/94. The rise for children is even steeper – from 1.4 million (10 per cent of all children) in 1979 to 4.2 million (32 per cent) in poverty in 1993/94. Over one decade and a half the composition of those in poverty has changed significantly: pensioners and couples with children now make up a smaller proportion of those in poverty, while lone parents and single people without children make up larger proportions. Not surprisingly, the unemployed and the group labelled 'other' (a rough indicator of economic inactivity as it encompasses people who are long-term sick and lone parents who are not in work) also account for a larger proportion of those in poverty in 1993/94 than in 1979.

TABLE 2.1: **Numbers and proportion of individuals living below 50% of average income before and after housing costs (includes self-employed)**

	Before housing costs		After housing costs	
	Nos: Millions	%	Nos: Millions	%
1979	4.4	8	5.0	9
1981	4.7	9	6.2	11
1987	8.7	16	10.5	19
1988/89	10.4	19	12.0	22
1991/92	11.7	21	13.9	25
1992/93	11.4	20	14.1	25
1993/94	10.7	19	13.7	24

The Breadline Britain surveys (Mack and Lansley, 1985; Gordon *et al*, 1995) provide an entirely different window on poverty, focusing on living standards rather than income. These surveys define poverty as when people have to live without the things which society as a whole regards as necessities – an 'enforced lack of socially perceived necessities' (Mack and Lansley, 1985). These are identified through public opinion surveys rather than by experts or people's behaviour. Households lacking three or more necessities were counted as being in poverty. According to this definition, in 1990 around 11 million (20 per cent of households) were living in poverty in comparison with around seven and a half million (14 per cent) in 1983. The 1990 survey graphically describes how around 10 million could not afford adequate housing (home was unheated or damp) seven million went without essential clothing (such as a warm waterproof coat) two and a half million children went without at least one of the things they needed, like three meals a day, toys or school activities, five million people were not fed properly (insufficient fruit and vegetables or two meals a day) (see Chapter 14) and six and a half million could not afford one or more essential goods, like a fridge, telephone, carpets (Gordon *et al*, 1995). The research is a rich source of data on other dimensions of poverty.

One of the criticisms that has been directed at HBAI and many other studies of poverty is that they provide snap-shots and do not look at poverty over time. The Government has been particularly keen to use a dynamic picture of low income in order to question the scale and severity of poverty in the UK. The *Guardian* headline 'Study "rebuts poverty myth"' (27 June 1996) encapsulates Peter Lilley's claim that a study of male earnings over time proved that the poor have not got poorer since 1979 (Ball and Marland, 1996). The research Lilley cites is limited: it focuses on men alone, on earnings and does not take account of housing costs. However, despite the political hyperbole it is important to look at the dynamics of poverty, not to discredit HBAI data, but to enable us to identify the barriers and exits from poverty. The evidence suggests that there is movement at the bottom of the income distribution, but it is very often of the revolving door kind – from unemployment to low pay to unemployment again. HBAI (DSS, 1996), drawing on work done by the Institute for Fiscal Studies, shows that although people in poverty do move from the bottom rung of the ladder, a large proportion do not move up very far (see Table 2.2). Between 1991 and 1994, 40 per cent of the bottom tenth (decile group) moved up one step to the second bottom decile; a further 18 per cent to the third bottom decile, and another 22 per cent to the fourth or fifth decile. Only 21 per cent moved into the top half of the income distribution. Around 10 to 15 per cent of the sample experienced poverty continuously – they were in the bottom three deciles in all four years. Close to half (43 per cent) had some experience of poverty over the period – they spent at least one year out of the four in the bottom three deciles. Lone parents and pensioners were least likely to be able to move from the lowest levels of income in contrast to households with someone in employment or self-employment or in receipt of disability benefits. Not surprisingly, the chances of moving up the income ladder decrease with the length of time spent at the bottom of the income distribution.

TABLE 2.2: **Destination of those moving up out of the bottom of the 1991 income distribution for the year 1994**

Position in 1994	Those in bottom 10% in 1991	Those in bottom 30% in 1991
Second decile	40%	n/a
Third decile	18%	n/a
Fourth decile	14%	38%
Fifth decile	(8%)	23%
Top five deciles	21%	38%

Source: *Households below Average Income, A statistical analysis 1979–1993/94*, HMSO, 1996, p76.

NO EVIDENCE OF 'TRICKLE DOWN'

> Everyone in the nation has benefited from increased prosperity – everyone (Margaret Thatcher MP, House of Commons, *Hansard*, 17 May 1988, col 796)

Despite Thatcher's grand claim, the evidence suggests that not everyone has benefited from the 'trickle down' effect. Inequality, whether measured by income, earnings, health, housing or wealth has grown since the late 1970s. Here three dimensions of inequality are touched upon: income, expenditure and geography. HBAI (DSS, 1996) documents the rising disparities in income over the 1980s; the real incomes after housing costs of the bottom tenth fell by 13 per cent, compared with a rise of 40 per cent for the average and a staggering rise of 65 per cent for those in the top tenth (see Table 2.3). Even excluding the self-employed, the poorest tenth had a fall in real income of 6 per cent after housing costs. In an international analysis of income inequality Atkinson (1996a) shows that the UK stands out as having one of the sharpest rises in inequality between 1977 and 1991.

TABLE 2.3: **Rises in real income between 1979 and 1993/94 (including self-employed) for each tenth of the population**

	Before Housing Costs	After Housing Costs
First (bottom)	6%	−13%
Second	13%	4%
Third	17%	10%
Fourth	20%	18%
Fifth	25%	25%
Sixth	29%	31%
Seventh	33%	36%
Eighth	37%	40%
Ninth	45%	49%
Tenth (top)	59%	65%
Total population	**39%**	**40%**

Source: *Households below Average Income, A statistical analysis 1979-1993/94*, HMSO, 1996, p114

Another way of looking at inequality is through expenditure rather than income. Atkinson (1989) argues that an income measure is about a right to a minimum level of resources, while expenditure is about a standard of living. Each approach reveals different aspects of inequality and has its strengths and weaknesses. Expenditure inequality has also grown sharply since 1979 though not as steeply as for income (Goodman and Webb, 1995). Goodman and Webb (1995) find that expenditure, in contrast to the income data, for the poorest tenth has risen. This may be due to a number of factors: the change in composition of the poorest tenth from pensioners to families with children who tend to have higher spending patterns, running down savings, increased levels of debt, the tendency of some self-employed to report low levels of income but have high levels of spending and volatility of income which characterises parts of today's labour market – those who have experienced a rapid fall in the incomes may still have relatively high spending patterns.

In the influential Rowntree Inquiry into Income and Wealth, Hills (1995) untangles the web of interconnected reasons for the UK's sharp rise in inequality over the 1980s. In particular, he identifies the marked rise in the dispersion of male earnings which is 'now wider than at any time in the century for which we have records'. Drawing on research by Gosling et al (1994), Hills (1995) shows that between 1966 and 1977 male wages at different levels rose at broadly the same rate. Between 1978 and 1992 the lowest wages were stagnant or falling while in real terms there was a rise of 35 per cent for the median and 50 per cent for the top. Between 1979 and 1993/94, the total weekly income, after housing costs, at July 1996 prices increased from £331 per week to £546 for the richest 10 per cent but fell from £78 to £67 for the poorest 10 per cent (DSS, 1996). There are similar though slightly more uneven patterns for women. The only narrowing of wage differentials was between male and female full-timers. The gap between high and low paid is due both to the growing importance of educational qualifications in determining fates in the labour market, and to changes in labour market institutions such as the decline in Trade Unions and wage regulation. Atkinson (1996a) also pinpoints the behaviour of firms: 'it has become socially acceptable to have larger differentials in the work place.' Another important cause of inequality is the unequal distribution of employment opportunities – what Gregg and Wadsworth (1994) have identified as the gap between the 'work rich' and the 'work poor'. The Rowntree Report also pinpoints the growing importance of self-employment income (which is both more unequal and more prevalent), investment income and occupational pensions in prising apart the incomes of those at the bottom and top still further. Finally, Hills (1995) found that key changes in benefit policy, in particular the breaking of the link between some benefits and earnings, and discretionary tax changes played an important role in undermining the effectiveness of the welfare state in narrowing income differences (see also Oppenheim and Lister, 1996).

Inequality affects place as well as income and expenditure. The Rowntree Report shows that between 1981 and 1991 there was little evidence of greater polarisation at district level but there was a widening of the gap at ward level (Green, 1994). Despite strong elements of continuity in terms of the pattern of poor and rich areas there was an increase in the concentration of poverty – in 1991, 8.9 per cent of wards had concentrated poverty compared to 7.5 per cent in 1981. These included Inner London, Merseyside, West Midlands, South Wales, the North East, Strathclyde and the coastline. The Oxford and Oldham study (Noble *et al*, 1994) also shows the growth of polarisation between small areas (enumeration districts) especially in Oldham and the ways in which benefit receipt and council housing tenure overlap.

The 1990 Breadline Britain survey adds new dimensions to this picture of division by area. In an analysis of the use of local authority services, Bramley (1995) finds that demand-led leisure services such as libraries, sports facilities, adult education classes, museums and galleries have what he calls a 'pro-rich' bias. The only exception is the bus service.

> These services are not only failing to compensate for other deprivations but problems of access to them are on balance worsening the deprivation of some households. Another way of looking at these services, in particular is that they represent examples of 'participating in the normal life of the community'... 'multiply deprived' households are less likely to participate in this 'normal life of the community'.

Bramley (1995) also identifies that poor people are particularly disadvantaged in relation to access and use of what he calls 'local public goods', for example, the cleanliness of the local area, the quality of the open space, access to school resources and the extent of home disrepair. The survey also examines the impact of poverty on both the experience and the fear of crime. It found that being a victim of crime was related to a number of factors: being in a single non retired household, poor quality housing and a history of poverty. Fear of crime, however, was strongly related to poverty and deprivation. The authors (Gordon *et al*, 1995) suggest that crime should be looked at in relation to social cohesion rather than poverty alone. The material on inequalities between areas and the quality of life in poorer areas indicates the importance of exploring a broader definition of social exclusion and inclusion (see the final section of this chapter).

THE IMPACT OF POVERTY AND INEQUALITY

The effects of poverty may be immediate, for example the sudden cutting of household expenditure following redundancy or separation, or they may be long term, affecting relationships within families or the future health and educational experiences of adults and children (Oppenheim and Lister, forthcoming).

A number of key themes underlie the qualitative studies of poverty drawn together by Elaine Kempson (1996). First, there is strong evidence that families reduce expenditure on basic necessities such as food or fuel; research by Kempson *et al* (1994) into 74 families living on low incomes identified the ways in which people cut down on essentials: 'families were forced to assign priorities within their necessities'. Second, people in poverty sharply curtail spending on items that broaden and enhance life, such as leisure and social activities. Children from less affluent homes were much more likely to go on holiday in the UK than abroad; to have shorter holidays; and to be more dependent on day trips from school for their experience outside home than children from more affluent homes (Middleton *et al*, 1994). Third, emotional and psychological consequences filter into the matrix of relationships within families. Ritchie's (1990) qualitative study of 30 unemployed families explored the psychological and social consequences of extended periods of unemployment among couples. Unemployment among men was associated with the anxiety of making ends meet and the loss of the 'provider' role. She also showed that the women were under the same or even more stress because they were responsible for budgeting and were concerned both about their husband's moods and their children's welfare: 'there seemed to be a deep sense of insecurity which was surrounding their family life and which, most crucially, posed some kind of threat to their children'.

Despite the pressures of living on meagre incomes people in poverty adopt a number of strategies for getting-by whether it is redistributing income or resources within the family when parents attempt to shield their children from poverty, or the support and help from extended family, friends, neighbours and the community.

It is not possible to do justice to the extensive material on the long term effects of poverty on adults and children's well-being, their physical and mental health and their educational chances (Kumar, 1993; Wilkinson, 1994; Holtermann 1995; OPCS, 1995). A quotation from Holtermann's (1995) analysis of the data on children illustrates how poor children are disadvantaged on nearly every measure of life-chances:

> Children from poor homes have lower life expectancy and are more likely to die in infancy or childhood; they have a greater likelihood of poor health, a lower chance of high educational attainment, a greater risk of unemployment, a higher probability of involvement in crime and enduring homelessness. Girls from poor homes are at greater risk of teenage pregnancy.

The impact of inequality has also been widely commented upon (Hills, 1995). The emphasis here is on the economic and social costs of inequality. At the heart of neo-liberal thinking was the view that inequality would generate economic growth. But there is little evidence to suggest that the scale of inequality is strongly linked to economic growth. Corry and Glyn (1994) stress that although the picture is complex, the steady economic growth of the 1950s and 1960s was associated with a period of declining inequality, the rise in inequality in the 1980s did not produce marked improvements and the international picture suggests that countries with less disparity of incomes have tended to grow faster. Not only has inequality apparently not yielded economic dividends it has also brought in its wake sharply rising social costs such as unemployment, reliance on social security, health costs associated with low income, crime and so on, each in turn carrying economic penalties. It has also imposed stresses on families who are caught between the economic imperative and the task of sustaining relationships. We are, in the words of the Rowntree Report, spending too much on the costs of failure rather than success (1995). Hutton (1995) eloquently encapsulates the damage wreaked by rising inequality:

> The collapse of social cohesion that comes when the market is allowed to rip through society has produced a fall in the growth rate; marginalisation, deprivation and exclusion have proved economically irrational ... Market rule has recoiled on the state's finances; as the polarisation of society has worsened, public spending on crime, health and specialist education has increased − and social security spending itself, even though rates are meaner in relation to average earnings, has ballooned as poverty drives millions through the drab waiting room of the rump welfare state.

THE WAY AHEAD

> *Rt Hon Tony Blair MP:* Does the Prime Minister accept it as a responsibility of government to reduce inequality?
> *The Prime Minister:* Yes.
> (House of Commons, *Hansard*, 9 February 1995, col 452)

> I believe in greater equality. If the next Labour Government has not raised the living standards of the poorest by the end of its time in office it will have failed. (Rt Hon Tony Blair MP, *Independent on Sunday*, 28 July 1996)

Four key challenges face a future government. The legacy of nearly two decades of high levels of deprivation will continue to shape people's life-chances in the future; many of the broader economic and social factors which have partly generated inequalities will persist; tight control of public spending especially in the run-up to a European single currency (whether Britain joins or not) will limit resources for regeneration; and public attitudes to paying higher taxes for public spending are ambiguous. *The British Social Attitudes Survey* (Taylor-Gooby, 1995) shows a growing recognition of the scale of poverty and yet a reluctance to pay higher taxes for services which particularly benefit the poorest. By contrast there is widespread support for increased taxes for spending on universal services such as health and education – though even here people identify themselves as paying sufficient tax already. These challenges are not insurmountable: the evidence from other countries shows that politics and policies can make a crucial difference to the scale of poverty and inequality.

There are a number of building blocks for reform. The first is to weld the economic and social together – each rebounds on the other (Commission on Social Justice, 1994). Policies to tackle poverty and inequality are not only about people in poverty – important though that is – they benefit society as a whole. The second is to address social exclusion as well as poverty. Social exclusion captures the complexity of the experience and processes of poverty (Lister, forthcoming). Room (1995) argues that social exclusion involves adopting multi-dimensional measures of poverty, looking at poverty over time and at community as well as individual/family/household resources. He also, importantly, develops the notion of enhancing individual and community assets, such as education, work, social skills, time, culture and of course financial assets: income and capital. Thus, one of the ways of tackling social exclusion is to re-build those individual and community assets. The third is to broaden the notion of redistribution to encompass education, skills, capacities and time as well as income and wealth, localities as well as individuals, the shift of resources over the lifecycle as well as between rich and poor. Finally, the fourth building block is to put taxation back onto the political agenda once the pre-election taboo is lifted. There are imaginative and potentially politically acceptable ideas for raising taxes such as looking at the rationale and distribution of tax reliefs and allowances, the 'marketing' (Hills, 1996) of taxes – linking them to particular forms of spending and green taxation (Tindale and Holtham, 1996).

These building blocks would provide the foundations for a National Strategy for Social Inclusion which would symbolise government commitment to tackling deprivation and also galvanise public support. It offers the opportunity to have an open debate about how we look at poverty and social exclusion and what range of solutions are possible and over what period. There is a wealth of research but it is not pulled together with an eye for policy and above all change. This approach would straddle different areas of policy at national and local level and not be confined to state provision alone. The process would also need to be democratic, including people in poverty in the process of thinking about solutions (CAP, 1996). Ireland, for example, has developed a national anti-poverty strategy which is linked into government institutionally and encompasses a consultative process on the ground. A national strategy could also address difficult issues of achieving a consensus about an official poverty line and targets to reduce poverty over the long term as suggested recently by Atkinson (1996b).

Confronting poverty and inequality is both daunting and promising. Daunting because of the scale of the problem; promising because the international picture suggests that other countries have been much more successful at containing poverty and inequality and also because there are many small scale local projects which tread new ground in tackling poverty. Given the focus of political parties on addressing the wider electorate it is crucial that outside players such as the Child Poverty Action Group, the children's charities, the Church and the Joseph Rowntree Foundation continue to keep poverty and inequality firmly on the political agenda.

REFERENCES

Atkinson, A B (1989) 'How should we measure poverty? Some conceptual issues' in Atkinson, A B (ed) *Poverty and Social Security*, Harvester Wheatsheaf.

Atkinson, A B (1996a) 'Income Distribution in an International Context', 1996 Annual Lecture, South Bank University.

Atkinson, A B (1996b) 'Drawing the Line', *Guardian*, 6 November 1996.

Ball and Marland (1996) *Male Earnings Mobility in the Lifetime Labour Market Database*, Working Paper Number 1, DSS.

Bramley G (1995) 'Poverty and local public services' in Gordon, D *et al* (eds) *Breadline Britain in the 1990s*, MORI and Domino Films.

Church Action on Poverty (1996) *Speaking from Experience, Voices at the National Poverty Hearing*, Church Action on Poverty.

Commission on Social Justice (1994) *Social Justice, Strategies for National Renewal*, Vintage.

Corry, D and Glyn, A (1994) 'The macro-economics of Equality, Stability and Growth, in Glyn, A and Miliband, D (eds) *Paying for Inequality, The Economic Cost of Social Injustice*, IPPR/Rivers Oram Press.

DSS (1996) *Households below Average Income, a statistical analysis 1979–1993/4*, HMSO.

Goodman, A and Webb, S (1995) *The Distribution of UK Household Expenditure 1979-1992*, Institute for Fiscal Studies.

Gordon, D *et al* (eds) (1995) *Breadline Britain in the 1990s*, MORI and Domino Films.

Gosling *et al* (1994) *What has happened to wages?*, IFS Commentary No 43, Institute for Fiscal Studies.

Green, A (1994) *The Geography of Income and Wealth*, University of Warwick Institute for Employment Research.

Hills, J (1995) *Joseph Rowntree Foundation Inquiry into Income and Wealth*, Volume 2, Joseph Rowntree Foundation.

Hills, J (1996) 'Tax policy: are there still choices?', in Halpern, D *et al*, *Options for Britain, A Strategic Policy Review*, Dartmouth.

Holtermann, S (1995) *All Our Futures: the impact of public expenditure and fiscal policies on children and young people*, Barnardos.

Hoover, K and Plant, R (1989) *Conservative Capitalism in Britain and the United States, A Critical Appraisal*, Routledge.

Hutton, W (1995) *The State We're In*, Jonathan Cape.

Joseph Rowntree Foundation (1995), *Joseph Rowntree Foundation Inquiry into Income and Wealth*, Volume 1.

Kempson, E (1996) *Life on a Low Income*, Joseph Rowntree Foundation.

Kempson, E, Bryson, A and Rowlingson, K (1994) *Hard Times, How poor families make ends meet*, Policy Studies Institute.

Kumar, V (1993) *Poverty and Inequality in the UK, The effects on children*, National Children's Bureau.

Lister, R (forthcoming) 'Inclusion and exclusion' in Kelly, G, Kelly, D and Gamble, A, *Stakeholder Capitalism*, Macmillan.

Mack, J and Lansley, S (1985) *Poor Britain*, Allen and Unwin.

McCormick, J and Oppenheim, C (1996) 'Options for change', *New Statesman/Society*, 26 January 1996.

Middleton, S., Ashworth, K. and Walker, R. (1994) *Family Fortunes, Pressures on parents and children in the 1990s*, Child Poverty Action Group Ltd.

Moore, J, Speech to Greater London Area Conservative Political Centre Conference, 11 May 1989.

Murray, C (1984) *Losing Ground*, Basic Books, New York.

Murray, C (1990) 'Rejoinder' in *The Emerging British Underclass*, Institute for Economic Affairs.

Murray, C (1994) *Underclass: the crisis deepens*, Institute for Economic Affairs.

Murray, C (1996) *Charles Murray and the Underclass*, Institute for Economic Affairs.

Noble, M *et al* (1994) *Changing Patterns of Income and Wealth in Oxford and Oldham*, Department of Applied Social Studies, University of Oxford.

Novak, M (1987) *The New Consensus on Family and Welfare*, American Enterprise Institute for Public Policy Research.

OPCS (1995) *The Health of our Children*, Decennial Supplement, HMSO.

Oppenheim, C and Harker, L (1996) *Poverty: the facts*, CPAG.

Oppenheim, C and Lister, R (1996a) 'The politics of child poverty 1979– 1995', in Pilcher, J and Wagg, S (eds), *Thatcher's Children?, Politics, Childhood and Society in the 1980s and 1990s*, Falmer Press.

Oppenheim, C and Lister, R (1996b) 'Ten years after the 1986 Social Security Act' in May, M *et al*, (eds) *Social Policy Review 8*, Social Policy Association.

Oppenheim, C and Lister, R (forthcoming) 'Poverty and family life' in Itzin, C (ed), *Home Truths*, Routledge.

Ritchie, J (1990) *Thirty Unemployed Families: their living standards in unemployment*, HMSO.

Room, G (ed) (1995) *Beyond the Threshold, The Measurement and Analysis of Social Exclusion*, The Policy Press.

Taylor-Gooby, P (1995) 'Comfortable, marginal and excluded, who should pay higher taxes for a better welfare state?' in Jowell, R *et al* (eds) *British Social Attitudes*, the 12th Report, Dartmouth.

Wilkinson, R (1994) *Unfair Shares, The effects of widening income differences on the welfare of the young*, Barnardos.

3 Earnings, taxation and wealth

Helga Pile and Catherine O'Donnell

The record rises in income inequality and poverty in Britain discussed in the previous chapter are among the dominant legacies of the Conservatives' four terms in office and put an end to the longer-term trend up to the late 1970s towards greater equality in the UK. This chapter examines how changes in the distribution of earnings, wealth and taxation have contributed to this rising inequality.

WORK AND UNEMPLOYMENT: THE GROWING DIVIDE

From the 1980s onwards there has been a growing divide not only between people in the labour market and those outside but also – in terms of income and security – between different groups within the labour market. The number of individuals under 60 living in households without work has more than doubled: from 4.1 million or 8 per cent in 1979 to 9.4 million or 17 per cent in 1993/94 (DSS, 1996). This has been accompanied by a widening gap in the incomes of households in work and those out of work, which has been caused mainly by the falling relative value of social security benefits (see Chapter 6). As a result there has been an increasing polarisation between so-called 'work-rich' and 'work-poor' households (Gregg and Wadsworth, 1994), and particularly between two-earner and no-earner couples.

Since 1979, for reasons discussed later in this chapter, it has become harder to move from unemployment into work: between

1979 and 1993 the proportion of people from workless households who made the transition from non-employment into work more than halved for couples from 25 per cent to 12 per cent (Gregg and Wadsworth, 1994).

Inequalities have increased also within the working population. The distribution of incomes has widened: between the high and low paid (see Table 2.3, Chapter 2), between men and women, between those with higher skill/qualification levels and those without, and between young (especially the lesser qualified) and older workers (Atkinson, 1996).

The growth of self-employment has contributed to overall income inequality because income disparity among the self-employed is greater than that of comparable groups of employees. While the self-employed in the highest income decile have a third more income than employees, in the bottom decile their incomes are almost a third lower. In the 1980s a significant number of young women entered self-employment, most commonly in service sectors which are characterised by low survival rates and marginal returns. Over the same period and often encouraged by schemes such as Enterprise Allowance and Business Start-Up (Meager *et al*, 1996) many unemployed people also entered the more precarious world of self-employment.

LOW PAY

Growing inequality has led to a sharp increase in the number of families living in poverty and low pay has been one of the major causes.

Research which has looked at changes in patterns of low pay between 1968 and 1994 confirms the increasing overlap between low pay and poverty (Webb *et al*, 1996). While this study confirmed that women still make up the majority of the low-paid, it also revealed a sizeable shift in the composition of low-paid men away from young people to those aged 25–49. This has an inevitable knock-on effect to the number of families and children living in poverty because, traditionally, these men would have been the sole or main family breadwinner. For most of the 1970s and early 1980s only around 3 or 4 per cent of low-paid individuals were in household poverty but by the early 1990s the proportion had touched 13 per cent (Webb *et al*, 1996). This suggests that a minimum wage would reduce poverty among those in work because, although it would impact on low-paid *individuals'* earnings, the proportionate gain would generally be higher at lower levels of *household* income (Sutherland, 1995).

Low-paid work has played an increasing role in the spread of poverty. Of the 13.7 million people living on incomes on or below half household average in 1993/94, 4.4 million lived in a household which had income from work (DSS, 1996b) (see Table 3.1).

Table 3.1: **Numbers of working poor in 1979 and 1993/94 (millions)**

	1979	1993/94
Self-employed	0.51	1.40
Single/couple all in F/T work	0.13	0.25
One in F/T work, one in P/T work	0.11	0.24
One in F/T work, one not working	0.45	1.20
One or more in P/T work	0.51	1.27
Total	1.71	4.36

Based on income after housing costs
Source: DSS, 1996

The Low Pay Unit's monitoring of the extent of low pay found that the number earning below the Council of Europe's decency threshold has increased by 10 per cent or 2.5 million since 1979 to stand at 10.4 million in 1996 (Low Pay Unit, 1996) (see Table 3.2). The number of men in full-time work earning less than the Council of Europe decency threshold has increased by over one million. While the *number* of women falling below this line has fallen, a higher *proportion* of women than men earn poverty wages. Over three-quarters of part-time workers earn less than the Council of Europe minimum, confirming the link between part-time work and poverty. In 1996:

- over 10 million people worked for a basic wage below the Council of Europe decency threshold;
- nearly 5 million workers were on a wage of less than half male median earnings (£4.42 an hour in 1996);
- 2 million people earned less than £3 an hour;
- 1.3 million people earned less than £2.50 per hour (Low Pay Unit, 1996).

Analysis of inequality measures based on the New Earnings Survey (NES) shows that:

- full-time male manual workers in the lowest earnings decile in 1996 earned 6 per cent less in relation to the median than they did in 1886 when records began;
- the lowest decile of all full-time male employees now earn 29.9 per cent of that earned by the highest decile, down from 43 per cent in 1979; the equivalent figures for full-time working women fell from 41.3 per cent to 32.6 per cent;
- the earnings of those in the highest decile rose by 25.3 per cent in real terms between 1986 and 1996, while average earnings for the lowest decile rose by only 13.7 per cent. (Low Pay Unit, 1996)

As well as the growth of low pay, these developments reflect record remuneration rises among the highest paid directors and managers whose pay it is claimed, is dictated by 'the market'. The *Independent on Sunday* (3 November 1996) plotted a graph of the earnings distribution in 1996 which would have covered 1,400 pages if the scale for the highest earners had not been compressed.

WOMEN, WORK AND PAY

Since 1979 women's labour market participation has increased while men's has decreased: there are now almost equal numbers of men and women in paid employment. But NES data show that while implementation of the Equal Pay Act together with government incomes policies enabled women's average earnings to catch up with men's during the 1970s, progress slowed throughout the 1980s. In the 1990s it has almost come to a halt. In 1996 women in full-time work still earned only 72 per cent of men's average weekly earnings and 80 per cent of their average hourly earnings. Women are far more likely to work part-time than men and earnings for part-time women employees are even lower. The rise in overall wage inequality has blocked any narrowing of the gender pay gap which a fall in overt discrimination or the rise in skill levels among women might have been expected to bring about (Harkness, 1996).

One of the key government employment policies which has had a negative impact on women's pay was the abolition of the Wages Councils in 1993. These had previously set minimum pay levels for three million low-paid vulnerable workers, the majority of whom

TABLE 3.2: **Number & proportion of employees with gross earnings excluding overtime below Council of Europe decency threshold (£6.31/hr, £239.16/wk), April 1996**

	1979		1982		1988		1994		1995		1996	
	million	%	million	%	million	%	million	%	million	%	million	%
Full-time												
women	3.00	57.6	2.75	55.6	2.91	55.0	2.71	49.7	2.69	49.5	2.73	49.4
men	1.64	14.6	1.83	17.7	2.77	26.7	2.76	29.9	2.83	30.4	2.88	30.8
all	4.64	28.3	4.58	30.0	5.68	36.2	5.47	37.0	5.52	37.2	5.61	37.6
Part-time												
women	2.99	79.0	3.04	80.5	3.50	82.2	3.70	76.6	3.63	75.9	3.89	79.3
men	0.17	62.2	0.46	63.9	0.68	79.5	0.80	72.2	0.79	67.2	0.89	74.1
all	3.16	78.0	3.50	77.0	4.18	81.0	4.50	76.7	4.42	72.2	4.78	78.6
Total	7.80	38.1	8.08	40.9	9.91	47.6	9.97	47.8	9.94	48.1	10.40	48.1

Source: Low Pay Unit, 1996.

were women. Abolition followed a programme of cuts which had began in 1979 with a reduction in the number of wages inspectors and continued until 1986 when minimum wage protection was withdrawn from half a million young people. Abolition of the Wages Councils has led to significant falls in the average pay rates in the sectors formerly covered, but with no parallel increase in employment levels – indeed there are signs that employment has actually fallen in some sectors (Low Pay Network, 1995).

THE DIVIDED LABOUR MARKET

Conservative Government policies have fostered a labour market which at the bottom is characterised by insecurity – with the lowest levels of employment protection of any industrialised country, low wages and low productivity – while at the top there have been ever-increasing levels of remuneration and benefits for executives and directors, which often bear scant relation to company performance. Since 1979 these policies have included:

- increasing the qualifying period for employment rights from six months to two years;
- the run-down and eventual abolition of the Wages Councils;
- the restriction of trades union power to represent and protect their members;
- privatisation of utilities and public services with subsequent reductions in employment, rates of pay and employment rights for many workers;
- the fostering of a contract culture where competitiveness is based on the continuous driving down of costs at the expense of wages, working conditions and quality;
- the development of an in-work benefit system (such as family credit) which, in 1996, cost the taxpayer £3.3 billion in subsidies to low-paying employers.

There is a deep division between the majority of employees who are still in permanent jobs (over 90 per cent with around 70 per cent in full-time permanent jobs) and a growing minority who are participating at the margins of the labour market often in low-paid, temporary and part-time jobs interspersed with spells of unemployment. Fifty per cent of those who leave the unemployment register to take work are back claiming benefits within a year (ONS, 1996a).

Policies which have encouraged the run–down of Britain's manu-facturing base and promoted the growth of 'flexible' service sector employment have meant that the net growth in employment during the 1990s has been largely confined to part-time and temporary jobs. In 1995/96, for example, there was a 3.2 per cent net increase in part-time jobs but only a 0.1 per cent increase in full-time jobs (IDS, 1996).

BARRIERS TO RE-ENTERING EMPLOYMENT

The Bank of England (1996) has acknowledged the price paid by those who are trapped in this flexible end of the labour market:

> The penalty attached to losing a permanent job may have increased. The minority of people who lose their job face a labour market increasingly characterised by part-time and temporary jobs. Only 20 per cent of unemployed people who found jobs in 1992/93 found permanent full-time jobs. And real earnings in new jobs taken by those out of work have barely risen since 1980.

This has been a key factor behind the growth of work-rich and work-poor households mentioned earlier. The growing dependence on means-tested benefits, described in Chapter 5, can provide a disincen-tive to taking low paid work – especially where there are children in the household – as one partner's earnings reduce or terminate the other's benefit entitlement. Rather than lifting people out of unem-ployment into work, benefits like family credit act more as a safety net for those already in employment. Only one in ten workers first claim this benefit as new job entrants. The majority of claims result from a change in circumstances, such as a downturn in earnings (Bryson and Marsh, 1996). The present strategy of disregarding some childcare costs for those in full-time work has failed: of the 660,000 families receiving family credit in 1995/96, only 3.5 per cent claimed the available help with childcare charges (DSS, 1996a).

TAXATION

Taxation can act as a mechanism for redistribution and a means of alleviating poverty. However, in recent years, tax policy itself has led to greater inequality and the combination of direct income tax cuts and indirect tax rises has made it a source of redistribution from the poor to the rich.

The system of personal taxation has undergone major revision since 1979 at the same time as there has been a change in the make-up of earnings. At one end of the spectrum capital income as a proportion of total income has increased; at the other end, there are growing numbers of households reliant solely or mainly on cash transfers (ie, benefits) caused by increased unemployment and low pay. The changing treatment of these types of income in the tax system is a major contributory factor to income inequality.

DIRECT TAXATION

The role of a progressive tax system, where each one gives according to her or his ability to pay, is to redistribute income from the richer to the poorer sections of society and thereby moderate inequality. However, the system of personal direct taxation in the UK has become significantly less progressive since 1979.

One of the Conservative Government's main aims has been to reduce direct taxation. The 11 tax rates which existed in 1979 (starting at 25 per cent and rising to a top rate of 83 per cent) had been flattened to only three (20 per cent, 23 per cent and 40 per cent) by 1996. The result has been a much greater decrease in marginal tax rates (the tax levied on additional income) for higher earners than for those on lower incomes. The same is also true of average tax rates (the amount taken in tax on total income). Average income tax rates for a single person on half average earnings went from 16.2 per cent in 1979 to 13.7 per cent in 1995, while the reduction for someone on five times average earnings was three times as large, from 43.9 per cent to 34.4 per cent. Poor families fared very badly: a married man on half average income claiming the full allowance actually saw his income tax burden rise from 10.1 per cent to 11.1 per cent (Inland Revenue, 1996).

Cutting tax rates gives the greatest benefits to the higher paid, both as a proportion of income and in cash terms. Tables 3.3 and 3.4 show how the effects of a 1 per cent cut in the basic rate of tax in the 1996 budget were distributed. Those on twice average earnings gained 20 times as much in cash terms as those on half average earnings. The cut in the basic rate of tax was of no benefit at all to the 3.2 million employees currently earning below the income tax threshold (ONS, 1996b) nor to those only earning enough to pay the lower rate of tax, who represent a fifth of all taxpayers. The wealthiest 20 per cent of taxpayers, on the other hand, accounted for over 56 per cent of the total cash handout associated with the basic rate cut.

TABLE 3.3: **Gain in income from a I pence reduction in the standard rate of income tax**

multiples of average earnings

¹/₄ x	¹/₂ x	I x	2 x
–	25p	£2.00	£5.01

Estimates based on NES, 1996

TABLE 3.4: **Effect of a I pence reduction in the basic rate of income tax at 1996/97 income levels**

Group of taxpayers (%)	Reduction in income tax (£ million)	Reduction as a percentage total income (%)
Top 10	520	0.4
11-20	380	0.6
21-30	270	0.5
31-40	190	0.5
41-50	130	0.4
51-60	80	0.3
61-70	40	0.2
71-80	10	under 0.1
81-90	0	0
Bottom	0	0

Source: *Hansard,* 19 November 1996, col 500

To those on low incomes the level of personal allowances is more important than lower income tax rates because it is this which determines the level of income at which they start to pay tax and as such is a crucial means of alleviating poverty. However, since 1979 the relative value of personal allowances has fallen, contributing to greater income inequality, particularly for families with children:

• The single person's tax free income has fallen from 20.4 per cent of average earnings in 1979 to 18.2 per cent in 1996/97.

- The married person's allowance has fallen from almost a third of average earnings (31.8 per cent) to under a quarter (24.7 per cent).
- The allowance for a married person with children was 36 per cent in 1979 compared to 24.7 per cent of average earnings in 1996/97 (Inland Revenue Statistics, 1996).

The gradual phasing out of the married couple's allowance has been responsible for the deterioration in the tax position of many families. While the aim of individualising tax treatment is important in terms of equal treatment of men and women, the failure to transfer the benefits to the single person's allowance was a cynical way of paying for tax cuts further up the income scale.

As a result of the many changes to direct tax rates and to personal allowances, 1.7 million low paid employees, earning little over £8,000 per year, paid tax at the basic rate in 1997.

NATIONAL INSURANCE

While income tax rates have fallen, national insurance (NI) contribution rates have risen – the standard rate increased from 6.5 per cent in 1979 to 10 per cent in 1994. It should be noted that although earnings under the lower earnings limit (£62 in 1996/97) are taxed at 2 per cent, around three million of the low paid are part-timers who earn too little to pay even this rate.

The NI system is particularly regressive because there is a ceiling on contributions (the upper earnings limit) which in 1997 stands at £465 per week. As a consequence someone earning £25,000 a year pays 23 pence in direct taxation for each additional pound he or she earns, whereas someone on £10,000 per year pays 33 pence for each extra pound. In real terms, the revenue from national insurance contributions has increased by over £3 billion since 1987 (*Hansard*, 4 July 1995, col 139).

INDIRECT TAXATION

> It's a perfectly fair tax. (Kenneth Clarke referring to VAT on fuel, *Daily Telegraph*, 9 September 1993)

Indirect taxation is much more regressive than direct taxation as it bears down heaviest on the poor who spend a higher proportion of their incomes on essential goods and services. Notwithstanding this fact, successive Conservative governments have shifted the balance of taxation from taxes on income to taxes on spending. In 1985 expenditure taxes raised 17 per cent *less* than taxes on income as a proportion of government revenue. By 1995 they raised 14 per cent *more* (ONS, 1996d). Their relative importance as a proportion of total tax revenue has consequently been reversed – indirect taxes account for 54 per cent and direct taxes 46 per cent in 1997/98 compared to 43 per cent and 57 per cent respectively in 1978/79 (Financial Statement and Budget Report, 1996).

The Conservative Government increased both the level and the scope of VAT. The standard rate of VAT rose from 8 per cent in 1979 to 15 per cent in 1981 and 17.5 per cent in 1992. Petrol, alcohol and tobacco have attracted excise duty increases above the level of inflation and new expenditure taxes have been introduced on, for example, insurance and air travel. The imposition of VAT on domestic fuel in April 1994 represented the biggest extension of the VAT base since it was introduced in 1973. Poor families with children were especially adversely affected because the bottom 20 per cent of income earners spend a higher proportion of their income on fuel than the top 20 per cent. Those on benefit were not fully compensated for the increased cost while the better off were encouraged to limit and delay their VAT liability by paying for fuel in advance. By 1995, VAT accounted for nearly 20 per cent of the income of the bottom decile compared to 8 per cent of the income of the top decile. This contrasts to around 15 per cent and 7 per cent respectively in 1985 (Giles and Johnson, 1994).

THE EFFECTS ON HOUSEHOLD INCOME

Changes in personal taxes between 1985 and 1995, both direct and indirect, have led to huge gains for better off households while for those at the lower end of the income distribution, the tax burden has increased. Between 1985 and 1995 the proportion of income taken in personal tax fell from 42 per cent to 38 per cent for the top decile, but increased from 22 to 25 per cent for the bottom decile. When gains and losses are analysed by family type, another picture emerges, one which shows that low income families with children, both in and out of work, have suffered most from the tax changes (Table 3.5).

TABLE 3.5: **Proportions losing from tax changes by family type (1985/95)**

Family type	Percentage losing	Percentage gaining
Single unemployed	58	21
Single employed	16	76
Lone-parent family	64	13
Unemployed couple without children	53	31
Unemployed couple with children	78	8
One earner couple without children	44	46
One earner couple with children	62	28
Two earner couple without children	28	65
Two earner couple with children	46	47
Single pensioner	16	48
Couple pensioner	29	51
All	37	47

Source: IFS, 1994

TAXES AND SOCIAL SECURITY

With a third of those in poverty living in a household with an income from employment, and in the absence of a minimum wage floor on earnings, more people in work have been dragged into dependence on means-tested benefits (see Chapter 5). The numbers dependent on means-tested in-work benefits has increased dramatically: the number of people living in households with work who also receive family credit increased from 302,000 in 1979 to 2,295,000 in 1995 (*Hansard*, 21 May 1996, col 185). As around a third of the poorest fifth of households rely on both benefits and income from work (*Hansard*, 14 March 1996, col 755) they are affected both by changes to the tax system and by benefits policy.

An analysis of the changes to both the tax and benefit systems since 1979 (Redmond and Sutherland, 1995) confirms that the combined effect of tax and social security changes through the 1980s has been to reduce low and middle incomes in relation to those at the top. Social security reforms since 1979 have reduced the level and coverage of benefits (see Chapter 6) and, along with the change in uprating policy, have exacerbated income inequality (Atkinson, 1994).

Social security's role in relation to the labour market has become one of pushing unemployed people into low paying employment. For example, the introduction of the jobseeker's allowance cut the period of national insurance benefit entitlement to the unemployed from twelve to six months and put even more stringent criteria on entitlement to force claimants to accept very low wages or lose their benefits (see Chapter 12). At the same time the topping up of such wages through income support or family credit have provided huge subsidies to employers. This cost the taxpayer nearly £4 billion in 1996/97 and it has been estimated that it might rise to nearly £6 billion by the year 2000 – equivalent to an extra 2 pence on the basic rate of income tax (Labour Party, 1996).

The lack of coordination between the tax and benefit systems has created a punitive poverty trap for those on in-work benefits, with some facing huge marginal tax rates: for every extra pound in earned income, up to 97 pence may be lost in tax, national insurance and benefit withdrawal. In the earnings top-up scheme being piloted at the time of writing, which extends family credit to couples without children, it has been estimated that withdrawal rates could reach 124 per cent (Redmond and Sutherland, 1995).

TAXES AND WEALTH

Overall, earnings from employment make up a decreasing proportion of non-benefit income. In 1978 wages and salaries accounted for 66 per cent of household 'market' income but this had dropped to 54 per cent by 1995. Especially important for the richest households has been the increase in income from rents, dividends and interest on savings, which represents 10 per cent of their household income (Atkinson, 1996). This has increased overall inequality because it is more unevenly distributed than earnings (Goodman and Webb, 1994).

Personal wealth nearly doubled in real terms between 1977 and 1992 and its distribution, which had been narrowing until the mid-1970s, has remained largely unchanged since 1979. The wealthiest tenth of adults still own around half of all personal wealth. The wealth owned by the richest 1 per cent of the population fell by 3 per cent between 1979 and 1993, but the share taken by the next richest 1 per cent increased by 1 per cent, and the share taken by the next 4 per cent of wealth owners increased by 2 per cent (Inland

Revenue, 1996). So the losses of the top 1 per cent were simply redistributed within the top 5 per cent of wealth owners. Meanwhile, half of the adult population still owns only 7 per cent of the nation's wealth, less than half of the share taken by the most wealthy 1 per cent.

Wealth in the form of interest-bearing accounts is the most common and evenly distributed, but their value can be very small. As we move up the wealth scale, the incidence of these accounts falls and that represented by residential property rises: wealthier groups hold the bulk of their wealth in shares and assets such as land. As well as being the most commonly held form of wealth, interest bearing accounts, are the most heavily taxed (Banks *et al*, 1994). Shares and equities have much more preferential tax treatment. The investment income surcharge was abolished in 1984 and tax free investment has been positively encouraged in recent years in the form of tax exempt special savings accounts (TESSAs) and personal equity plans (PEPs) which are concentrated among higher income households.

Meanwhile, the scope of the two major taxes on wealth, inheritance tax and capital gains tax, has been progressively restricted since 1979. In 1995 these two taxes accounted for 2.4 per cent of total government revenue compared to 3.1 per cent in 1979.

While transfers in the form of access to benefits for the poor are restricted, transfers in the form of tax allowances on wealth and profits have been extended. In 1996/97 tax relief on occupational and personal pensions amounted to £10 billion. Profit and share-related schemes received £1 billion in allowances and another £1 billion was foregone on inheritance and capital gains tax allowances. The only form of allowances falling in value from 1995 to 1996 was mortgage interest relief, which is one of the allowances most likely to benefit even those on low incomes (Inland Revenue, 1996).

These trends in the growth and taxation of personal wealth since 1979 have added to income inequality, albeit in a less significant way than direct and indirect tax changes, and have served to tip the balance of taxation further in favour of richer households. The overall effect of changes in the structure of taxation shows that the poorest fifth paid more of their income in tax – 27 per cent in 1983 versus 39 per cent in 1995 – than the richest fifth – 41 per cent in 1983 versus 36 per cent in 1995. The basic principle of fairness and progressivity in the tax system has been abandoned and, since 1979, tax policy has increasingly become a mechanism for increasing inequality.

CONCLUSION

Urgent change is needed in both the tax and social security systems to redress the adverse impact they have had on levels of poverty and inequality since 1979. Such changes include:

- reforms in capital taxes so that unearned income makes a bigger contribution to the system;
- reform of direct taxes so that they reflect ability to pay by, for example, substantially increasing personal allowances, reducing the starting rate of tax, extending the reduced rate band and introducing higher rates for higher incomes. The upper earnings limit on national insurance contributions should be abolished;
- reform of the indirect tax system in particular reducing the rate of VAT on fuel as a matter of priority;
- reform of the social security system to make sure that, along with labour market policy, it acts as a mechanism of social protection and integration rather than a means of intensifying social exclusion.

While all these measures are necessary, by themselves they would not redress the underlying causes of inequality. The problems of poverty and inequality must be tackled at source through the introduction of a national minimum wage and improved access to work for the excluded via better training, childcare and employment policies.

REFERENCES

Atkinson, A (1994) *Seeking to Explain the Distribution of Income,* STICERD.
Atkinson, A (1996) 'Seeking to explain the distribution of income', in Hills (ed), *New Inequalities: The Changing Distribution of Income and Wealth,* CUP.
Bank of England (1996) *Inflation Report,* August, Bank of England.
Banks, J, Dilnot, A and Low, H (1994) *Distribution of Wealth in the UK,* IFS Commentary No 45.
Bryson, A and Marsh, A (1996) *Leaving Family Credit,* DSS.
DSS (1996a) *Family Credit Quarterly Statistics,* Press Release, February, DSS.
DSS (1996b) *Households Below Average Income 1979-1993/4,* HMSO.
Giles, C and Johnson, P (1994) 'Tax reform in the UK and changes in the progressivity of the tax system', *IFS,* Vol 15 No 3, pp64-86.
Goodman, A and Webb, S (1994) 'For richer for poorer: the changing distribution of income in the UK, 1961-91', *IFS,* vol 15, no 4, November, pp29-63.
Gregg, P and Wadsworth, J (1994) 'More work in fewer households' in

Hills (ed) *New Inequalities: The Changing Distribution of Income and Wealth*, CUP.

Harkness, L (1996) 'The gender earnings gap: evidence from the UK', *IFS*, Vol 17, No 2, May, pp1-36.

Her Majesty's Treasury (1996) *Financial Statement and Budget Report 1997/8*, HMSO.

Hills, J (1995) *Joseph Rowntree Foundation Inquiry Into Income and Wealth*, Vol 2, Joseph Rowntree Foundation.

Hutton, W (1995) *The State We're In*, Jonathon Cape.

IDS (1996) *Is the Labour Market Really All That Flexible?*, Report 724, Incomes Data Services, November.

IFS (1994) 'More indirect taxes', *IFS Update*, Spring/Summer, p3.

Inland Revenue (1996) *Inland Revenue Statistics*, HMSO.

Labour Party (1996) *The Cost of In Work Benefits*, Labour Party Press Release, December.

Low Pay Network (1995) *Wages Council Abolition: The Official Statistics*, The Low Pay Network.

Low Pay Unit (1995) Arguments for a National Minimum Wage, TUC.

Low Pay Unit (1996) 'Coming apart at the seams', *The New Review*, No 42, November/December, pp8-10.

Meager, N, Court, G and Moralee, J (1996) 'Self employment and the distribution of income', in Hills, J (ed), *New Inequalities: The Changing Distribution of Income and Wealth*, CUP.

ONS (1996a) *Family Expenditure Survey 1995/96*, HMSO.

ONS (1996b) *Labour Force Survey*, Spring, Quantime.

ONS (1996c) *Labour Market Trends*, October.

ONS (1996d) *UK National Accounts*, HMSO.

Redmond and Sutherland, H (1995) *How Has Tax and Social Security Policy Changed Since 1978? A Distributional Analysis*, University of Cambridge.

Sutherland, H (1995) 'Minimum wage benefits', *New Economy*, 214, pp214-19.

Webb, S, Kemp, M and Millar, J (1996) *The Changing Face of Low Pay in Britain*, University of Bath.

4 Poverty and social exclusion in Europe

Robert Walker

It is increasingly apparent that the traditional concept of poverty provides an inadequate description of the circumstances of the tens of millions of people who do not receive an adequate share of Europe's growing wealth.

Typically the poor have been contrasted with the non-poor as if the two groups comprised fixed classes in an hierarchically organised society. While class continues to influence life chances, it is equally true that many poor people swap places with the non-poor and even, albeit much less frequently, with the affluent. As a consequence, the proportion of the European population who experience a shortfall in resources is far greater than indicated by much cited poverty rates. On the other hand, the number of people who are condemned to a lifetime of penury is thankfully considerably smaller than one might guess by taking the same poverty rates at face value.

It is probable that poverty has always been characterised by much social mobility. It is also possible, however, that the pace of social dynamics has accelerated in recent times. The various demands of technological development, world trade and political ideology have certainly created a labour market characterised by less stable forms of employment. The prospect of a 'job for life' has become anachronistic in many parts of the labour market, while the risk of hard times around the corner has begun to spread to groups of skilled, unionised and white-collar workers who were previously largely immune to the vagaries of labour demand (Walker, 1996a).

The traditional concept of poverty smacks, too, of a late Victorian, liberal view of society in which 'a mass of atomised individuals

[were] engaged in competition within the market place' and where 'the goal of social policy was to ensure that each person had sufficient resources to be able to survive in this competitive arena' (Room, 1995). It is true that the market still enjoys pride of place and that other social institutions come a poor second, that individual self reliance is contrasted with dependency on the state, that obligations to work are increasingly enforced and that tax cuts are given higher priority than improved public services. But the welfare institutions developed over the last century remain largely intact and continue, by their very presence, to convey rights to the majority of the population which in some countries are enshrined in law. Poverty, with its focus on the lack of disposable income, does not take account of the denial, or non-realisation, of these citizenship rights (Room, 1991).

As indicated in the Introduction to this volume, social exclusion, although a weasel term that can sometimes seem to mean anything and everything (Walker, 1995a), does draw attention to the denial of rights and to the failure of the various social systems that underpin modern life (Berghman, 1995):

> the democratic and legal system which promotes civic integration; the labour market which promotes economic integration; the welfare state system, promoting what may be called social integration; the family and community system, which promotes interpersonal integration.

Unlike the term poverty, the use of which encourages the practice of 'blaming the poor', social exclusion emphasises society's role in *excluding* certain people from full participation. It is ironic, therefore, that European discourse should have alighted on the concept of social exclusion at a time when market trends, including the creation of a single European market and currency, are generating more inequality and insecurity and there is an apparent loss of support for social protection (Freeman, 1996; Walker and Simpson, 1993).

This chapter begins with the traditional, static measures of poverty before attempting to marshal evidence on social exclusion and poverty dynamics. While aspiring to include all 15 Member States of the European Union, data limitations mean that this is rarely possible.[1]

---

1. See Walker and Simpson (1993) and Bradshaw and Chen (1997) for more information on Eastern Europe.

THE INCIDENCE OF POVERTY

There is not space to rehearse arguments about the best measure of poverty. Suffice it to say that all the measures used are relative; some are income based indices – which index potential command over resources – and others expenditure based – that indicate the extent to which people are sharing the living standards of their peers.

COUNTING THE POOR

Figure 4.1 presents poverty rates for 11 European countries at three points during the 1980s based on analyses undertaken by the European Commission. The threshold used is individual expenditure below 50 per cent of the national equivalised average. At no time and in no place were less than 5.9 per cent of people counted as poor (Belgium in 1985), while the European average rested at around 15 per cent. Higher rates were evident in the geographically more peripheral countries, notably those bordering on the Mediterranean, but also in Britain. During the early 1980s poverty fell in Spain, Greece and France but rose markedly in Britain and to a lesser extent elsewhere. Poverty rates at the end of the 1980s were typically higher than in 1985 although a fall was recorded in The Netherlands.[2]

Poverty estimates are notoriously sensitive to the definition used and Table 4.1 compares figures for the late 1980s based on expenditure and total income. In most countries the poverty rate is higher when expenditure is used which suggests that the non-poor have more to spend than is indicated by their cash income. However, the reverse is true in The Netherlands, and especially in Britain, where poorer people seem to spend a disproportionately high proportion of their income (see Chapter 3). Indeed, on the basis of incomes, Britain in the late 1980s had the highest poverty rate in Europe but came fifth behind Italy, Spain, Greece and Portugal when expenditure was used.

---

2. According to micro level data, poverty in Britain grew at three times the rate shown in Figure 4.1 (Hagenaars, de Vos and Zaidi, 1994).

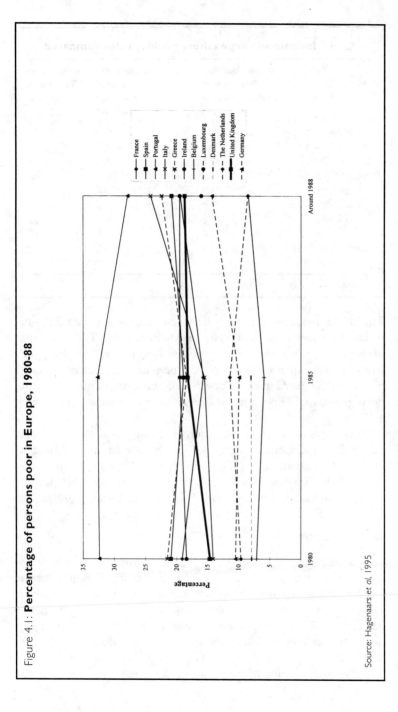

Figure 4.1: **Percentage of persons poor in Europe, 1980-88**

Source: Hagenaars *et al*, 1995

TABLE 4.1: **Income and expenditure poverty rates compared**

	Income less than 50 per cent of national average equivalent	Expenditure less than 50 per cent of national average equivalent	Less than 50 per cent for both
United Kingdom (1988)	22.4	17.0	12.4
Portugal (1990)	20.2	26.5	14.5
Greece (1988)	18.6	20.8	–
Ireland (1987)	14.2	16.1	7.6
France (1989)	14.0	14.9	6.2
Spain (1988)	12.9	17.5	6.8
Italy (1988)	12.8	22.0	10.7
The Netherlands (1988)	7.4	6.2	1.7
Luxembourg (1987)	5.1	9.2	2.2
Belgium (1987-8)	–	7.5	–

Source: Ramprakash, 1994

The above measures of poverty deliberately discount the substantial variations in living standards between Member States. Taking account of these by defining poverty in relation to average European Community expenditure (in 1985) presents a radically different picture of the distribution of poverty: on this basis 70 per cent of the Portuguese, and 33 per cent of Greeks were defined as poor (Figure 4.2).

Returning to an income measure, but one based on households rather than individuals, Figure 4.3 shows that Britain retained its unenviable reputation as a high poverty country into the first years of the 1990s. Indeed, over twice as many households were poor in Britain than in Belgium, Denmark, Italy, The Netherlands or Sweden.

WHO IS POOR?

One is used to thinking of the poor being comprised largely of the elderly, the unemployed and, to a lesser extent, of single parents. Generally this is true throughout Europe but Figure 4.4, which shows the risk of poverty by family type, offers an alternative perspective. While older people constitute the largest group among the poor it is evident that in most countries social insurance means that pensioners are no more at risk of experiencing poverty than other groups (although, importantly, they may experience it for

Figure 4.2: **Percentage of persons with expenditure less than 50 per cent of EC mean equivalent expenditure, 1985**

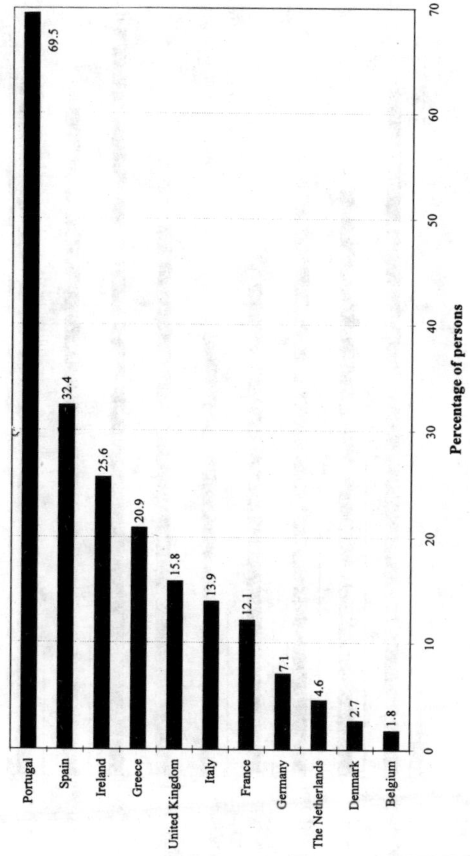

Country	Percentage of persons
Portugal	69.5
Spain	32.4
Ireland	25.6
Greece	20.9
United Kingdom	15.8
Italy	13.9
France	12.1
Germany	7.1
The Netherlands	4.6
Denmark	2.7
Belgium	1.8

Source: EC, 1990

Figure 4.3: **Households with incomes below 50 per cent of average national equivalent income**

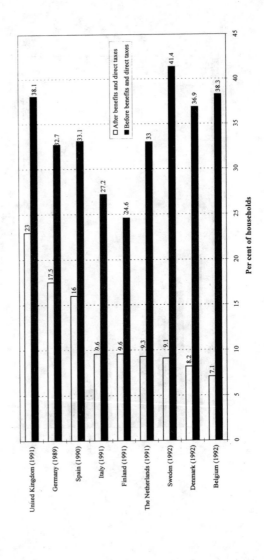

Source: Bradshaw and Chen, 1997

Figure 4.4: **Types of household having equivalent post benefit and direct tax income below 50 per cent of the national average**

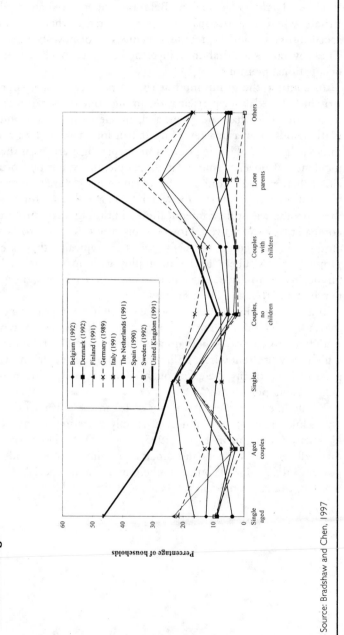

Source: Bradshaw and Chen, 1997

longer). The exceptions are lone pensioners in Sweden and Finland, and the elderly in general in Belgium, and most dramatically, in Britain where it is occupational pensions rather than compulsory social insurance which provide a lifeline out of poverty in old age. The coverage of social insurance, however, is much wider than occupational pensions.

In contrast, the group most at risk of poverty is lone parents. In Britain (where labour participation among lone parents is unusually low) more than half are poor and, in Germany, Spain and The Netherlands, over a quarter. Only Italian lone parents face a lower than average risk of being poor. More surprising, perhaps, is the high incidence of poverty among single people, many, but by no means all, of them young. Around a fifth of single people are in poverty in seven of the nine countries for which there are data. A proportion of these people will still be in education and thus their poverty may be comparatively short lived. However, disadvantage tends to coalesce around single people in many societies: typically they are disproportionately likely to be unemployed, homeless, mentally or physically ill, to have a criminal record or to have experienced family disruption as a child or subsequently.

It is worth noting that the presence of children noticeably increases the risk of couples being in poverty in Britain and Italy. In the Scandinavian countries, perhaps as a result of the family policies for which they are renowned, children have no impact on the risk of poverty. In Germany, the effect of children is actually to decrease the risk of being poor.

While unemployment is a major factor in the poverty of families with children, low pay is almost invariably more important, even in Germany (Strengmann-Kuhn, 1995). The extent of low pay varies markedly across Europe, constrained by minimum wages and union power (OECD, 1996), but is highest in Britain, especially among women, young people and workers in retailing (Table 4.2).

TABLE 4.2: **Low pay in European countries**

Percentage of full time workers who earn less than two-thirds median full time earnings

	Sex		Age		Industrial sector		Total
	Men	Women	Under 25	55 and over	Manufacturing	Wholesale/ retail	
United Kingdom (1994)	12.8	31.2	45.8	22.9	17.8	36.1	19.6
France (1995)	10.6	17.4	49.5	10.5	11.5	22.6	13.3
Germany (1994)	7.6	25.4	50.4	5.4	10.6[1]	22.9	13.3
Austria (1993)	7.0	22.8	19.5	9.6	10.9	23.8	13.2
Italy (1993)	9.3	18.5	27.0	7.4	14.2[1]	24.2	12.5
Netherlands (1994)	–	–	–	–	10.8	24.4	11.9
Belgium (1993)	3.9	24.2	22.2	4.9	5.1	15.7	7.2
Finland (1994)	3.3	8.7	27.1	4.4	4.0	11.1	5.9
Sweden (1993)	3.0	8.4	18.7	2.9	–	–	5.2

1. Manufacturing and construction
Source: OECD (1996)

POVERTY DYNAMICS

The story so far has been based on a series of snapshots. No account has been taken of the turnover of the poor population or whether this varies from one country to another. If countries do differ in these respects it may be that we are not comparing instances of the same kind of phenomenon.

PREVALENCE OF POVERTY[3]

Comprehensive analysis of poverty dynamics must await the 'Europanel' initiated by Eurostat in 1994. However, some facts are already known. For example, as Oppenheim discussed earlier, it is clear that

---

3. As a technical term, prevalence is defined as the proportion of the population who experience poverty over a given period of time. It is the longitudinal equivalent of the cross-sectional measure of incidence. For a fuller discussion, see Walker (1994).

significant numbers of poor families escape poverty at least temporarily from one year to the next and are replaced by variable flows of newcomers. The British Household Panel Study shows that one half of individuals with incomes below half average will have moved out of 'poverty' a year later, although only three per cent of these will enjoy an above average income. Moreover, the dynamics of the poverty population did differ between countries at least in the late 1980s. Turnover at that time – that is, flows in and out of poverty (Table 4.3, columns 4 and 5) – seemed particularly marked in The Netherlands and Lorraine (in France) compared with Germany, Ireland or Luxembourg which suggests that the average time spent in poverty was less in the two countries.

TABLE 4.3: **Poverty dynamics among families with children in European countries, mid to late 1980s**

Country	Poverty rate[1]	3 year poverty rate[2]	3 year rate as percentage of annual rate	Percentage becoming poor each year[3]	Percentage leaving poverty each year[4]
	(1)	(2)	(3)	(4)	(5)
France (Lorraine)	4.0	1.6	40	2.0	27.5
Germany (all)	7.8	1.5	24	3.1	25.6
(German)	6.7	1.4	21	2.7	26.9
(Foreigners)	18.0	4.0	22	5.9	20.0
Ireland	11.0	na	na	na	25.2
Luxembourg	4.4	0.4	9	1.7	26.0
The Netherlands	2.7	0.4	15	na	44.4
Sweden	2.7	na	na	0.7	36.8

1 Percentage with incomes of less than 50 per cent of median national equivalent income.
2 Poor in each of three years. This is not the same as long-term poverty since a family leaving in year T1 and counted as being poor in one of the three years might have been poor in every previous year.
3 Percentage of those with incomes of 60 per cent or more of the median in year T having an income of less than 50 per cent of the median in T+1.
4 Percentage of those with incomes of less than 50 per cent of the median in year T having an income of 60 per cent or more in year T+1.

Source: Duncan et al, 1993

The time that people spend in poverty is a function of the total volume of poverty existing in a country and its distribution across the population. Although in the late 1980s the poverty rate in The Netherlands, for example, was only about half that in Ireland, the figures in Table 4.3 suggest that the proportion of the Dutch population that experienced poverty at *some* time was a good deal closer to the level in Ireland. The reason for this is that, other things being equal, short spells of poverty mean that a fixed volume of poverty is spread more evenly over a larger proportion of the population than is the case when poverty is long-term, and necessarily concentrated on a small number of people. In 1990s Britain, twice as many people experience poverty at some time over a four year period (31 per cent) than will be counted as poor in any given month.[4]

PATTERNS OF POVERTY

The factor that may not be equal in the above comparison between Dutch and Irish poverty is the extent to which the same people suffer repeated spells of poverty. Information is not readily available for The Netherlands or Ireland, but the evidence in Britain and elsewhere suggests that repeated spells are a frequent occurrence (Jarvis and Jenkins, 1996). Moreover, the patterning of spells may in fact constitute different experiences or types of poverty (Ashworth, Hill and Walker, 1994).

Researchers in both Germany (Buhr et al, 1991) and Sweden (Salonen, 1993) have isolated different social assistance careers using long runs of administrative data that may reflect these different patterns of poverty. Over a five year period Salonen identified people who needed assistance to cover a single short-term contingency, occasional users claiming once or for very short spells, sporadic users requiring assistance on several occasions, recurrent claimants making repeated long lived claims and permanent users. Occasional, sporadic and recurrent users respectively comprised 42, 19 and 21 per cent of the total caseload.

Adequate information has yet to become available in Britain that might enable the conceptual differentiation of poverty and facilitate comparison with other European countries. However, we know that 29 per cent of people who leave poverty return within a year,[5] and that just under a fifth of lone parents and unemployed recipients of income support reclaim benefit within six months (Shaw et al, 1996). It is also evident that, in Britain as elsewhere, short and repeated

---

4. This figure understates the number of people experiencing months in which income falls beneath 50 per cent of average income since months between the four annual waves of the BHPS are excluded from this analysis.

5. Poverty defined as 50 per cent of average equivalent income; figure recalculated from Jarvis and Jenkins, 1996.

spells of poverty are much more common than the persistent or permanent poverty implied by traditional class-based concep-tualisation. Just 4 per cent of people were income poor in each of the first four years of the British Household Panel Study; this represents only 14 per cent of those who were poor at any time between 1990/1 and 1993/4 (Jarvis and Jenkins, 1996).[6]

However, attention has nevertheless tended to focus on persistent poverty, partly because of concern that it is associated with crime, social unrest, the development of an underclass, and the abuse of welfare benefits. Long-term poverty is difficult to measure but Table 4.3 (column 2) shows the proportion of families that were poor in three consecutive years during the 1980s. It is evident that long-term poverty was higher in France and Germany than in either Luxembourg or The Netherlands. The corresponding figure for Britain, five or so years later, is at least double that in Germany and seven times that in The Netherlands (Jarvis and Jenkins, 1996).[7]

TRIGGERING POVERTY

Research has begun to move beyond generic causes of poverty (broadly divided between theories that emphasise structural causes of poverty and those that give greater weight to individual charac-teristics) to focus on the factors that precipitate spells (Figure 4.5).

A study of five European countries during the late 1980s revealed that a reduction in employment within the household was an important factor in all of the countries. This was also often associated with life-course changes such as retirement or childbirth. However, the degree of inter-country variation is striking and not instantly explicable. Note, for example, the importance of falls in employment triggering poverty in Sweden and Luxembourg. One might initially presume that contingencies associated with reduced employment were relatively more common in Sweden and Luxembourg than elsewhere, or that their social welfare systems were less well developed to cope with them. However, an alternative proposition might be that the welfare systems in these two societies had systems that were

---

6. Strictly, at the time of any of the four survey interviews between 1990/1 and 1993/4.

7. Jarvis and Jenkins estimate that 7 per cent of persons in families with children were poor throughout a three year period but the measure of poverty used is 50 per cent of the mean (£127) which is more generous than the median (£109) used by Duncan *et al*, 1993.

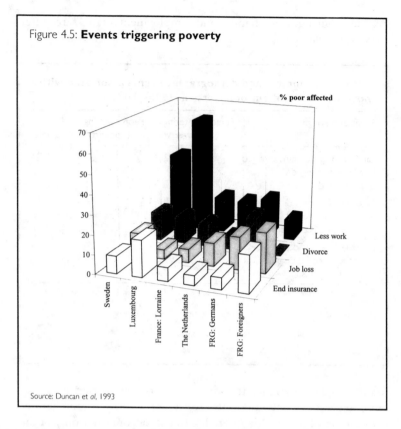

Figure 4.5: **Events triggering poverty**

Source: Duncan et al, 1993

better able to protect people against the other social risks, such as unemployment, which triggered a higher proportion of new spells of poverty in Germany and The Netherlands.

The importance of institutional factors is further reinforced by the impact of social insurance rules in Luxembourg and among foreigners in Germany; in each case a fifth of new spells of poverty appear to have been triggered by the exhaustion of insurance entitlement.

Unfortunately there is as yet no directly comparable information for Britain. What we do know, however, is that people moving into poverty are much more likely than other people to have recently experienced changes in their economic or family status or both (Table 4.4). Economic change is the more important, perhaps implicated in three or four times as many episodes of poverty than the loss of an adult through death, separation or leaving home, although changes in family and employment status are often inextricably linked.

TABLE 4.4: **Economic and demographic events associated with movements in and out of poverty in 1990s Britain**

Event occurring	Persons entering poverty[1]	People leaving poverty[2]	Total sample[3]
Family economic status changed	43	32	24
Family type changed	14	11	9
Both changed	10	6	4
Number of earners decreased	30	15	13
Earners remained the same	56	67	76
Number of earners increased	14	18	11
Number of adults decreased	14	6	6
Adults remained the same	79	85	86
Number of adults increased	7	9	8

1 Having income equal or above 50 per cent of mean national equivalent income in year T1 but below it in T+1.
2 Having income less than 50 per cent of mean national equivalent income in year T1 but higher in year T+1.
3 Average of the three transitions between four survey waves.

Source: Jarvis and Jenkins (1996) based on analysis of the British Household Panel Survey.

Many people experience the kind of events which trigger poverty but comparatively few suffer poverty as a result. Any comprehensive explanation of poverty therefore has to take account not only of the probability that any particular event occurs, but also of the probability that the event triggers a spell of poverty.

ROUTES OUT OF POVERTY

Figure 4.6 and Table 4.4 reveal that employment provides the most effective route out of poverty. The British data suggest that nearly forty per cent of people leaving poverty do so as a result of one or more members of their family obtaining work or increasing their hours of employment. Similar or higher numbers appear to do likewise in other European countries (Figure 4.6), although it is notable that in the late 1980s marriage accounted for a tenth of moves out of poverty in Germany. In Britain, family changes appear to play a minor role and, indeed, stability in household composition may have a benign influence. In Germany, and to a lesser extent in

The Netherlands, a small though significant number of people escape poverty as the result of receiving social insurance; this is a cause for concern since it points to delays in the payment of benefits (Leisering and Walker, 1997).

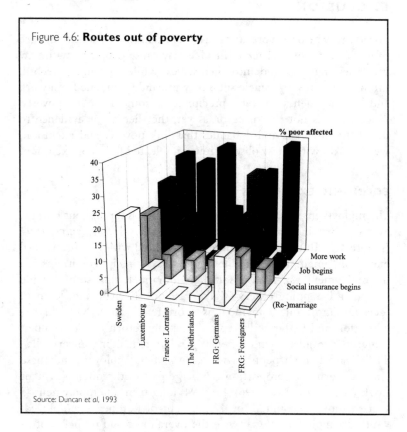

Figure 4.6: **Routes out of poverty**

Source: Duncan et al, 1993

Insofar as these findings show that significant numbers of people escape from poverty, they counter the more fatalist approaches to poverty management which view alleviation as the only attainable policy goal. They are also consistent with the growing consensus which emphasises proactive policies that aim to assist people to return to employment.[8] On the other hand, a proportion of those

---

8. Employment may not be an acceptable solution to poverty among the older people or those with disabilities. Insertion policies need to take note of the large number of jobs that are acquired through informal networks (Bottomley, McKay and Walker, 1997).

who leave poverty are destined to return and may simply be living out a specific form of occasional or recurrent poverty.

EXCLUSION

Poverty may be both a precursor of social exclusion and a consequence of it (Walker, 1995a). Lack of finance may cause people to withdraw into their families and into themselves, while a criminal record, immigrant status or homelessness may preclude someone from work and self-sufficiency, thereby precipitating some form of poverty. Since there is not the space or, as yet, the theory[9] or evidence to detail the processes and dynamics that link poverty and exclusion, we make do with a few observations on selected forms of exclusion.

ECONOMIC EXCLUSION

Unemployment remains at historically high levels throughout Europe, even in Britain where rates have fallen considerably since 1993 (Figure 4.7). But while undoubtedly associated with increased social exclusion, unemployment does not always precipitate it. Instead unemployment serves as a social membrane letting some people escape and trapping others (Walker, 1996b). Even in the depth of recession most unemployment is short term. Those with higher education and better skills typically rapidly return to work (albeit sometimes to jobs paying lower wages and demanding lower skills). They leave behind people with less to offer employers and these come to form a disproportionately large part of the unemployment stock (Ashworth *et al*, 1996). In 1994, long term unemployment (a year or more) accounted for 47 per cent of Europe's unemployed, youth unemployment was twice the overall rate and 60 per cent of those aged over 55 had been out of work for over a year and about 15 per cent for four years or more (EC,1995).

The options facing the unemployed are limited. Across Europe 50 per cent of the unemployed who find work return to temporary jobs (20 per cent in Britain, 85 per cent in Spain) although such work constitutes only 10 per cent of all employment; just 7 per cent of people with temporary jobs do not want a permanent post (EC,

---

9. Although see Jordan (1996) who has begun the process of theorising, focusing on the working of exclusive social groups within the framework of public choice theory.

Figure 4.7: **European unemployment 1973–96***

Percentage rate

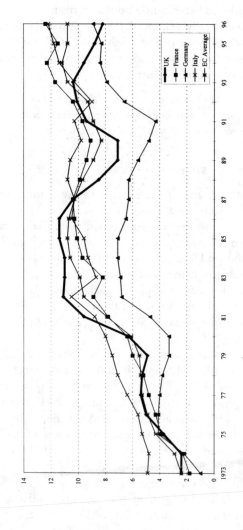

EC average relates to 9 until 1983, 12 until 1991 and then 15.

There are some discontinuities in the other series in the same years.

* August (seasonally adjusted)

1995). Ten per cent of men and 38 per cent of women return to part-time work; the fact that the former figure is two and a half times the overall proportion of men working part-time suggests that working part-time is not the outcome of unrestricted choice. Indeed, there is evidence in Britain that, despite active job search, the long-term unemployed benefit little from upturns in the economy as new jobs go to the already employed, the recently unemployed or to new entrants to the labour market (Ashworth *et al*, 1996). In Germany the chances of finding work among those out of work for two years can drop to one in ten (Kronauer, 1995):[10]

> Effectively excluded from the formal labour market, a proportion of the unemployed will engage in the informal economy, thereby risking prosecution and, thus, multiple exclusion.

SOCIAL EXCLUSION

Social assistance and homelessness are two indicators of social exclusion. These are now considered.

In Britain (and Ireland) social assistance has always been an important component of social welfare. Elsewhere in Europe, social insurance and (in Denmark) tax financed provisions have played the pivotal role as mechanisms of social solidarity and social cohesion. For someone to need to apply for social assistance is to fall outside the scope of such structures and the moral framework which they exemplify and may be taken as a prima facie case of social exclusion (Spicker, 1996).

Dependence on social assistance has increased markedly throughout Europe since 1980 although it still remains most important in Britain (Figure 4.8). The main reason for the growth of social assistance is rising unemployment causing more people to exhaust (or not acquire) entitlement to insurance benefits. In Germany and The Netherlands and some other countries it can also be attributed to cuts in social insurance benefits (Eardley *et al*, 1996). All countries have also witnessed increased spending on the basis of disability (although this reflects more generous provisions as well as substitution for inadequate unemployment protection). Similarly, lone parents make up an increasing proportion of social assistance claimants in many countries while at the same time claims from older people have generally been falling. Reunification and migration from Eastern

---

10. Measured over an 18 month period.

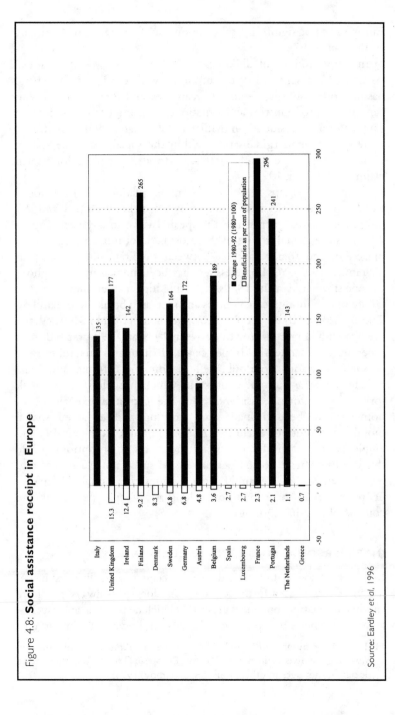

Figure 4.8: **Social assistance receipt in Europe**

Source: Eardley *et al*, 1996

Europe has put significant pressure on social assistance in Germany (Buhr *et al*, 1997).

In many, though not all contexts (Walker, 1995b), receipt of social assistance represents a loss of autonomy with the locus on control passing to the social assistance bureaucracy and social workers who can, in certain countries and situations, even impose obligations to support on non-resident kin (Millar and Warman, 1996). Sometimes, there is further marginalisation within the social assistance system itself as when, for example, staff cease to assist or place long term claimants (Walker, 1995b).

However, perhaps the most extreme manifestation of social exclusion is homelessness which may affect between 1.8 and 2.7 million individuals across the European Twelve in any year (Figure 4.9). It is the denial of one of the most basic of human rights and a breach of the social contract between the state and its citizens (Avramov, 1995). Yet homelessness has been increasing throughout Europe since at least the 1980s, reflecting higher unemployment, the failure of community care policies and increased break-up of families. Taking as a base those people who were sheltered and re-housed, the average annual rate of growth between 1989 and 1994 ranged from 5 per cent in Flanders to 16 per cent in Britain and Luxembourg.

Such variations no doubt reflect different national and local policies and the cultural context in which homeless people seek formal and informal assistance. But the common experience of homelessness, beyond inadequate housing and enforced spatial mobility, is multiple exclusion from community care, health and employment that erodes autonomy and closes down options. While this exclusion may not be permanent, as successful placement and resettlement schemes around Europe demonstrate, for many homeless people the road to re-inclusion is long and steep, especially in the context of housing shortages.[11]

INTERPERSONAL AND CIVIC EXCLUSION

In the same way that poverty does not necessarily result in exclusion (or vice versa), one form of exclusion does not always predicate another. Mediating influences presumably include personal and psycho-logical tendencies but institutions have been shown to be important.

11. In 1991 the number of households exceeded the number of 'good quality' dwellings in five countries out of the European Twelve but there were localised shortages in other countries (Avramov, 1995).

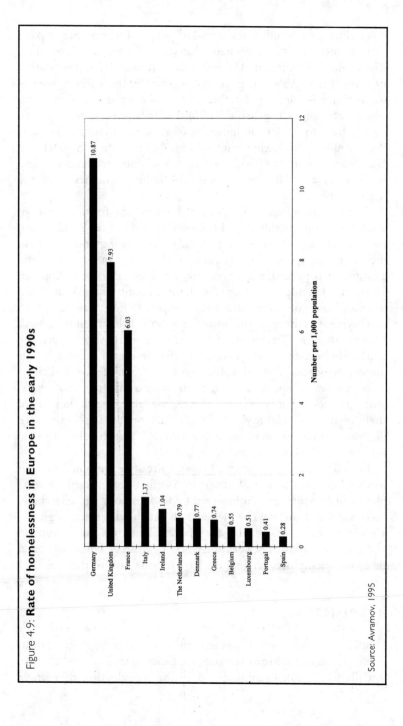

Figure 4.9: **Rate of homelessness in Europe in the early 1990s**

Source: Avramov, 1995

German and Swedish unemployed people, for example, make a clear distinction between insurance based benefits and social assistance. The former are legitimated by reference to reciprocity and restitution in ways that make them generally acceptable; the latter is seen as stigmatising (excluding) because of its connotations with poverty and destitution (Clasen *et al*, 1996). In Britain, most unemployed people have to accept the indignity of assistance that may be made slightly more bearable by being ubiquitous. Likewise, in Sweden and Germany training and work experience schemes confer status and hope, whereas in Britain government training schemes share the stigma of benefit.

Families are differentially protected against the financial costs of unemployment in different European countries. In Sweden and Germany families have to forgo holidays and eating out; in Britain they cut down on eating (Clasen *et al*, 1996). In each case the adjustment is painful, and necessarily involves some restrictions on socialising. Unemployed people in all three countries feel humiliated by their lack of work and long maintain their attachment to employment as the way back into 'the system'. It has been suggested, though, that in Germany the majority of men who experience extremely long-term unemployment give up on the regular labour market (Kronauer, 1995). Unable to participate in the 'work society' or to find an accepted role, some retreat into isolation and others, with the support of wives and relatives, are 'able to uphold parts of their own social identity'. In Britain, the temptation is to work illicitly in order to supplement low benefits, and thereby to risk a form of civic exclusion (Jordan *et al*, 1992).

Indeed, Britain's unemployed mostly already experience another form of civic exclusion. Whereas in Sweden, for example, unemployment benefits are administered by trade unions and elsewhere, such as in Germany and The Netherlands, the social partners negotiate a social wage, in Britain the unemployed are largely de-unionised and have no say in the world of work. Consistent with the liberal tradition unemployed individuals have to look out for themselves.

RESPONSES

Despite Europe's wealth, poverty and exclusion in their various forms are rampant. Moreover, they are likely to increase and change, initially as a result of adjustments to the introduction of a single currency and later in response to demographic pressures (Walker and Simpson, 1993). Occasional and recurrent poverty may well spread among people of working age and permanent poverty could return to afflict older people as has already happened in Britain (Walker, 1995b). Additional reliance on social assistance may corrode the communal solidarity inherent in social insurance and further erode public support for social welfare.

But there is light within the gloom. A flexible labour market could act to redistribute poverty in the form of comparatively short spells over a larger proportion of the population. To the extent that permanent poverty is lessened and more people have an obvious stake in social security, this could act to reduce economic and civic exclusion. It might even encourage support for collective responses over individualistic ideology.[12]

In the longer term, social protection will be required at the European level to protect institutions and society as much as individuals (Berghman, 1996). Some economic readjustments which may be deemed necessary, notably the need to clear the labour market of inefficient workers, are nevertheless likely to be beyond the competence of Member States which are hemmed in by tight fiscal constraints. European institutions will be required to redistribute resources to be spent by Member States or other institutions according to the subsidiarity principle (Leibfried and Pierson, 1995).

In the more immediate future, reconceptualising poverty and exclusion as processes rather than states will, as shown above, result in a better understanding of the nature of the problems to be addressed. It also opens the door to policy strategies that are proactive and preventive rather than reactive and ameliorative. Figure 4.10 illustrates the scope for policies to stimulate and support transitions between different forms of work, between unemployment and employment, between education and employment, and between employment and domestic activities and retirement. In the past such transitions occurred only once in a person's life. Increasingly this will not be the case and creatively facilitating such transitions could help to achieve personal and collective goals, reducing poverty and exclusion in the long and short term.

---

12. Similar pressures could produce the opposite result. To the extent that shorter spells of poverty are easier than longer ones to bridge through the mechanism of personal saving, individualised private insurance might be preferred by the ideologue.

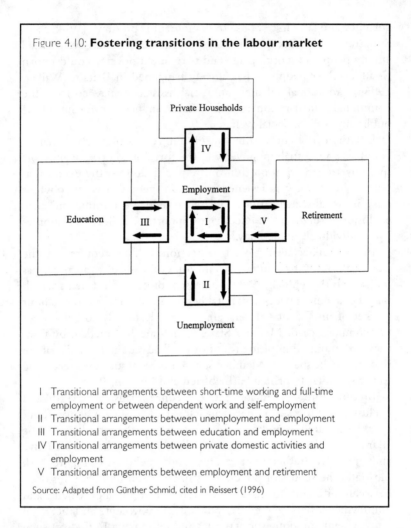

Figure 4.10: **Fostering transitions in the labour market**

Private Households

IV

Employment

Education III I V Retirement

II

Unemployment

I Transitional arrangements between short-time working and full-time employment or between dependent work and self-employment
II Transitional arrangements between unemployment and employment
III Transitional arrangements between education and employment
IV Transitional arrangements between private domestic activities and employment
V Transitional arrangements between employment and retirement

Source: Adapted from Günther Schmid, cited in Reissert (1996)

REFERENCES

Ashworth, K *et al* (1996) 'Time spent on income support by unemployed claimants', in Gregg, P (ed) *Labour Market and Income Dynamics*, Centre for Economic Performance.

Ashworth, K, Hill, M, and Walker, R (1994) 'Patterns of childhood poverty', *Journal of Policy Analysis and Management*, 13, 4.

Avramov, D (1995) *Homelessness in the European Union*, Feantsa, Brussels.

Berghman, J (1995) 'Social exclusion in Europe' in Room, G (ed) *Beyond the Threshold*, Policy Press.

Berghman, J (1996) *Social Protection and the Internal Market*, Paper presented at the 1996 Joint ETUC/ETUI Annual Conference, Brussels 7-8 November.

Bottomley, D, Walker, R and McKay, S (1997) *Unemployment and Jobseeking*, HMSO, forthcoming.

Bradshaw, J and Chen, J (1997) 'Poverty in the UK: a comparison with nineteen other countries', *Benefits*, 18

Buhr, P *et al* (1991) *Passages through Welfare*, Centre for Social Policy Research, Discussion Paper, 3, Bremen.

Buhr, P and Weber, A (1997) 'German social assistance after the fall of communism' in Leisering, L and Walker, R (eds) *The Dynamics of Modern Society*, Policy Press.

Clasen, J *et al* (1996) *Barriers to Employment and the Threat of Social Exclusion*, Centre for Research in Social Policy, Working Paper 273.

Duncan, G *et al* (1993) 'Poverty dynamics in eight countries', *Journal of Population Economics*, 6, pp295-234.

Eardley, T *et al* (1996) *Social Assistance in OECD Countries: Synthesis Report*, HMSO, Department of Social Security, Research Report, 46.

EC (1995) *Employment in Europe*, European Commission COM(95) 381, Luxembourg, p381.

Freeman, R (1996) *Work and Social Protection in the Age of Flexibility*, Paper presented at the 1996 Joint ETUC/ETUI Annual Conference, Brussels 7-8 November.

Hagenaars, A, de Vos, K, and Zaidi (1994) *Poverty Statistics in the Late 1980s*, European Commission (Eurostat), Luxembourg.

ISSA (1990) *Poverty in Figures: Europe in the early 1980s*, European Commission (Eurostat), Luxembourg.

Jarvis, S and Jenkins, S (1996) *Changing Places: Income Mobility and Poverty Dynamics in Britain*, ESRC Research Centre on Micro-social Change, Working Paper 96-19.

Jordan, B *et al* (1992) *Trapped in Poverty?*, Routledge.

Jordan, B (1996) *A Theory of Poverty and Social Exclusion*, Polity Press.

Kronauer, M (1995) *Exclusion on the Labour Market: Towards a new 'underclass'*, Paper given at a Conference on Empirical Poverty research, Bielefeld, 17-18 November.

Leibfried, S and Pierson, P (eds) (1995) *European Social Policy: Between Fragmentation and Integration*, Brookings Institution, Washington DC.

Leisering, L and Walker, R (1997) 'Social assistance dynamics: Anglo-German similarities and differences', submitted to the *Journal of European Social Policy*.

Lucifora, C *et al* (1996) *An International Comparison of Earnings Mobility: The Case of Italy and France*, Paper presented at a seminar on Labour Market Changes and Income Dynamics, Centre for Economic Performance, London, 18-19 March.

Millar, J and Warman, A (1996) *Family Obligations in Europe*, Family Policy

Studies Centre.

OECD (1996) *Employment Outlook*, OECD, Paris.

Ramprakash, D (1994) 'Poverty in the Countries of the European Union', *Journal of European Social Policy*, 4, 2, pp117–28.

Reissert, B (1996) *How are Social Protections Systems Coping with Change? A comparative approach*, Paper presented at the 1996 Joint ETUC/ETUI Annual Conference, Brussels 7–8 November.

Robbins, D (1994) *National Policies to Combat Social Exclusion Third Report of the EC Observatory on Policies to Combat Social Exclusion*, European Commission, Brussels.

Room, G et al (1991) *National Policies to Combat Social Exclusion: First Report of the EC Observatory on Policies to Combat Social Exclusion*, European Commission, Brussels.

Room, G et al (1992) *National Policies to Combat Social Exclusion Second Report of the EC Observatory on Policies to Combat Social Exclusion*, European Commission, Brussels.

Room, G (1995) 'Poverty and social exclusion', in Room, G (ed) *Beyond the Threshold*, Bristol.

Salonen, T (1993) *Margins of Welfare*, Hällestad Press, Torna.

Shaw, A et al (1996) *Moving off Income Support: barriers and bridges*, DSS Research Report 53, HMSO.

Spicker, P (1996) *The French Perspective On, and Understanding Of, Exclusion and Inclusion*, Paper presented at the ESRC Seminar on the Concepts of Social Exclusion, London, 15 March.

Strengmann-Kahn, W (1995) *Working or Living on State Transfers?*, Paper given at a Conference on Empirical Poverty Research, Bielefeld, 17–18 November.

Townsend, P (1993) *The International Analysis of Poverty*, Harvester Wheatsheaf.

Walker, R (1995a) 'The dynamics of poverty and social exclusion', in Room, G (ed) *Beyond the Threshold*, Policy Press.

Walker, R (1995b) 'Routes in and out of poverty over the life course' in Bayley, R, Condy, A and Roberts, C (eds) *Policies for Families: Work, Poverty and Resources*, Family Policy Studies Centre.

Walker, R (1996a) 'Rethinking poverty in a dynamic perspective' in Andress, H-J (ed) *Poverty Research in a Comparative Perspective*, Bielefeld: publication of conference papers.

Walker, R (1996b) *Unemployment, Welfare and Insurance*, Paper presented to the Geneva Association Seminar on Employment and Insurance, London, 15 May.

Walker, R and Simpson, R (eds) (1993) *Europe: for richer or poorer?*, CPAG.

ACKNOWLEDGEMENTS

Thank you to Sharon Walker for preparing the diagrams and Catherine O'Donnell (Low Pay Unit) for drawing my attention to data on low pay.

5 The growth of means testing
David Piachaud

The basic rate of income tax is now at its lowest rate for 60 years (see Chapter 3). By contrast, the extent of means testing is at a level never previously attained in British history. This chapter reviews the policies of Conservative governments since 1979 towards means testing. What were the policy intentions and what were the results? Has social security become more focused on those in need? Is it better run? Have incentives been improved?

CONSERVATIVE INTENTIONS

The 1979 Conservative Manifesto was largely supportive of social security.

> Child benefits are a step in the right direction ... One-parent families face much hardship so we will maintain the special addition for them ... Much has been done in recent years to help the disabled, but there is still a long way to go.

The Manifesto pledged to: 'do all we can to ... restore the incentive to work, reduce the poverty trap and bring more effective help to those in greatest need.' The 'earnings rule' – in effect a means test on retirement pensions – was to be phased out. There was no mention in the Manifesto of two of the most important changes that followed the 1979 election – the shift from earnings-indexation to price-indexation of pensions – and the abolition of the earnings-related supplement to unemployment benefit, sickness benefit and invalidity benefit.

The 1983 Conservative Manifesto was similarly supportive in tone: 'Our record shows the strength of our commitment'. The election was soon followed by the 'Fowler' review of social security which began: 'To be blunt the British social security system has lost its way'. The suggested approach to reform was to ensure that 'resources must be directed more effectively to the areas of greatest need', that the system should be simpler and better administered and that it 'must be designed to reinforce personal independence ... to widen, not restrict, peoples' opportunity to make their own choices; to encourage, not discourage, earning and saving'.

The Fowler reforms, enacted in the 1986 Social Security Act, were extolled in the 1987 Conservative Manifesto. The 1992 Manifesto recorded a 40 per cent increase in real expenditure on social security and went on:

> This extra help is more clearly focused on those groups with the greatest needs ... We have also sought to provide those on social security with better incentives to earn, and gain independence. All too often the old system created barriers to work and penalised the thrifty.

Thus, over the four terms of Conservative government, there has been increasing emphasis on directing resources to areas of greatest need. On the other hand a means-tested system has always been treated with caution. As the Fowler Green paper argued:

> A wholly means-tested approach to social security – including pensions and child benefit – would at best meet only one of the main objectives of social security to concentrate help on those who need it most. This approach would, by discouraging self-help and reducing incentives, undermine the importance of individual provision. Nor, in the Government's view, would a system which provided no benefits as of right to pensioners or families with children be acceptable. (Cmnd 9517, 1985, para 6.9)

So much for the intentions. What has been the record?

THE GROWTH OF MEANS TESTING

In 1979, 4.4 million people were provided for by supplementary benefit; in 1995, 9.8 million people, one-sixth of the population, depended on its successor, income support. Whereas 81,000 families received family income supplement in 1979, by 1995, 648,500 families were receiving its successor, family credit. In 1994/95, 31 per cent of households had at least one member who was in receipt of one or more of the major income-related benefits. There is no doubt that the number dependent on means-tested benefits has increased dramatically.

Expenditure on income-related benefits has also increased much faster than that for other benefits, from 17 per cent of all benefits in 1978/79 to some 30 per cent in 1995/96. Most remarkable has been the growth of family credit on which expenditure increased ten-fold (in money terms) in the decade up to 1995/96; in November 1995 there were 650,000 recipients getting an average amount of £55 per week. Total expenditure on family credit is now nearly £2 billion per annum, compared to child benefit expenditure of under £7 billion. Half of family credit recipients work in catering, cleaning, hairdressing and other personal services – services now heavily subsidised by the state.

THE PATTERN OF GROWTH

While means testing increased under successive Conservative admini-strations, this expansion was far from uniform. There has not been a consistent approach to the main groups dependent on social security.

Among older people the number on supplementary benefit/ income support as a proportion of those on retirement pension declined from 23 per cent in 1979 to 17 per cent in 1993.

The proportions of those receiving income support varies between groups of beneficiaries (see Table 5.1); the majority of short-term sick people, lone-parent families and unemployed people who were receiving benefits now depend on income support. Even during the 1990s dependence on income support has increased for most groups, as shown in Table 5.1.

TABLE 5.1: **Proportion of beneficiaries receiving income support**

	1990/91	1994/95
Elderly people	15%	18%
Long-term sick/disabled people	24%	30%
Short-term sick people	48%	61%
Lone-parent families	66%	65%
Unemployed people	79%	86%

Source: Cm 3213 (March 1996) Table 7.

THE TARGETING OF SOCIAL SECURITY

Has the increase in dependence on means-tested benefits resulted in social security being more effectively targeted on lower income groups? This question is analysed in Table 5.2 which is derived from the annual account of the incidence of taxes and benefits.

TABLE 5.2: **Distribution of cash benefits**

	Quintile groups of households ranked by equivalised disposable income					
	1	2	3	4	5	All
(a) Cash benefits as % of average cash benefits						
1979	177	136	90	57	40	100
1994/95	151	145	103	63	38	100
(b) Cash benefits as % of disposable income						
1979	78	35	16	8	4	17
1994/95	79	51	23	10	4	20
(c) Equalised disposable income as % of average equivalised disposable income						
1979	47	67	89	117	80	100
1994/95	39	59	82	114	206	100

Sources: Author's calculations based on:
a. *Economic Trends* (March 1991) Table 1 (Appendix 4).
b. *Economic Trends* (December 1995) Table B.

Table 5.2(a) shows that the bottom quintile received much more than the average in cash benefits in both years but that, in 1994-95, it was much less relative to the average than in 1979. Taking the bottom two quintiles together, in 1979 they received 63 per cent of all cash benefits but in 1994/95 only 59 per cent of the total. More cash benefits were received by the third and fourth quintiles in 1994/95 but receipt by the top quintile declined. Overall, cash benefits have not become more effectively targeted.

Table 5.2(b) shows that cash benefits became more important generally, rising from 17 to 20 per cent of disposable income; in all quintiles save the top one, cash benefits rose as a proportion of disposable income.

Table 5.2(c) shows the increase in inequality of equivalised disposable income. The bottom four quintiles all fell relative to the average; there was a large increase in the top quintile. There has been a marked increase in inequality which was only slightly mitigated by the growth of social security.

THE WORKING OF MEANS TESTS

A common theme of Conservative intentions from the 1979 Manifesto onwards has been to simplify the system. How far have they improved take-up and reduced costs of administration; two beneficial outcomes that might have been expected to accompany a simpler system?

In Table 5.3 official estimates of take-up are shown both in terms of the proportion of those thought eligible who apply (caseload) and the proportion of potential expenditure paid out (expenditure).

TABLE 5.3: **Take-up of benefits**

	1979	Caseload 1993/94[c]	Expenditure 1993/94[c]
SB/income support	71[a]	79-88	89-95
Housing benefit	n.a.	88-96	92-97
FIS/family credit	51[b]	71	81

a. Official Report, 30 November 1983 WA Cols 533-6
b. Social Security Advisory Committee Report, 1983
c. *Social Security Statistics*, 1996, Tables H4.01–H4.03.

Although estimates of take-up present many difficulties (Marsh and McKay, 1993) and their comparison over time is still more difficult, it does seem that take-up rates for income support are now higher than they were for supplementary benefit and those for family credit are higher than they were for family income supplement. On the other hand, take-up rates for the main means-tested benefits remain substantially short of 100 per cent and, given the increase in eligibility, the number (as opposed to the proportion) of eligible non-claimants has probably risen.

Costs of administration are shown in Table 5.4. Despite the search for simplification and the pursuit of efficiency, the costs of administering means-tested benefits remain many times those of the main national insurance and non-contributory benefits. Unemployment benefit (now jobseeker's allowance) is the one national insurance benefit which is relatively expensive to administer. The cost emanates from the many checks and controls in the administration of all benefits to the unemployed, which are there to ensure they are actively seeking and available for work.

TABLE 5.4: **Costs of administration**

	Average weekly administration costs per beneficiary	Administrative costs as percentage of benefit expenditure
Non-means-tested benefits		
Retirement pension	£0.60	1.1%
Child benefit and one parent benefit	£0.40	2.2%
Sickness and invalidity benefit	£3.50	4.3%
Unemployment benefit	£6.20	11.7%
Means-tested benefits		
Family credit	£1.75	3.8%
Income support	£5.55	10.2%
Social fund	–	46.3%

Source: Cm3213 (March 1996) Figure 8.

EFFECTS ON INCENTIVES

One of the recurrent themes in Conservative Manifestos and policy documents has been the need to improve incentives and encourage paid work and saving. Among the main changes in the 1986 Social Security Act was the shift in the method of calculating the main means-tested benefits to avoid the worst extremes of the poverty trap. How far have incentives been improved?

The short answer is that they have not: overall, incentives for large numbers are worse than in 1979. The main reason is increased dependence on income support which, for most recipients, results in little or no gain whatsoever from any extra earnings or from any income from savings or occupational pension. While there have been some improvements such as the introduction of a childcare allowance for those on in-work benefits, other factors have worked against this, such as the increased number on low earnings and the increases in direct and indirect taxation (see Chapters 2 and 3). The number of earners facing marginal net income deduction rates of

100 per cent or over has fallen substantially, as shown in Table 5.5. But the number facing a poverty trap of over 60 per cent or over 80 per cent effective marginal tax rates has substantially increased.

TABLE 5.5: **Poverty trap for earners**

Marginal net income deduction rates	1985	1995/96
60% and over	450,000	630,000
80% and over	290,000	420,000
100% and over	70,000	10,000

Source: Cm 3213 (March 1996) Figure 19.

To illustrate this, in April 1995 a married couple with two children (aged four and six) in council housing faced the following situation:

Gross earnings	*Net income (after housing costs)*
£50 pw	£126.89
£210 pw	£137.04

Thus an increase of £160 in earnings (or from 13 to 56 hours worked at an hourly rate of £3.75) achieves a net increase of £10.15 per week – equivalent to a 94 per cent tax rate. It is true that at no point does the effective marginal tax rate exceed 100 per cent but this is achieved at the price of the extension of the poverty trap over a wide range of earnings; in 1995 one-quarter of employees earned below £210 per week.

Another potential effect of extending means testing has been on family formation and family fission as Morgan (1995) and Parker (1995) have discussed. Whereas income tax has become more individualised, social security has become more means-tested, based on joint family income; this may encourage family break-up (see Chapter 7) as couples are treated less generously than individuals.

Overall, the incentives resulting from the extension of means testing have markedly worsened since 1979.

CONCLUSION

The period since 1979 has seen a major extension in means testing. There has not, however, been a clear, consistent and comprehensive shift towards an income-tested social security system. For certain groups, notably older people, there has been no shift towards means testing (though large numbers do not claim their entitlements): for others, notably unemployed people, the insurance basis of social security has virtually collapsed. If there had been a consistent policy towards all social security – with all social security benefits income tested, rather than picking on the unemployed and low-paid – then the impact of means testing would have been more broadly shared. It is hard to avoid the conclusion that the more politically vulnerable and expendable have been more harshly treated in order to curb public expenditure and limit any potential political damage.

Even though means testing has been extended there has been no serious attempt to overcome non-take-up, for example by enlisting the assistance of the Inland Revenue, local authorities or employers. Again, a desire to limit public expenditure must be part of the explanation. Much more fundamentally there has been little attempt to limit the need for means-tested support. Much of the growth and pressure on social security has been the result of the massive increase in unemployment and earlier withdrawal from the labour market since 1979. Yet the training, economic regeneration and macro-economic policies which could have led to more employment and limited dependence on social security – as Beveridge realised, but many have forgotten – have been woefully inadequate. Means-tested benefits, despite increased expenditure, have been altogether inadequate to offset the social costs of mass unemployment.

The effects on incentives give rise to the most serious gap between declared intentions and actual results. The growth of means testing, currently operating on a trial basis with an 'earnings top-up' for people without children on low earnings, has occurred at the same times as – and in part because – the extent of low pay and job insecurity has increased. More employed people are having their pay supplemented by means-tested benefits, making them more dependent on the state.

Put simply, decisions on social security have in general undermined incentives to work and to save and made it harder for individuals to stand on their own feet. The current mean-minded approach that has led to the extension of means testing described here is an approach that has achieved little, has imposed severe costs, and offers no real hope for the future.

REFERENCES

CM 3231 (March 1996) Social Security Departmental Report, HMSO.

Cmnd 9517 (1985) *Reform of Social Security*, HMSO.

Economic Trends (December 1995) *The Effects of Taxes and Benefits on Household Income 1994/95*, HMSO.

Economic Trends (March 1991) *The Effects of Taxes on Benefits and Household Income 1988*, HMSO.

Marsh, A and McKay, S (1993) *Families, Work and Benefits*, Policy Studies Institute.

Morgan, P (1995) *Farewell to the Family?*, Institute of Economic Affairs.

Parker, H (1995) *Taxes, Benefits and Family Life*, Institute of Economic Affairs.

This chapter is an extended and updated version of the paper that appeared in *Benefits*, Issue 15, January 1996.

6 Cutting social security
Marilyn Howard

As earlier chapters have indicated, the social security landscape has been changed in ways probably undreamed of in 1979. Many significant changes have been made with only limited Parliamentary scrutiny. Since 1992 the pace of change has speeded up considerably, to the extent that the Secretary of State for Social Security, Peter Lilley, boasted during the 1996 uprating debate that he had introduced 12 bills over the previous four years (House of Commons, *Hansard*, 28 November 1996, col 490).

It is sobering to reflect on the progress of an agenda put together by five Conservative MPs from the 1992 Parliamentary intake (The 'No Turning Back' Group, 1993). Believing that state benefits should be 'primarily for the poor − not for wealthy widows or even the wealthy disabled', their ultimate aim was for a means-tested 'whole person benefit' to replace the range of existing benefits. Those of their recommendations which had been adopted, or were in the process of being implemented at the time of publication include:

- tackling social security fraud by introducing a time-sensitive smart card linked to a central computer network;
- reducing the period of contributory benefits to the unemployed from one year to six months;
- equalising the state pension age for men and women to 65 (eventually 67);
- phasing out the earnings-related element of invalidity benefit;
- taxing invalidity benefit as income;
- encouraging the private sector to operate innovative schemes for

the long term unemployed, such as 'workability';
* market-testing benefits administration.

This chapter examines the most important changes which have been made to the social security system since 1979 under the broad (and sometimes overlapping) themes of targeting benefits; reducing benefit levels; promoting personal responsibility; policing claimants; and (hidden) cuts.

TARGETING BENEFITS

David Piachaud (Chapter 5) provides evidence to show that British social security has become increasingly means tested but that not all groups have been equally affected. The following section illustrates how unemployed people and those who are sick and disabled have particularly lost out in terms of eligibility and entitlement in the search for a more efficient targeting strategy. In 1983 the then Secretary of State for Social Security, Norman Fowler, initiated a review of various aspects of the social security system, the conclusions of which led to the major restructuring of means-tested benefits in the 1986 Social Security Act. Yet by 1993, Peter Lilley, the new Secretary of State, said the system needed reviewing again. His goals were the same as Fowler's: to make the system 'better focused' and to keep expenditure within 'the nation's ability to pay' (Lilley, 1993). These two major reviews, together with a number of other smaller policy initiatives have led to substantial changes in both the eligibility and contribution conditions for benefit.

ELIGIBILITY

Originally the test for unemployed people to claim national insurance (NI) benefit was dependent only upon an adequate contributions record and proof of availability for work. This rule was first tightened in 1980 with administrative changes requiring the completion of a questionnaire upon initial claim and every six months thereafter (Ogus, Barendt and Wikeley, 1995). A new condition was added in 1989 to make claimants show they were also 'actively seeking work' as well as available for it. This was introduced as an anti-fraud measure based on the assumption that not all claimants were making strenuous efforts to find work. The period during which claimants could search for work on terms and conditions similar to their last job was restricted to 13 weeks. The jobseeker's allowance, introduced in October 1996, followed these trends to their logical conclusion. Receipt of benefit is now conditional upon signing a jobseeker's agreement which details jobsearch activities. Failure to comply with the terms of the agreement can lead to the issue of a jobseeker's direction to undertake a particular task, or attend a training scheme, with the threat of benefit sanctions for non-compliance. It is anticipated that, when in full operation, the jobseeker's allowance will save the Government £240 million per year (*Guardian*, 11 February 1996).

People with a long-term sickness or disability have also been 'targeted'. Following concern that the number of claimants had grown – from 557,000 in 1978 to 1.7 million in 1995 – at a time when the nation's health had improved, invalidity benefit, which itself had been administered much more rigorously in its last three years, was replaced in 1995 by incapacity benefit. Incapacity benefit is based on a 'functional' assessment of incapacity for work, on the assumption that under this criterion more claimants would be found capable of work than before, thus generating substantial benefit savings. It was anticipated by Lilley that 220,000 existing incapacity benefit claimants and 55,000 new claimants would fail the new, tougher test. In October 1996 the DSS estimated that, by the year 2000, incapacity benefit would have saved £2.3 billion annually, although savings were £135 million less than originally planned by late 1996 (National Insurance Fund Account 1995/96, HCP 221, 21 January 1997).

DISENTITLEMENT

Targeting has not only entailed tightening the eligibility conditions, it has also removed or restricted benefits for particular claimant groups. For instance, since 1988 most young people aged between 16–18 have had no entitlement to income support unless belonging to a restricted group (such as lone parents or disabled) and/or where they can prove severe hardship. In 1990, unemployment benefit and means-tested benefits were withdrawn from full-time students in favour of student loans. Recent entrants to the UK were excluded from means-tested benefits in 1994 through the operation of the habitual residence test, which affected even British citizens returning from voluntary service overseas. A report by NACAB (1996) found that five times as many people as expected, including 5,000 British people, failed the new habitual residence test. Even more draconian rules were introduced in early 1996 to prevent asylum-seekers receiving a range of benefits unless they had declared themselves as such at the port of entry (Chapter 8). This development led to the Red Cross distributing food parcels to destitute asylum-seekers in London: the first time they had undertaken such action in this country (*Guardian*, 19 December 1996).

CONTRIBUTION CONDITIONS

A form of targeting has also taken place with changes to contribution conditions. Partial benefits, payable where only part of the national insurance contribution conditions were met, were removed in 1986 for short term benefits like unemployment benefit and sickness benefit. The most significant change occurred in 1988, after which contributions had to be satisfied within either of the two complete tax years before the claim; previously, contributions paid in any tax year could give entitlement. As a result of these and other changes fewer people have been eligible for contributory unemployment benefit. In 1987, 34 per cent of claimants were denied unemployment benefit because they did not meet the contribution tests, and 48 per cent because they had used up their entitlement. By 1994, twice as many people failed the contribution tests (62 per cent) and 32 per cent had used up their entitlement (Murray, 1996).

REDUCING BENEFIT LEVELS

Conservative governments have been particularly concerned that levels of benefit should not erode the incentive to work. As a result, benefit rates have been reduced, even for those having to satisfy the tougher conditions of entitlement discussed earlier. Alongside lower benefits for people out of work, the Government's approach has been to boost in-work incomes through improvements to family credit, including the introduction of a pilot scheme extending this type of earnings top-up to people without children.

The merging of contributory and means-tested benefits with the introduction of jobseeker's allowance (JSA) allowed several changes to benefit rates; there are no increases for dependants paid with contribution-based JSA; young people under 25 receive a lower rate, and contribution-based JSA is only payable for six months instead of

12. There has been a levelling down of both means-tested and contributory benefits. The replacement of supplementary benefit with income support in 1988 brought about 'rough justice' for many claimants through the change from weekly additional requirements to premiums for claimant groups. Personal allowances were reduced for people under 25, in effect replacing the previous distinction between householders and non-householders.

Earnings-related supplements, payable with contributory benefits, have been virtually abolished. The additional pension payable with invalidity benefit was only paid in full until 1985, when its value was reduced by the amount of the age allowance payable. This was followed in 1991 by the removal of any future entitlement. The introduction of incapacity benefit in 1995 ended additional pension entitlement for new claimants, and the additional pension for existing claimants was frozen at 1995 levels. The value of incapacity benefit was reduced in other ways – age allowances cease for new claimants aged over 45, the long term rate is not paid until the end of the first year of incapacity (rather than 28 weeks), increases of benefit for adult dependants are restricted, and the benefit is taxable.

Occupational pensioners have had their entitlement to unemployment benefit reduced. In 1980, unemployment benefit was abated for people with occupational pensions of £30 or more who were aged 60-65; this age limit was reduced to 55-60 in 1988. The Government raised the occupational pension threshold to £50 with the introduction of JSA, but abolished the age threshold so that all claimants can have their contribution-based JSA reduced if their pension is above £50 per week.

ACKNOWLEDGING THE CUTS: TRANSITIONAL PROTECTION

Conservative governments have protected some existing claimants from the worst effects of these reductions in benefit entitlement. The introduction of income support was accompanied by a complex set of regulations to ensure that claimants previously on supplementary benefit were no worse off at the point of change. However, this has meant that some claimants have had their entitlement frozen for many years (110,000 in 1990; House of Commons, *Hansard*, 28 February 1991, cols 660/1). Similar transitional protection has been used for regulation changes such as the redefinition of full time work from 24 to 16 hours in 1992, and the introduction of incapacity benefit in 1995. Transitional protection also accompanied the frequent changes to housing benefit and help towards local taxes which occurred throughout the 1980s, which would otherwise have left existing recipients worse off.

It could be argued that the payment of transitional protection is an acknowledgement of the financial losses resulting from these structural changes. However, even this limited protection was not provided in 1996, when pensioners on the reduced earnings allowance were moved onto the retirement allowance at a lower rate.

PERSONAL RESPONSIBILITY

THE RESPONSIBILITY TO PROVIDE FOR CHILDREN

The intention of the Child Support Agency (CSA) was to 'ensure that parents honour their legal and moral responsibility to maintain their own children whenever they can afford to do so' (DSS, 1990) However, the value of state support for children has fallen as the value of child benefit has been eroded in monetary terms. Unlike other benefits, child benefit was not uprated in line with inflation until 1991 and between 1988 and 1991 it was frozen. As a result, its value fell by 4 per cent in real terms for the first child and 22 per cent for subsequent children, saving the Government an estimated £900 million gross at 1995/96 prices (Oppenheim and Harker, 1996). As Oppenheim and Harker (1996) point out, the real value of child support (ie, child benefit versus the old family allowances and child tax allowances) for a family paying basic rates of income tax was worth less in 1996 than 30 years ago.

The Conservative Government's concern with the growing number of lone parents on benefit was first shown with the introduction of the Child Support Agency in April 1993. The stated objective of the CSA was to ensure 'both parents ... honour their legal and moral responsibility to maintain their own children whenever they could afford to do so' (DSS, 1990). However, in practice, the CSA acted as a money collector for the Treasury:

> While the duty to pay child maintenance applies to all absent parents, the legal requirement placed on parents with care to give their permission to pursue maintenance applies only to those in receipt of income support, family credit and disability working allowance. The

latter formed 97 per cent of the cases dealt with by the CSA in its first year. (Knights, 1994)

While much of the adverse publicity given to the early years of its operation centred on poor administration (culminating in the replacement of the Chief Executive) and the impact of the new system on absent parents and their second families, less attention was paid to the fact that:

> While there may be small numbers of women who have managed to find paid work and so leave income support as a result of receiving maintenance ... any ... gains for the few have been achieved at an unacceptable cost ... for many more families. (Knights, 1994)

In the 1996 Budget the Government announced its intention to freeze lone parent benefit and the lone parent premium paid with income support, with the intention of narrowing the gap between benefits payable to one- and two-parent families, despite new research evidence suggesting that the needs of the former are at least as great as for couples with children (Berthoud and Ford, 1996).

RESPONSIBILITY FOR ONESELF

Support which was previously given by the state has been progressively taken out of the social security system. The Fowler Review acted as an impetus for this change by providing incentives for people to take out private pensions in preference to the embattled SERPs scheme. From October 1995, the level of assistance with mortgage interest given to owner-occupiers on income support has been limited explicitly to encourage home-owners to take out private insurance to cover the costs of a mortgage during periods of unemployment and sickness, although such cover may offer poor value for money and exclude some from cover completely (Burchardt and Hills, 1997). In March 1997, the Government announced plans to transfer from the current pay-as-you-go pensions scheme to individual cash funded pensions, with a view to phasing out the state retirement pension for younger people.

Provision to cover short term sickness has been progressively shifted to employers. The obligation of employers to make payments to sick employees in the first eight weeks of sickness through statutory sick pay from 1983 was extended, in 1986, to 28 weeks. The cost to employers was borne via reductions in their national insurance contributions until 1992 when reimbursement was reduced to 80 per cent, followed by the abolition of reimbursement in 1994. The earnings-related additional pension payable with invalidity benefit was abolished for new incapacity benefit claims in 1995 on the basis that it duplicated occupational and private cover.

INCREASED BENEFITS POLICING

A more coercive benefits regime has been developed especially for unemployed claimants, together with a renewed emphasis on fraud.

BENEFIT SANCTIONS

The maximum period of disqualification for voluntarily leaving work was extended from six to 13 weeks in 1986 and doubled to 26 weeks in 1988. In practice, the development of compulsory 'remotivation' courses like the Jobplan workshop and Restart courses have led to an increase in the numbers sanctioned for non-attendance, from 4,700 in the first half of 1993 to 37,400 by late 1994 (Murray, 1996). Similarly, the numbers disqualified for failing to actively seek work increased tenfold between 1990/91 and 1994/95 to 21,600 (Murray, 1996). The jobseeker's direction is likely to make most similar schemes compulsory.

Sanctions under JSA are harsher and will bite more sharply as hardship payments during periods of disqualification are more restrictive than previously. Single and childless couples will receive no payment for the first two weeks, with no access to crisis loans from the social fund for living expenses. Even 'vulnerable' groups have to prove hardship before any payment can be made. In 1996 the Government introduced, on a pilot basis, 'Project Work' for people aged between 18 and 50 who have been unemployed for two years, whereby 13 weeks of Jobsearch is followed by a 13 week compulsory work programme. The extension of this nationally is to be a major proposal in the Conservative Party manifesto in the 1997 election.

FRAUD

As indicated earlier in relation to the actively seeking work test, fraud control has always been an important feature within the social security system. However, this element of administration has become most extreme since November 1993, when a Fraud Strategic Board was set up across the DSS and its agencies to launch a five year 'Security and Control' programme, including a fraud review of each benefit. A fraud hotline with a 'Beat a Cheat' advertising campaign was introduced in August 1996, shortly after the Freeline benefit information service for claimants and potential claimants was closed for 'efficiency savings'. A Fraud Bill, published in November 1996, provided for a range of new powers to allow the exchange of information across the data banks of different agencies. The intended legislation would have created new offences with tougher penalties including imprisonment for up to seven years, and would have given the power to review benefit where fraud was suspected and to suspend payment where there was doubt as to the validity of a claim (such as housing benefit) or when a claimant failed to attend a medical examination as part of a fraud investigation into receipt of disability benefits. This Bill fell, however, with the dissolution of Parliament in March 1997.

CUTS HIDDEN FROM VIEW

Some social security changes have taken place with less publicity than the substantive changes described above. Examples include the failure to uprate benefits, limited Parliamentary scrutiny of amendments, and changes to administration.

UPRATING

One of the first and most significant reforms made by the Conservative Government in the 1980 Social Security Act was to change the formula for uprating benefits in line with prices not earnings. While government claimed that this more restricted formula protects claimants against inflation, the retail prices index fails to reflect the different patterns of consumption between rich and poor (Bradshaw and Lynes, 1995). This has been exacerbated by the trend towards greater indirect taxation, which is regressive (Chapter 3) and increased charges, for example on prescriptions and local authority services. Some elements of the benefits system, such as the capital limits and earnings disregards on means-tested benefits, have not been uprated for years. This failure to uprate is another way of excluding people from benefit and of deliberately allowing inflation to erode payments such as the child dependants' increases payable with long-term contributory benefits, which would be too unpopular to cut openly (Bradshaw and Lynes, 1995).

Most importantly, the less favourable uprating rules means that the standard of living of people on benefit is falling behind that of those in work. In 1979 a single person entitled to unemployment benefit including the earnings-related supplement received benefit equivalent to 31 per cent of average earnings; by 1993 the value of unemployment benefit in similar circumstances had more than halved to 14 per cent (Convery, 1994). The single person's pension is more than £22 per week lower than it would have been if the link with earnings had not been broken.

MINIMAL SCRUTINY

The use of primary legislation giving the Secretary of State extensive regulation-making powers accelerated in the 1990s. On occasions the Government proceeded with regulations against the advice of the Social Security Advisory Committee, with whom it is obliged to consult by law. By tradition, regulations cannot be amended, only approved or rejected wholesale. Some regulations can slip through unnoticed if subject to a 'negative' resolution under Parliamentary procedure, and some regulations came into force before they were debated by Parliament – this happened six times in 1995/96 (House of Commons, *Hansard*, 3 December 1996). The Conservative Government has been criticised for introducing 'enabling' Acts, which left the detail of legislation to regulations. For example, the Select Committee on the Scrutiny of Delegated Powers put pressure on the Government to place more detail on the face of the Jobseekers Bill. Similarly, the Child Support Bill gave the Secretary of State 94 regulation-making powers, only 12 of which would be subject to scrutiny under 'affirmative' Parliamentary procedures. The enabling nature of the Bill, together with pressures of time and complexity of the subject matter, 'allowed the detail of legislation to escape without the attention it deserved' (Garnham and Knights, 1994). The discretionary social fund, operated by Directions and Guidance issued by the Secretary of State, conferred on him 'a power to create a code of subdelegated legislation which was not subject to any parliamentary scrutiny whatsoever' (Wood, 1994). The system remains, despite judicial challenges and critical research evidence (Huby and Dix, 1992).

CPAG has been at the forefront of testing the legality of government powers to change social security in this way. However, even successful test cases have tended to be reversed through amending regulations – even when challenges have been based on European law, as in the Newton case (payment of mobility allowance abroad: see Wood, 1994) – or through 'anti-test case rules' introduced to ensure that success for one individual at Commissioner level should not result in payment of benefit arrears to other claimants. Pending the outcome of an appeal by the Secretary of State against a successful claimant, the Secretary of State used further powers to suspend payment of benefit to other claimants who had established entitlement under the particular point of law which was the subject of the appeal.

ADMINISTRATION

Over the past 18 years, the policy and operational processes within the DSS have been progressively hidden from view, from the department splitting from health in 1988, to the 'Next Steps' agencies created in 1991 which split the policy functions (DSS) from operations (Benefits Agency). In practice, this separation has weakened accountability and has allowed Ministers to hide behind the Agencies. At one point answers to MPs' Parliamentary Questions were referred to Agency Chief Executives and not even printed in *Hansard*. The final *coup de grace* was a proposal to sell off the delivery and administration of benefits (*Sunday Telegraph*, 29 September 1996) and to contract out the administration and adjudication functions of the Benefits Agency Medical Service to the private sector from April 1997.

An erosion of procedural rights can make it more difficult to assert substantive rights to benefit. The announcement in February 1996 of a 25 per cent cut in the running costs of the DSS agencies over the following three years – proposals for which, in a letter to the Chief Financial Secretary to the Treasury, Peter Lilley said 'filled him with despair' and 'would have a devastating impact' – has already led to changes in the appeal procedures, tighter time limits for claiming, and limited backdating. A further proposal to pay benefits only from the date that all relevant information was provided, rather than from the date of original claim was under consideration when the General Election was called. The Benefits Agency has been making other cuts at the 'luxury end of customer service', including scrapping the free Benefits Advice Line, reduced office opening hours and scrapping benefit buses (*Guardian*, 1 March 1996). Such changes may save not only on administration costs but on actual benefit spending by further reducing benefit take-up (Chapter 5).

CONCLUSION

It would be unfair to suggest that there have been no improvements to benefits since 1979; for instance, the introduction and extension of child care disregards and extended payments of housing benefit to those starting work. However, gains for one group of claimants have often been made at the expense of others. For example, the improvements to some disability benefits (disability living allowance and disability working allowance) have been accompanied by a reduction in help paid to people injured at work and to people experiencing short-term sickness.

Despite the many large and small cuts made in the social security budget overall, spending has still risen, mainly because unemployment has remained high (Chapter 12) and deregulation has led to a massive increase in rents and therefore in housing benefit costs. The challenge for any new government is to tackle these underlying causes while creating a more flexible benefit system.

REFERENCES

Berthoud, R and Ford, R (1996) *Relative Needs: variations in the living standards of different types of household*, PSI.

Bradshaw, J and Lynes, T (1995) *Benefit Uprating Policy and Living Standards*, SPRU.

Burchardt, T and Hills, J (1997) *Private Welfare Insurance and Social Security: pushing the boundaries*, Joseph Rowntree Foundation.

Butler, E and Pirie, M (1995) *The Fortune Account; the successor to social welfare*, Adam Smith Institute.

Convery, P (1994) *Unemployment Benefits: values decline*, Unemployment Unit, Working Brief no 53, April.

DSS (1990) *Children Come First: The Government's proposals on the maintenance of children*, vol 1, Cm 1263.

Garnham, A and Knights, E (1994) *Putting the Treasury First; the truth about child support*, CPAG.

Huby, M and Dix, G (1992) *Evaluating the Social Fund*, DSS Research Report, No. 9, HMSO.

Knights, E (1994) 'The truth about child support: CPAG's monitoring of the Child Suport Agency', *Benefits*, Issue 11, September/October.

Lilley, P (1993) Foreword to *The growth of social security*, DSS, HMSO.

Murray, I (1996) *Desperately Seeking … A Job*, Unemployment Unit.

NACAB (1996) *Failing the Test – CAB clients' experiences of the HRT in social security*, NACAB.

The 'No Turning Back Group' of Conservative MPs (1996) *Who Benefits? Reinventing Social Security*, Conservative Political Centre.

Ogus, A, Barendt and Wikeley, N (1995) *The Law of Social Security*, Butterworths.

Oppenheim, C and Harker, L (1996) *Poverty: the facts*, CPAG.

Wood, P (1994) 'An overview of CPAG's campaigning strategy', *Legal Action*, September, pp6-8.

Section Two

DIMENSIONS OF POVERTY AND SOCIAL EXCLUSION

7
Gender
Jane Millar

At the end of the 1970s the two groups with the highest risk and the longest durations of poverty were both female: older women living alone and lone mothers. As we move towards the end of the 1990s this is still true.

The official statistics on low-income households and on benefit receipt provide a glimpse of this. The latest statistics on *Households below Average Income* (DSS, 1996a) show that, in 1993/94, about 22 per cent of all households had incomes, after meeting housing costs, of less than half the average. Among single pensioners the proportion with less than half the average was 30 per cent, and among lone-parent households it was 58 per cent. Although these figures do not separately identify women and men (routine breakdown of such statistics by gender is still not available), it is known that both groups – single pensioners and lone parents – are predominantly women.

The income support statistics also suggest that many of these women are long-term benefit recipients. In May 1995 there were almost 1.2 million single women aged over 60 receiving income support, including just over half a million women aged 80 and over (DSS, 1996b). Most had been on income support for several years and few had income from any other sources, apart from their benefits.[1] In

---

1. Again, however, the published statistics do not provide a gender breakdown. Of those aged 60 and receiving income support about two-thirds are women, about three-quarters had been in receipt of income support for at least two years and only 18 per cent had any non-benefit income. The continuing lack of a routine breakdown of statistics by gender limits our knowledge and capacity to understand the different economic situations of women and men.

the same year, just over one million lone mothers were receiving income support, including almost 650,000 women who had been in receipt for at least two years. Like the older women, most were reliant upon income support for all their income; those few receiving child support would have had that deducted from benefit, as would be any earnings above £15 per week.

Figures from the *Family Expenditure Survey* show how far below the average are the incomes of these women. In 1994/95 average weekly household disposable income was about £300, for lone parents it was about £150, and for single pensioners only about £79 (CSO, 1996). Jarvis and Jenkins (1995), in their analysis of poverty dynamics, found that the types of family most likely to stay on a low income between 1991 and 1992 were lone-parent families and elderly single pensioners. Thus, despite the lack of detailed statistics, for these two groups of women the picture is fairly clear: they have a very high risk of poverty, many of them are in receipt of income support and often have no other source of income, they are likely to remain income support recipients for relatively long periods, and so their incomes change little over time. Long-term persistent hardship marks the lives of these women, especially the older women.

These women have been largely left behind in the economic race of the 1980s and 1990s. But so too have many others. As average incomes and living standards have risen, those on low incomes – including benefit recipients – have seen their real incomes and living standards in decline.[2] Not only have the incomes of the poorest stayed stagnant or fallen, but their access to public services has also declined. Policies of privatisation – in transport, in basic amenities such as water, gas and electricity – have often led to higher prices (Chapter 13). Charges for services – such as prescriptions, home helps, dental care – are levied on all but the very poorest. The state has also become more intrusive into the lives of the poorest – more people face means tests, not just for benefits, as discussed in Chapter

---

2. The *Households Below Average Income* statistics show that the real median income of the bottom decile (excluding the self-employed) rose by 8 per cent if income is measured before deducting housing costs, but fell by 6 per cent after housing costs are taken into account (DSS, 1996a, p3). This does not mean that the same people have seen their incomes fall (although as discussed below these family types do tend to stay poor). It does, however, mean that, for example, lone mothers in the mid-1990s are worse off as a group than they were in the late 1970s. So anyone becoming a lone mother today faces a worse financial situation than her counterpart 15 or so years ago.

5, but also for other services, and the child support legislation requires people to provide some very detailed and intimate information about their lives.

Trying to identify the real 'gainers' and 'losers' from all these changes is a complex, if not impossible, task: more so if we want to compare men and women. In general, men have probably gained more than women from changing tax policies (which have reduced the direct tax burden on the higher paid) and men have also been better able than women to take advantage of increased, and subsidised, opportunities to 'opt out' of state systems. But poor men, like poor women, have seen their benefits reduced, their rights restricted, and their characters and motives attacked. In this chapter the extent of poverty among different groups of women and men, and the impact of government policies on those at the bottom of the income distribution are considered.

WOMEN AND POVERTY

'Female-headed households', such as lone mothers and single women pensioners, are only the most visible tip of the iceberg of women's poverty. If we could see more clearly then we would certainly find many more women living in, or on the margins, of poverty. Some of these women are to be found in the statistics as members of poor families: married women, for example, living with husbands who are unemployed or economically inactive. In May 1995 there were about 670,000 married couples below pension age receiving income support, including about half a million with dependent children (DSS, 1996b). Because of the impact of means-testing (Chapter 5) most women in such circumstances are not themselves employed, and the consequent growth in the number of 'no-earner' households has been a striking factor in rising income inequalities (Gregg and Wadsworth, 1994; Joseph Rowntree Foundation, 1995).

Another group of poor women are those who do have jobs but with earnings that are not enough to support them. These are the women who make up the vast majority of low-paid workers. Dex *et al* (1994) calculate that about four million women in Britain are low paid, equivalent to about a third of the female workforce. Webb *et al* (1996) use a lower threshold for defining low pay but they too find that women predominate among the low paid. They estimate that, in 1994, about 3.2 million women were low paid and that women account for about seven in ten low-paid workers. These women are poor in the sense that they could not support themselves, and certainly not children or other dependants, on their own earnings alone. But these women are not visible in poverty statistics unless they also live in poor households. Indeed, the view that low-paid women are not in 'real' poverty remains strong in some quarters, and has provided a continuing justification for rejecting the idea of a minimum wage, because 'a large majority of those on lowest wages are second earners in a family or household in which other members are already earning higher wages' (DSS, 1995, para. 2.10).

This perception – that women are protected against poverty because they live with male partners – ignores the importance of financial independence (or at least the possibility of such independence) as a dimension of income adequacy. Relying upon others financially can be a risky business, as many formerly-married women find out when they separate or divorce. Not only do they lose their current source of income (very few women now receive maintenance for themselves after divorce) but often they also lose their rights to pension entitlements that are considered as 'belonging' to their former husbands. A recent survey of divorcing women found that most (63 per cent) said that they had not even discussed pensions as part of the divorce settlement (Prior and Field, 1996). Women part-timers also make up the bulk of those who are not contributing to the national insurance fund (because they earn below the lower earnings limit), and who are not members of occupational or private pension schemes. As things stand, many of these women will live in poverty when they are old.

Even more invisible to poverty statistics are married women who are not employed but who live with employed, and relatively well-off, husbands. On family-based poverty measures these women are not poor. On individual-based poverty measures some would be, since they have no independent income of their own (except perhaps child benefit or, in some cases, private income sources). Webb (1991) calculates the 'independent' income of individuals living with others (ie, that portion of household income that 'belongs' to the individual). He finds that, in 1991, average weekly independent income was £200 for men and exactly half that, £100, for women. Actual living standards will, of course, depend on how income is pooled in practice. It is difficult to get firm evidence on this but Vogler and Pahl (1993) have calculated that only one in five married couple households use fully egalitarian ways of pooling their income. The rest use various different ways of managing their money but in general women are less likely than men to have their own personal spending money. Davies and Joshi (1994) have calculated that if we measured poverty on the basis of individual incomes rather than assuming equal sharing of household income, then 52 per cent of married women would be under the poverty line, compared with 11 per cent of married men.

In some ways, however, the most invisible of poor women are also, paradoxically, the most visible – women who are homeless and living on the streets. Such people do not get counted in the income statistics (which cover only those who live in private households) and accurate estimates of numbers are difficult to come by. The 1991 Census counted about 2,700 people sleeping rough but this is almost certainly an underestimate (Oppenheim and Harker, 1996). Men are more likely to be sleeping rough than women but women, because of their responsibility for children, are more likely to be accepted as homeless by local authorities (whose duty to provide housing applies only to those with children). In 1994 about 69,000 households with children were accepted as homeless by local authorities. Many of these households would spend time in temporary accommodation, most commonly in bed and breakfast hostels (about 11 per cent of households in temporary accommodation) or in women's refuges (about 23 per cent) (Oppenheim and Harker, 1996).

The visible tip of women's poverty – the lone mothers and elderly sole women – is thus only one element of the true total. A more complete picture would also include women in 'no-earner' families, low-paid women, non-employed women completely dependent on others, and homeless women. A more complete picture would also probably tell us that some types of women face far higher risks of poverty than others (class, race, disability and region all play a part) and that women's chances of escaping poverty over time are often limited. And it would also tell us that women bear the major brunt of poverty in terms of their own living standards and health. Because women are generally responsible for domestic work and childcare, the burden of 'managing' poverty falls mainly upon them. They must try and make insufficient income stretch to meet needs and can often do this only by going without themselves, or by going into debt, or by trying to juggle what money they have across competing demands. Mothers try and ensure that their children have adequate nutritious food, often going without themselves to achieve this (Dowler and Calvert, 1995; Kempson, 1996). There may be significant consequences for women's health (Graham, 1996). Kempson (1996) has recently reviewed the findings from over 30 studies of how people cope on low incomes. She finds no sign of an 'underclass' of poor people with different attitudes and aspirations from the mainstream. What she does find is much evidence of people struggling hard to manage on what they have, and to improve their situations.

MEN AND POVERTY

Our knowledge of the true extent of poverty among men is also somewhat patchy. The visible tip of the iceberg of men's poverty is made up of those men who are registered as unemployed. In October 1996 there were about 1.62 million men in the 'claimant count' of the registered unemployed, of whom about 638,000 had been unemployed for at least one year (DfEE, 1996). However, the 'claimant count' is based on a very restricted definition of unemployment which includes only those who are actually in receipt of benefits, thus excluding many men who have no jobs and who would like to work, but who are not eligible for benefits, as well as those who are on training or other government schemes. Convery (1996) calculates that the number of men of working age who are 'economically inactive' rose from about 1.9 million in spring 1984 to 2.7 million in the spring of 1996. This is equivalent to about 15 per cent of all working age men. But, even on the restricted definition used by the Government, male unemployment is a major problem and a major cause of family poverty. In 1995 there were almost 620,000 children living in families receiving income support because of unemployment (DSS, 1996b).

As with women, however, this highly visible group is just a part of the broader total. In the case of men this encompasses three main groups: older men who are no longer in work, young men just entering the labour market, and the increasing numbers of men to be found in low-paid jobs. Men aged between 50 and 65 have been increasingly squeezed out of the labour market in the past 20 years. In 1979 the majority of men in this age range were employed – 88 per cent of those aged 50–59 and 70 per cent of those aged 60–64. By 1994 these employment rates were down to 73 per cent and 43 per cent respectively (OPCS, 1996). Many older men have more or less withdrawn from the labour market, some taking a comfortable early retirement on the back of an occupational pension but others knowing that – because of where they live, or their health, of their lack of skills now in demand – they are unlikely ever to work again. At the other end of the age-range the job opportunities for young men have also closed up. In 1979, 60 per cent of male school-leavers aged 16–17 were employed; now the figure is only 46 per cent (OPCS, 1996) with most of the rest on various government training schemes, and earning very little. As many as 85 per cent of unemployed 16–17-year-olds (about 120,000 people) do not receive any income from benefits at all (Chatrik and Convery, 1996).

Low pay, once a problem almost entirely confined to young people and to women in part-time jobs, has spread across the labour market to encompass an increasing proportion of men. Webb *et al* (1996) calculate that the proportion of male employees who are low paid has risen from about 8 per cent of the male workforce in the late 1960s to about 13 per cent today. In addition, whereas in the 1960s most of these low-paid men were either young entrants to the labour market or men coming up to retirement, today a significant proportion (about one third) of men receiving low pay are aged 25 to 49. These are men who are likely to be married with dependent children. Receipt of family credit (paid to low-wage earners with children) has more than doubled since it was introduced (to replace family income supplement) in the mid 1980s, and in November 1995 there were about 265,000 working men in receipt.[3] The capacity for men to be 'breadwinners' for their families, to earn enough to support themselves, their wives and children, is receding fast. Even the well-paid professional classes are likely to find two earners necessary, especially when paying off a mortgage.

THE IMPACT OF GOVERNMENT POLICIES

Blame for the increase in inequality and poverty that has been such a feature of the past two decades cannot all be laid at the Government's door. Long-run employment and demographic trends have played a significant part (Joseph Rowntree Foundation, 1996). Nevertheless, government policies have largely failed to prevent poverty and have sometimes exacerbated the problem. This is true in somewhat different

---

3. There were also 94,000 women in couples, about 11,000 lone fathers and almost 280,000 lone parents,

ways for women and for men. Women have been very directly affected by a wide range of policies, because of their multiple roles as mothers/carers/paid workers. Thus policies such as the freezing of child benefit throughout most of the 1980s had a very direct impact on women. Other reductions in benefits – such as the linking of the basic pension to prices rather than to earnings (Chapter 6), the cutbacks to SERPS, the introduction of income support and the social fund – have also affected women disproportionately. Some cuts have been directly targeted on women. The freezing of one-parent benefit and of the income support premiums for lone mothers, which came into effect following the 1996 Budget, will mean that these small payments will ultimately disappear. The abolition of reduced rate national insurance contributions in 1986 excluded more women from the possibility of claiming national insurance benefits.

The abolition of the Wages Councils, which were responsible for setting minimum rates of pay for workers in certain industries (Chapter 3), is likely to have affected about two million women workers. The privatisation of welfare provisions has affected women in a number of ways: privatisation of services has meant job losses for many women who were working in the public sector and those who have transferred to the private cleaning and catering companies have seen their pay and conditions deteriorate. Because of their part-time and discontinuous employment patterns, women have less access than men to private and occupational pension and sickness schemes (May and Brunsdon, 1996). The privatisation of 'care' through policies of community care has meant a greater burden of care falling upon 'carers', many of whom fail to qualify for the invalid care allowance (McLaughlin, 1991).[4]

But it also true that generally women have had rather 'less to lose' from welfare state restructuring and reductions than men. As has been well documented, the social security system was created with the needs of men rather than those of women in mind (as various contributors to Baldwin and Falkingham, 1995, show). So, when thinking of the impact of government policy on women, we also need to consider what has *not* happened, as well as what has. In particular the failure to recognise the needs of working women – despite the increase in the numbers of such women – has increased

---

4. Glendinning (1987) provides a more detailed analysis of the way in which Conservative policies have 'impoverished' women.

the difficulties that women face in combining home and family. The failure to achieve equal pay between men and women, the failure to protect the rights of part-time workers, the failure to address the lack of adequate and affordable child-care – all these make the lives of working women stressful and costly. The positive policies that have been enacted – the extension of maternity leave to women employed for six months, the extension of family credit to part-time workers, the introduction of a 'disregard' of part of the costs of child-care for some family credit recipients, the introduction of child-care vouchers for nursery-school age children – are indeed beneficial to the women who can make use of them, but the restrictions and qualifications ensure that this is only a minority. The majority of British working women must make the best of things by their own efforts and, where they can, with the help of partners and families.

Men, however, have seen a number of the rights and benefits that they did have reduced or removed, especially in respect of national insurance benefits. The policies that have affected men of working age most directly are probably the changes to long-term sickness and unemployment benefits. These benefits, along with pensions, were at the centre of the Beveridge welfare state: paid to all those entitled on the basis of their contributions, not means-tested and not discretionary. These rights have been significantly eroded since 1980, when the earnings-related supplement to unemployment benefit was abolished and the benefit itself was made taxable (this came into effect in 1982). Atkinson and Micklewright (1989, p126) calculated that there were at least 38 'significant' changes made to unemployment benefit between 1979 and 1988 and concluded that 'the system has undergone major changes of principle without any widespread public recognition'. Specifically, the shift was from a contributory to a means-tested system of support (Chapter 5), and the final abolition of unemployment benefit and introduction of jobseeker's allowance in October 1996 has almost completed this process.

It is estimated by the Low Pay Unit that 165,00 people will lose entitlement to unemployment benefit and 70,000 will not qualify for income support (Low Pay Unit, 1996). Early press reports suggest that implementation has been difficult, with long delays in processing claims (*Guardian*, 11 November 1996) and a significant number of people, between 10,000 and 15,000, dropping out of the unemployment count in the first month because of failure to qualify for jobseeker's allowance (*Independent*, 14 November 1996).

The reform of invalidity benefits has also meant a substantial reduction in the number of claimants. Incapacity benefit was introduced in 1994 and replaced the existing invalidity benefit with a flat-rate benefit (paid at three rates, depending on length of time in receipt). One of the key changes involves the 'all work test', which means that a person must be judged to be incapable of any kind of work at all, not just the type of work they have done in the past. It was predicted that up to 320,000 claimants would fail this test and thus be found fit for work in the first two years and savings of over £1.5 billion were estimated. Implementation (as with jobseeker's allowance) has been somewhat slower than predicted but about 39,000 were assessed as fit for work (and therefore ineligible for benefit) in the first six months of operation (*Poverty*, Spring 1996).

CONCLUSION

Policies aimed at creating a 'free' labour market and a 'targeted' social security system, alongside a stress on 'family responsibility', have hit poor people hard and made the task of achieving an adequate and secure income very much harder. Women and men have been affected in somewhat different ways, because of their different employment and family situations. Women have been most affected by changes to means-tested benefits while men have particularly lost out through reductions in national insurance provisions. Labour market deregulation has contributed to an increase in the extent of poverty among those in work, and led to an explosion in in-work benefit receipt. Socially divisive policies, such as the child support legislation, have not only led to increasing conflict between some men and some women at the individual level, but have also contributed to more general feelings of uneasiness, if not despair, about the future of the family. Blaming the victim has reached new heights. The stereotypical figures of the 'single mother', with her 'babies on benefit' who grow up to be 'delinquent youth', not least because of the failure of the 'absent father' to provide support, are indeed an insult to those many poor women and men struggling to achieve an adequate standard of living in 1990s Britain.

REFERENCES

Atkinson A B and Micklewright J (1989) 'Turning the screw: benefits for the unemployed 1979-1988' in Atkinson A B (ed) *Poverty and Social*

Security, Harvester Wheatsheaf.

Baldwin, S and Falkingham, J (eds) (1995) *Social Security and Social Change: New Challenges to the Beveridge Model*, Harvester Wheatsheaf.

Chatrick, B and Convery, P (1996) '120,000 young unemployed people have no income', *Working Brief*, Issue 77, August/September, pp15-17.

Convery, P (1996) 'How many people are unemployed?', *Working Brief*, Issue 78, October.

CSO (1995) *Family Spending: a report on the 1994/95 Family Expenditure Survey*, HMSO.

Davies, H and Joshi, H (1994) 'Sex, sharing and the distribution of income, *Journal of Social Policy*, 23, 3, pp30-40.

Department of Social Security (1995) *Piloting change in social security: helping people into work*, DSS.

Department of Social Security (1996a), *Households Below Average Income: 1979–1993/4*, HMSO.

Department of Social Security (1996b) *Social Security Statistics 1995*, HMSO.

Dex, S, Lissenburgh, S and Taylor, M (1994) *Women and Low Pay: Identifying the Issues*, Equal Opportunities Commission.

DfEE (1996) *Monthly Digest of Statistics*, DfEE, September.

Dowler, E and Calvert, C (1994) *Diet, choice and poverty*, Family Policy Studies Centre.

Glendinning, C (1987) 'Impoverishing women' in Walker, A and Walker, C (eds) *The Growing Divide*, CPAG.

Graham, H (1996) 'The health experiences of mothers and young children on income support, *Benefits*, Issue 17, October, pp10-13.

Gregg, P and Wadsworth, J (1994) *More work in fewer households*, NIESR Discussion Paper no 72.

Jarvis, S and Jenkins, S (1995) *Do the poor stay poor? New evidence about income dynamics from the British Household Panel Survey*, ESRC Research Centre on Micro-Social Change, University of Essex, Occasional Paper 95-25.

Joseph Rowntree Foundation (1995) *Inquiry into Income and Wealth*, Joseph Rowntree Foundation.

Kempson, E (1996) *Life on a low income*, Joseph Rowntree Foundation.

Low Pay Unit (1996), *The New Review*, LPU.

May, M and Brunsdon, E (1996) 'Women and private welfare' in Hallett, C (ed) *Women and Social Policy: an introduction*, Harvester Wheatsheaf.

McLaughlin, E (1991) *Social Security and Community Care: the case of invalid care allowance*, HMSO.

OPCS (1996), *General Household Survey*, HMSO.

Oppenheim, C and Harker, L (1996) *Poverty: the facts* (third edn), CPAG.

Prior, G and Field, J (1996) *Pensions and Divorce*, HMSO.

Vogler, C and Pahl, J (1993) 'Social and economic change and the organisation of money within marriage, *Work, Employment and Society*,

7, 1, pp71-95.

Webb, S (1991) 'Women and the UK income distribution: past, present and prospects' in Lindley, R (ed) *Labour market structures and prospects for women*, Institute of Employment Research, University of Warwick.

Webb, S, Kemp, M and Millar, J (1996) *The changing face of low pay in Britain*, Centre for the Analysis of Social Policy, University of Bath.

8 Ethnic inequality and social security policy

Alice Bloch

The number of people, living in Britain, from a minority ethnic community has increased over the last decade from 2.5 million people, or 4.5 per cent of the total population in 1985, to 3.2 million people or 5.7 per cent of the total population in 1994 (Haskey, 1996).

- The Indian community is the largest single minority ethnic community in Britain and makes up 28 per cent of the total ethnic minority population.
- The Pakistani and the African-Caribbean communities each comprise 16 per cent.
- The Black African community forms 9 per cent.
- The Bangladeshi community forms 6 per cent.
- The Chinese community forms 4 per cent.
- Other Black and Asian groups, including those of mixed origin make up 21 per cent of the total minority ethnic population in Britain. (Haskey, 1996)

As the number of people from minority ethnic communities increases in Britain, it becomes more difficult but more essential for the social security system to be able to address their diverse needs. This chapter will examine the reasons why people from minority communities might find themselves more dependant on social security benefits than their white counterparts. It will also explore the way in which changes to the social security system, over the last decade, have affected benefit entitlements among different groups and the steps taken to recognise the information needs of benefit claimants.

UNEMPLOYMENT

The labour market demonstrates the most basic operation of racial inequality. Black workers experience much higher levels of unemployment than white workers and, when in paid employment, are more likely to be in occupations with low pay and low status (Ginsburg, 1992).

Around 6 per cent of all those of working age belong to an ethnic minority group. The unemployment rate for people from ethnic minority groups is just over double the rate of unemployment found among members of the white population: 18.7 per cent and 8.2 per cent respectively. There are large variations in the employment rates of people from different communities although the overall rates of unemployment have changed little since 1984. The highest rates of unemployment are still found among those from the Pakistani, Bangladeshi and Black communities, especially those who describe their ethnic group as Black African (Sly, 1996). Table 8.1 shows the average unemployment rates, by sex and ethnic group, in the period 1994/95.

TABLE 8.1: **Average unemployment rates 1994/95, by ethnic group and sex**
Percentages

Ethnic group	All	Men	Women
White	8.2	9.5	6.4
Black Caribbean	20.8	23.3	17.0
Black African	29.9	30.8	28.8
Indian	11.7	12.4	10.9
Pakistani	24.5	25.1	*
Bangladeshi	40.3	37.7	*

*Less than 10,000 in cell so estimate not shown. In 1994 the combined rate of unemployment for Pakistani and Bangladeshi women was 24 per cent.

Sources: Sly, F (1996) and Sly, F (1995).

The most significant feature of employment patterns since 1984 are the differences found between white women and women from minority ethnic communities. Between 1984 and 1995, the employment rate for white women increased from 59 per cent to 68 per cent while the proportion of working women from minority ethnic communities increased only marginally, from 44 per cent in 1984 to

46 per cent in 1994. Moreover, men and women from minority ethnic communities are more likely than are white people to find their employment trends linked very closely to the economic cycle (Sly, 1996). This is not a new phenomenon: the economic slumps during the 1970s and early 1980s had a disproportionate effect on Black unemployment (Ginsburg, 1992).

Variations in rates of unemployment are very marked among different age groups and among different communities. Among 16–24-year-olds, the rate of unemployment for young Black men stands at three times that of young white men (51 per cent versus 18 per cent). In the 25 to 34-year-old age group, with the exception of Indian people, rates of unemployment among people from minority groups is around twice that found in the white population, although there is little difference in rates of unemployment between Indian people and white people. In the age group 35 to 44, Black men continue to have the highest level of unemployment and it is only in the 45 to retirement age group that Pakistani and Bangladeshi men have higher rates of unemployment than Black men (Sly, 1995).

EMPLOYMENT SECTORS AND LOW PAY

Ginsburg (1992) argues that 'the most fundamental aspect of racial inequality is to be found in the labour market'. People from minority ethnic communities, who are employed, tend to be employed in certain industries and sectors and white people are more likely to work in the private sector than are those from minority ethnic groups (62 per cent and 57 per cent respectively). Overall, around a quarter of white people and people from minority ethnic communities work in the public sector, although again there are marked differences between communities. While a quarter of those from all minority ethnic communities are employed in the public sector, 41 per cent of Black people worked in the public sector compared to 19 per cent of Indian people and 12 per cent of Bangladeshi or Pakistani people. Pakistani and Bangladeshi people were more likely to be self-employed (22 per cent) than were people from Indian (18 per cent), white (15 per cent) and Black (7 per cent) communities (Sly, 1995).

People from minority ethnic communities are more likely to work in low paid jobs with poor terms and conditions of employment than white people. For instance, 30 per cent of men from ethnic minorities worked in distribution, hotels, catering and repairs compared to 16 per cent of white men. They, therefore, have been significantly affected by the abolition of the Wages Councils discussed in Chapter 3. The differences between women are less pronounced; around a quarter of all women, regardless of their ethnic group, work in distribution, hotels, catering and repairs. However, 15 per cent of women from minority ethnic communities work in medical, health and veterinary services compared with only 9 per cent of white women (Amin and Oppenheim, 1992).

There are differences in the sectors and industries in which different minority communities are employed. While 4 per cent of all employees worked in hotels and catering, among Bangladeshi and Chinese employees the proportions were 41 per cent and 38 per cent respectively. On average, 5 per cent of employees worked in hospitals or medical care institutions. However, there is a concentration of Africans (14 per cent), Chinese (13 per cent) and African-Caribbeans (13 per cent) working within the hospital and medical care sector (Jones, 1993).

Given the sorts of jobs that people from minority ethnic communities obtain, it is not surprising that there are strong wage differentials among different ethnic groups. Data from the *Labour Force Survey*, in 1994, shows that average hourly pay among those in full time work was £7.44 among the white population and £6.82 among ethnic minority communities. Table 8.2 shows that people from the Pakistani and Bangladeshi communities tend to be least well paid.

TABLE 8.2: **Average hourly earnings of full-time employees by ethnic group and sex**

Ethnic origin	£ per hour		
	All	Men	Women
All origins	7.42	7.97	6.39
White	7.44	8.00	6.40
Black	6.92	7.03	6.77
Indian	6.70	7.29	5.77
Pakistani/Bangladeshi	5.39	5.47	5.15

Source: Sly, F (1995)

Given the higher rates of unemployment among people from minority ethnic groups, compared to their white counterparts, as well as the tendency for employment to be cyclical and often low paid, it is not surprising that people from minority ethnic communities can find themselves dependent on social security. However, changes to the social security system since the late 1980s continue the trend of restricting their benefit entitlement.

IMMIGRATION AND WELFARE

The welfare state was designed on the principles of a homogeneous white society with a male breadwinner supporting his family. The social security system revolved around the notion of contributions and because contributions are earnings related, people in low-paid work and those in and out of employment, which as we have seen tends to represent a greater proportion of people from minority ethnic communities, tend to find themselves dependent on means-tested benefits (Alcock, 1993).

In the last decade, a number of changes to social security have impacted harshly on people from minority ethnic groups. The changes include: Social Security Act 1986, Social Security Act 1988, Immigration Act 1988, residency tests, the public funds and sponsorship tests, the habitual residence test (1994) and the Social Security (Persons from Abroad) Miscellaneous Amendment Regulations contained in the Asylum and Immigration Act 1996.

People from minority ethnic communities who arrived in Britain as adults are disadvantaged in terms of their final pension entitlements since SERPs is now assessed on a lifetime's earnings rather than, as prior to 1986, on the 'best 20 years' rule (Chapter 6), as are those who spend extended periods abroad and therefore not in paid employment. Changes in the contributions base of unemployment benefit (now contribution-based JSA) also disadvantages people from minority ethnic communities because they are more likely than others to have broken employment histories.

There are three special rules which are attached to benefit entitlement for means-tested benefits and which are more likely to affect people in ethnic minority groups (Dean, 1996). First, there are rules surrounding immigration status, so that dependants of people already settled can come and live in Britain only if they can prove that they will have no recourse to public funds. Since the Aliens Act (1905) immigration legislation has restricted access to welfare through the concept of 'no recourse to public funds' (Miles and Clearly, 1993). The Aliens Act (1919) first linked immigration to employment status (Holmes, 1991). The trend of linking immigration to welfare entitlement and/or labour market activity has increased during the course of the twentieth century. For example, the Immigration Act (1988) introduced the public funds test for dependants of people who had settled in Britain before 1973. Under the Act, all British and Commonwealth citizens, who were settled in Britain and wanted their spouses and/or children to join them, had to sponsor them and prove that they would not need any public funds.

The second rule is the residence directives test which exempts from some benefits, any nationals from European Economic Area states who are not economically active, such as students and lone parents (Dean, 1996).

The third rule is concerned with the system of residency tests. In 1994, the Government introduced the habitual residence test as a condition for claiming income support, housing benefit and council tax benefit. Although the habitual residence test was supposed to target European 'benefit tourists', the reality is different (Kreel, 1994). The test has actually affected British nationals who have lived abroad and are now returning to the UK, as well as those who have settled in the UK but have gone abroad for a few months. According to Bolderson and Roberts (1995, p13) : 'It may have a disproportionate effect on British citizens who are Black who will find themselves more closely scrutinised than those who are white.'

Residency rules also restrict entitlement to the main disability benefits. In order to be eligible, an individual has to have been resident in Britain for six consecutive months during the preceding one year period. Again, this is more likely to impact on people from minority ethnic communities, who may travel abroad to visit sick or other relatives, than on others.

The most recent change to social security to affect people from minority communities is the Social Security (Persons from Abroad) Miscellaneous Amendment Regulations (1996) which were contained in the Asylum and Immigration Act (1996). The amendment removed entitlement to social security benefits for asylum-seekers who apply for asylum in-country rather than at the port of entry and from those asylum-seekers who are appealing against a Home Office decision on their case. Under the changes, anyone who has been sponsored by relatives is excluded from claiming benefits for five years, unless the sponsor dies. Clearly, the amendments impact most harshly on asylum-seekers, an already vulnerable group, and it is estimated that around 10,000 asylum seekers were affected by the changes in the period between February and September 1996 (Refugee Council, 1996b).

Prior to the 1996 amendments, around two-thirds of asylum-seekers entering Britain applied for asylum in-country, that is once they were already through immigration control and in Britain (HMSO, 1995). The proportion applying for asylum in-country dropped to 63 per cent after the legislation came into force, so there has been very little change in the pattern of asylum-seeking (Refugee Council, 1996a). Research demonstrates that asylum-seekers who apply in-country do so very soon after their arrival in the UK (Refugee Council, 1996a). Indeed, a survey of refugees in east London found that 92 per cent of asylum-seekers who applied in-country came to Britain with the intention of seeking asylum and 71 per cent made their application within one week of entering the country (Bloch, 1996b).

The impact of the legislation has been far reaching, especially in light of the number of people who seek asylum each year. In 1994 there were nearly 33,000 asylum applicants and this increased to nearly 44,000 in 1995. According to Carter (1996):

> The immediate impact of benefit withdrawal has been to cause intense hardship. Many people are moving between friends, relatives, casual acquaintances, church groups, community organisations, voluntary advice agencies and statutory authorities in a desperate attempt to secure food, clothing and shelter.

The situation is intensified by the fact that asylum-seekers are not allowed to apply for a work permit until they have been living in the UK for six months. The process of obtaining a work permit may be a slow one. A Home Office survey of refugees and asylum-seekers found that 86 per cent of those who applied for permission to work had to wait between six months and a year for a decision to be made, while 14 per cent had to wait a year or longer (Carey-Wood *et al*, 1995). This means that most asylum-seekers are unable to work in Britain for more than a year after their arrival and, without access to benefits, they have no source of income available to them.

MEETING DIVERSE NEEDS

The Benefits Agency and the Department of Social Security recognise the need to cater for the ethnic, cultural, religious and linguistic diversity of their customers. The creation of the Benefits Agency in 1991 brought with it decentralisation, more local autonomy, a greater concern for customer service and the recognition that 'people from ethnic minorities have particular needs' (Benefits Agency, 1991). A number of service delivery initiatives aimed at minority communities have been introduced with varying degrees of success. Initiatives include translated leaflets, interpreters, Ethnic Freeline Service and advice sessions at local voluntary or community organisations.

Translated leaflets, for distribution among the local offices of the Benefits Agency, have been produced by the Department of Social Security. However, research has shown that little use is made of translated leaflets, owing to a lack of knowledge about them and because among some communities and groups literacy skills are limited making the blanket production of translated leaflets of little value (Bloch, 1993).

Some local offices provide an interpretation service while some have Language Line, a telephone language service, in the reception areas of the local office. In reality, however, most people tend to rely on family, friends or a representative from a voluntary organisation to provide them with language assistance where necessary. The reasons for this are two-fold. First, not all offices provide interpretation services and where they are provided, it is virtually impossible to provide language support for the range of community languages in any single locality. Secondly, where local offices do provide interpreters, there is a lack of information and knowledge about the service within the targeted community (Bloch, 1994).

Another initiative that was developed was the Ethnic Freeline Service. The service provided information and advice about benefits in a number of different community languages. However, the service was not widely known about, reactions to it as a service were mixed and it failed to recognise the heterogeneous information needs of different communities. For example, Punjabi and Urdu speakers found the line useful as there was a preference for telephone advice. In the case of the Chinese community, the Freeline service was not very effective as there was a preference for face-to-face oral information (Bloch, 1994). Although the service was of value to some groups, it has now been closed down along with the other freeline information services.

Some local offices undertake outreach work in local voluntary organisations and this is seen as a very effective way of providing information and advice to customers from minority ethnic communities. An effective model is where an officer from the Benefits Agency makes regular visits to local community centres in order to provide information and advice about benefits and to provide help through the claiming process. The extent of the outreach service is necessarily limited, owing to resource constraints, as it requires a large staffing commitment (Bloch, 1993). Moreover, Law *et al* (1994) emphasises the fact that an active voluntary sector does not take away the need for the Benefits Agency to develop accessible multi-cultural services aimed at empowering people rather than reinforcing dependency on advisors.

The support of voluntary and community groups in the provision of information and advice is particularly important for refugees and asylum-seekers who are less likely to have family and friends in Britain than are people from other minority communities since their migration is involuntary and often unplanned as a result of an acute situation in their country of origin (Bloch, 1996b). Research in east London found that 74 per cent of refugees and asylum-seekers who were claiming benefits had received help making their claim and that four in ten had received help from a voluntary sector adviser, four in ten from a friend from their own community and two in ten from a family member. No one had received help from an officer of the Benefits Agency (Bloch, 1996b). Thus, there is a need for the Benefits Agency to collaborate with voluntary organisations and groups and religious networks in the delivery of services to minority ethnic customers. This would mean that the services were more appropriate to the needs of heterogeneous communities.

One of the effects of inadequate information and advice about benefits can be low take-up and this is especially prevalent among those whose first language is not English (Ritchie and England, 1985). But information and advice is not the only reason for a lack of take-up; cultural factors which attach shame and stigma to claiming benefits also come into play. Research carried out in Leeds found that, among the Chinese, Pakistani and Bangladeshi communities, there was stigma attached to claiming benefits and in some cases it resulted in a decision not to claim (Law, 1996).

IMMIGRATION AND SOCIAL SECURITY

In spite of the efforts made by the Benefits Agency to try and meet the information and advice needs of diverse communities, there is still a long way to go. Initiatives need to be better targeted in order to meet the needs of specific communities within any one locality and welfare rights advisors have expressed a fear that increased local autonomy could serve to perpetuate the disparity that exists in the level of services offered to people from minority ethnic groups nationally (Singh, 1992). In reality, efforts to save money have resulted in the curtailment of information and advice services such as the Ethnic Freeline Service and resource intensive outreach work. A commitment to improve service provision for everyone, regardless of race or ethnicity, means that resources must be made available.

There is widespread concern about the propensity of staff from the Benefits Agency to ask for documentation from members of ethnic communities and the resulting links between immigration control and welfare policies (Alcock, 1993; Law, 1996). According to Ginsburg (1992):

> This contributes to a political atmosphere surrounding the welfare state in which the legitimate claims of welfare need amongst Black people may be seen as suspect.

Moreover, some people from minority ethnic communities may be deterred from claiming benefits for fear that their eligibility and therefore their immigration status will be questioned (Bloch, 1993). In some instances, especially in the case of asylum seekers, people may be forced to travel without documents or with false documents and this may affect their benefit entitlement. Carter (1996) cites the case of a Somali woman:

> A Somali woman, 3 children and grandchildren whose mother had been killed, had been living in a Kenyan refugee camp. They fled to the UK in December 1995 seeking asylum and using a fake passport with the identity of a Kenyan woman. The DSS refused income support because of false identification. The immigration services say they will treat her as Kenyan.

Since the implementation of changes in social security entitlements for asylum-seekers, evidence suggests that many asylum-seekers are put off claiming benefits because they are unsure of their eligibility and due to a fear of officialdom (Carter, 1996). This is particularly worrying given that most asylum-seekers are not financially independent when they arrive in UK and have an immediate need for food, clothing and housing (Amnesty International, 1996).

CONCLUSION

The disparity between white people and people from minority ethnic communities in terms of levels of employment and low pay has continued during the course of the last decade. Conservative governments have maintained a policy of welfare curtailment over the last 18 years. Changing rules have ensured that increasing numbers of people from minority ethnic groups are excluded from social welfare which is a pre-requisite for citizenship (Twine, 1994). The policy of stricter immigration controls and the reduction in welfare benefits and services, all serve to limit citizenship and therefore maintain an unequal society where some people are included as full citizens, with access to all the social and economic institutions in society, while others are not.

REFERENCES

Alcock, P (1993) *Understanding Poverty*, Macmillan.

Amin, K and Oppenheim, C (1992) *Poverty in Black and White: Deprivation and ethnic minorities*, Child Poverty Action Group and The Runnymede Trust.

Amnesty International (1996) *Slamming the Door: The demolition of the right to asylum in the UK*, Amnesty International.

Benefits Agency (1991) *Introducing the Benefits Agency*, HMSO.

Bloch, A (1993) *Access to Benefits: The information needs of minority ethnic groups*, Policy Studies Institute.

Bloch, A (1994) 'Improving access to benefits for minority ethnic groups', *Benefits*, Issue 9, p3-6.

Bloch, A (1996a) 'Refugees in Newham', in Butler, T and Rustin, M (eds) *Rising in the East*, Lawrence and Wishart.

Bloch, A (1996b) *Beating the Barriers: The employment and training needs of refugees in Newham*, London Borough of Newham.

Bolderson, H and Roberts, S (1995) 'New restrictions on benefits for migrants: xenophobia or trivial pursuits?' *Benefits*, Issue 12, January, p11-15.

Carey-Wood, J, Duke, K, Karn, V and Marshall, T (1995) *The Settlement of Refugees in Britain*, Home Office Research Study 141, HMSO.

Carter, M (1996) *Poverty and Prejudice*, Commission for Racial Equality and the Refugee Council.

Dean, H (1996) *Welfare, Law and Citizenship*, Harvester Wheatsheaf.

Ginsburg, N (1992) *Divisions of Welfare: A critical introduction to comparative social policy*, Sage.

Gordon, P and Newnham, A (1985) *Passport to Benefits: Racism and Social*

Security, Child Poverty Action Group and Runnymede Trust.

Haskey, J (1996) 'The ethnic minority populations of Great Britain: their estimated sizes and age profiles', Population Trends, Number 84, HMSO, pp31-39.

HMSO (1995) 'Asylum statistics United Kingdom 1994', Home Office Statistical Bulletin, HMSO.

Holmes, C (1991) A Tolerant Country: Immigrants, refugees and minorities in Britain, Faber and Faber, London.

Jones, T (1993) Britain's Ethnic Minorities, Policy Studies Institute.

Kreel, J (1995) 'Habitual residence test: some new developments', Benefits, Issue 13, pp29-30.

Law, I (1996) Racism, Ethnicity and Social Policy, Prentice Hall/Harvester Wheatsheaf.

Law, I, Karmani, A, Deacon, A and Hylton, C (1994) 'The effect of ethnicity on claiming benefits: Evidence from Chinese and Bangladeshi communities', Benefits, Issue 9, pp7-11.

Miles, R and Clearly, P (1993) 'Migration to Britain: Racism, state regulation and employment', in Robinson, V (ed) The International Refugee Crisis: British and Canadian responses, Macmillan in association with the Refugee Studies Programme, Oxford University.

Refugee Council (1996a) The State of Asylum: A critique of asylum policy in the UK, The Refugee Council.

Refugee Council (1996b) Update: The impact of the social security regulations, Refugee Council, October 1996.

Ritchie, J and England, J (1985) The Hackney Benefit Study: A study to investigate the take-up of means tested benefits within the London Borough of Hackney, Social and Community Planning Research, unpublished report.

Singh, J (1992) 'The benefits agency: new deal for non-English speaking claimants', Benefits, April/May.

Sly, F (1995) 'Ethnic groups and the labour market: analyses from the Spring 1994 Labour Force Survey', Employment Gazette, June, The Employment Department, HMSO, pp251-62.

Sly, F (1996) 'Ethnic minority participation in the labour market: trends from the Labour Force Survey 1984-1995', Labour Market Trends, Volume 104, Number 6, HMSO, pp259-70.

Twine, F (1994) Citizenship and Social Rights, Sage.

Poverty and schooling: choice, diversity or division?

George Smith, Teresa Smith and Gemma Wright

We must restore to every child, regardless of background, the chance to progress as far as his or her abilities allow. (*Conservative Party Manifesto*, 1979)

I am not prepared to see children in some parts of this country having to settle for a second-class education (John Major, Foreword to *Choice and Diversity*, DfE, 1992)

… years later 93 per cent [of British pupils] are still locked into a second-class system of education. (George Walden, Conservative MP, 1996[1])

Education played little more than a walk-on role in the 1979 election campaign. But by then the Conservative party had already harnessed to its cause the rising anxiety over educational standards, first clearly articulated in the 'Black Papers' of the late 1960s/70s, thereby capturing a critical part of the developing educational agenda of the 1980s. It was not until the 1987 election that education became a key issue, foreshadowing the first major tranche of school reforms in 1988. By 1997 education had moved to the very centre of all the major parties' campaigns. The waves of concern over educational standards and quality had by now been whipped to a real storm – at least judged by media content and coverage – beating on schools, education authorities and increasingly, government.

---

1. To be fair, George Walden is making a comparison between the private and state sectors of education, while John Major simply has the state sector in mind.

Yet paradoxically, in terms of formal qualifications, staying on rates and access to higher education, there has been significant improvement since 1979: the proportions of 15-year-olds in England getting 5+ GCSE grade A–C rose from 24 per cent in 1979 to 44 per cent by 1995; the proportions getting two or more A levels from 14 per cent to 29 per cent, and the 'age participation index' for higher education from 12 per cent to over 30 per cent of the relevant age group even though the Government's ambivalence on whether these increases are real improvements or merely further evidence of falling standards (this time, by examiners) seriously undermines any confident claims they might have made.

The decade, too, since 1987 was marked – at least for England and Wales – by more educational legislation and centrally directed change, explicitly aimed at raising standards, than at any other comparable period. But, if anything, this avalanche of legislation has brought greater uncertainty by removing or weakening some of the major landmarks of the past, and creating new institutions and agencies (SEAC, NCC, SCAA, OFSTED, TTA, FAS – to identify just some of those with a central role) that, in trying to establish their sometimes overlapping roles, have tended – at least in the short term – to destabilise things further. The result by 1997 is a far more fragmented, divided and demoralised educational service, even though it still somehow produces better results.

Over the same period there has been a sharp increase in economic and social polarisation (as shown by other contributions to this volume), not just in society at large but in the way different neighbourhoods and localities have gained or lost in the far more competitive environment of the 1980s and 1990s. The growing proportion of families with children in the poorest income groups, and their increasing concentration in particular urban areas has had a major impact on locally delivered services, such as education.

This is the backdrop for our brief review of poverty and schooling. On any count poverty affects a very large and still rising number of children (see Chapter 2). On the most restricted criterion, the number of children actually receiving a free school meal (much less than those eligible, let alone those who have not claimed, and since 1988 available only to families on income support) was 821,400 children in England in 1991 (about 11 per cent of school pupils). By 1995 this had risen to 1,235,746 children, just under 17 per cent (19 per cent of primary age children, 13 per cent of secondary and 36 per cent of those in special schools) – a rise of about 50 per cent.

Other estimates give a much higher figure, for example, figures from the Households Below Average Income (HBAI) show 30 per cent of children are now growing up in households without a full-time adult earner.

This review, which focuses mainly on pre-school and school level education, with more limited information on further and higher education, addresses three main questions. First, what is the impact of growing social and economic divisions on education for low income families? Second, how far do educational policies reduce or amplify this impact? And finally, what is now the cost for parents of a 'free' educational service?

THE POLICY BACKGROUND

Broadly, educational reforms can be grouped into two main types. First come the centralising changes that have increased the power of government and its direct involvement in educational provision, in place of the long-standing 'partnership' between central government, local authority and school. This is seen most dramatically in the introduction of the statutory National Curriculum and assessment system following the 1988 Act. It is encapsulated in the first two clauses of the 1993 Act, which detail the Secretary of State's general responsibilities over education in England and Wales. It is seen too in the national system of regular school inspections following the 1992 Act, and in the annual 'league tables' of secondary school examination results.

But second, there are the changes that have apparently increased decentralisation within the system, sharply reducing the power of LEAs. The emphasis on parental choice was first expressed in the 1980 Act, but then spelt out as a central element in later policy, particularly the Parents' Charter. Local management of schools (LMS) under the 1988 Act requires local authorities to devolve increasing proportions of the total budget to schools, thereby reducing the power of the local authority to deliver services independently, and linking a school's funding directly to the number of pupils on roll. Both the 1986 and 1988 Acts substantially increased the responsibilities of individual school governing bodies. Further there was provision under the 1988 Act for schools to 'opt out' of local authority control and become grant maintained (GM). This became a central focus of the 1993 Act – the goal to increase 'choice and diversity'. The creation of 'City Technology Colleges' (CTCs), and the designation of existing schools as 'specialist' also formed part of the policy of creating diversity.

In combination, these changes were explicitly designed to shift the school system towards a more market based approach, based on per capita funding. The individual school must respond to its 'local market' by attracting parental choice and support. Schools that are successful and increase or hold their 'market share' are likely to flourish; those with a declining share will go to the wall. The power of the local authority to intervene to protect weaker schools is very much reduced, through loss of direct control over school funding (now more than 90 per cent devolved to schools) and the possibility that more schools will opt out if they disagree with local authority decisions.

Yet it is not a free market. Schools' greater autonomy is highly restricted by a much tighter framework of control laid down by central government. Nor do schools have leverage over the total size of their budget. Parents' choice is limited by available space or indeed there being a choice of local schools. If it is a 'market' at all, or a 'quasi-market', it is highly regulated and controlled, if not quite 'engineered'.

The idea of a 'market' puts the onus for success or failure squarely on the individual pupil, parent or school. It is up to them to maximise their chances, and to take action if they are blocked. But this takes no account of differences in capacity to take advantage of such opportunities, and the strong links between social background and educational performance, that were at the centre of many of the pre-1979 education reforms. Another casualty of these reforms has been those parts of the educational system that had a broader social or welfare purpose. The National Curriculum and 'league tables' have also tended to squeeze out the broader objectives of education, in favour of more easily measured examination or test results.

THE NEW 'MARKET' SYSTEM

RESOURCES FOR EDUCATION

Has the new 'market' system delivered adequate resources for schools? DfEE *Statistical Bulletin* 5/96 indicates that public spending on education in the UK is now roughly the same proportion of GDP as it was in 1979/80 (5.1 per cent), though it had been more than 6 per cent of GDP in the mid 1970s, and is now well below that of most comparable OECD countries (OECD, 1996). However, judged against general inflation this is an increase in 'real terms' of 33 per cent. Comparisons appear even more favourable for per-pupil expenditures because of the large fall in pupil numbers during the 1980s – there were over 1 million fewer pupils in maintained schools in England by the late 1980s than in 1979/80, though numbers have risen steadily since 1990 (another 400,000 pupils by 1994/95). DfEE figures for England show a 55 per cent increase in primary per-pupil funding over the period 1979/80 to 1994/95, 49 per cent for secondary, and 89 per cent for pupils in special schools. So why are levels of dissatisfaction so high – why are the 'shires marching'?

First, overall expenditure on schools has grown rather less rapidly, by about 25 per cent since 1979/80 for the UK as a whole, but less if we widen the time window to the 1970s (in fact by about 14 per cent since 1975). Secondary schools fared particularly badly with something under 4 per cent more than 1975. There is a fall in the proportion of GDP spent on schools from around 3.7 per cent in 1975 to just over 3 per cent by 1993/4 (0.7 per cent of GDP in 1993/4 was about £4.5 billion).

Secondly, expenditure *per pupil* rose quite sharply in this period (taking general inflation into account) until the early 1990s (Figure 9.1a). However, if we use the CIPFA derived educational cost inflation index (Figure 9.1b), which takes account of teacher costs, then per-pupil funding has been falling quite steeply since 1990 at secondary level and, slightly later at primary level. Secondary funding per pupil was by 1994/95 back to levels last seen in 1986/87, and will have fallen further since then. This is likely to be the time frame used by those directly affected, not the more distant comparisons with 1979.

The results are seen in rising class sizes in the 1990s (though lower teacher 'contact ratios' played a part) and locally in the loss of teachers. Capital funding for school building fell sharply in the late 1970s and is still less than half the level it was in the mid 1970s. Judged against current expenditure, capital building represented nearly 9 per cent of recurrent expenditure in 1975/76, but less than 5 per cent in 1993/94. The long term pattern of capital underfunding and inadequate maintenance is seen in the state of school building and the enormous backlog of work.

Finally, there are striking contrasts with the private educational

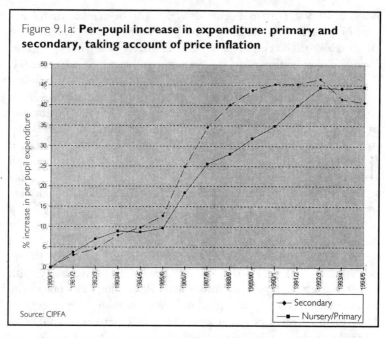

Figure 9.1a: **Per-pupil increase in expenditure: primary and secondary, taking account of price inflation**

Source: CIPFA

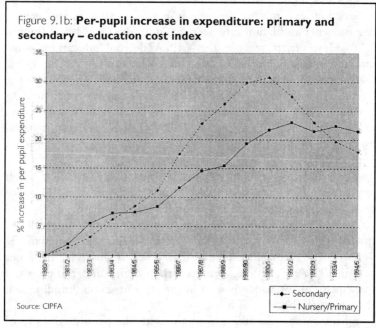

Figure 9.1b: **Per-pupil increase in expenditure: primary and secondary – education cost index**

Source: CIPFA

market. Private school day fees at secondary level are typically twice those of state sector costs for equivalent pupils, and capital expenditure probably three to four times higher per pupil.

DISTRIBUTION OF RESOURCES

Has the new market distributed resources in line with social needs? Complex and changing formulae now determine both the way central government funds are allocated to local authorities and how local authorities allocate funds to their schools under the LMS system. As funds have tightened and local authorities have had less and less scope to raise their expenditure on schools (or indeed anything else), these sometimes obscure mechanisms have become much more important. The Additional Educational Needs (AEN) formula, used by government to allocate resources to local authorities, is now based on three indicators of social need. It currently affects about 17 per cent of the total budget for schooling, though this has fallen back from 24 per cent of the total budget in 1990. The weightings for these needs factors are frequently altered. Changing the weighting given to the ethnic minority indicator in 1994 substantially reduced the budgets available to many inner urban areas with large ethnic minority populations. The overall results for different areas still remain hard to justify in educational terms (in 1996/97 Harrow has a higher AEN score – implying greater needs and therefore more resources – than Barnsley, and Westminster more than Birmingham or Liverpool).

Local authorities can build into their LMS formula some weighting for social needs. While a few allocate 10 per cent or more of the school budget in line with social or special needs, most allocate much less, and some negligible amounts. Analysis of school budgets suggests that the premium going to schools in the 10 per cent most disadvantaged areas in the country is typically about 5 per cent higher per pupil than other schools in the same type of LEAs (Smith, 1996). Ironically, these figures suggest that central government social needs allocations via AEN do not reach through *pro rata* to individual schools with high needs.

ACCESS AND CHOICE

Has the new 'market' created a fairer basis for access and choice? Parental choice has been built into the British education system since the 1944 Education Act, where pupils were to be educated in accordance with the wishes of their parents. But the legislation of the 1980s turned preferences into a market, in which parents are to act as consumers 'buying' educational 'goods'. Parents have a right to choose which school they want for their child; and schools are intended to offer a wider range – GM or LEA, specialist schools, and more support for assisted places in the private sector. However, this market may reinforce existing advantages and disadvantages, rather than ensure equal access to all. The evidence so far suggests that 'choice' and 'diversity' has not benefited all parents and children equally.

First, the principles of 'open enrolment' and 'the right to choose', established by the 1988 Education Reform Act and spelt out in the Parents' Charter published in 1991, assume access to good information and a certain self-confidence about working the system. In practice, many less active or motivated parents lose out in the scramble for scarce places at popular schools, and in the sharply rising levels of admissions appeals (up by 58 per cent in the primary sector and 35 per cent in the secondary sector between 1991/92 and 1994/95). Nominally more choice has produced higher levels of discontent. The Audit Commission's 1995/96 survey of parents showed that although parents overwhelmingly wish to express their preference, 40 per cent thought there was no real choice as there were 'no other suitable schools'. Nationally, about one in ten parents did not get their first choice – and in some areas this was as high as one in three (Audit Commission, 1996).

Second, there are GM schools, announced in the 1987 Conservative Manifesto and included in the 1988 Act. But these made up only 4 per cent of all schools in 1994/95 (although nearly one in five secondary pupils were in such schools). But these schools, with exceptions, are more likely than LEA schools to exercise some form of selection, through informal interview or formal test results or primary school reports. This is selection by the school, not the parent.

Third, there is specialisation by school – the creation of CTCs in 1986 and the extension in 1993 of specialisation to existing schools focusing on technology and languages and now sports and the arts. So far, this is a minority interest: CTCs provide for about 1 per cent of the secondary school population, and the specialist schools programme now covers 181 technology or language colleges. Selection of pupils and specialisation by school were intertwined in the 1997

Education Bill which included proposals to allow GM schools to select up to half their pupils, specialist schools up to a third and LEA schools up to a fifth. Both were a deliberate reversal of a comprehensive access policy, and are unlikely to favour children in poorer families – although there are schools that prove the exception. Few GM schools serve neighbourhoods that could be defined as disadvantaged. And specialist schools are expected to raise considerable sums from private sponsorship – notoriously more difficult to achieve in poorer areas.

Fourth, there is the Assisted Places Scheme, established under the 1980 Education Act to restore the direct grant principle to 'bright children from modest backgrounds'. The Conservatives are committed to doubling the 34,000 places offered in 1995 and planned to extend the scheme to primary schools. But to what extent does the scheme benefit children from disadvantaged backgrounds? Studies demonstrate that many students come from one-parent families in reduced circumstances or from families with some connection with the independent sector. Expansion of the scheme will at best only expand choice for a minority of children from poor areas.

The final example is preschool provision. The Government claims that day care for 23,000 families on low incomes has been boosted by the benefits disregard introduced in October 1994 allowing child-care costs to be offset against earnings (DfEE, 1996b); average daycare costs, however, are considerably higher than the £57 per week maximum. Up to now, preschool cover has been low (Britain is still near the bottom of the league table of publicly funded provision), and more than any other educational service, access has depended on where you live. The 1995 figures for England showed 53 per cent of children under five in school (27 per cent in nursery schools or classes). But this hides very large differences, ranging from the North region at the top of the league with 77 per cent of children under five in school (44 per cent in nursery schools or classes), to the South West at the bottom with only 38 per cent in school (10 per cent in nursery schools or classes). These inequalities are even more pronounced if we look at local authorities rather than regions (although there is evidence that authorities serving more disadvantaged areas have made determined efforts to expand 'compensatory provision').

The market analogy is clearest in the case of preschool education vouchers, introduced as a pilot scheme for four-year-olds in four local authorities in 1996 and extended nationwide in 1997. The voucher scheme is intended to increase parental choice by expanding provision by raising demand and by more diverse provision through encouragement for private and voluntary providers. Parents receive vouchers worth £1,100 for every four-year-old. Vouchers for all provides a new subsidy for the better off, and reduces the scope for focusing high quality pre-school provision on those most in need. Results so far suggest that more than half the parents in the pilot authorities are choosing to use their vouchers in state provision, and a quarter choose the private sector, while playgroups are hard hit.

EXCLUDED PUPILS AND FAILING SCHOOLS

Markets require regulation. How far have the regulatory arrangements worked in a socially fair way? The 1997 Education Bill aimed to further strengthen schools' powers of exclusion, linked to home-school agreements. Since 1990, rates of exclusion, particularly permanent exclusion or 'expulsion', have risen very rapidly. Latest figures show that approximately 13,500 children were permanently excluded in England in 1995/96, an increase of 8 per cent over the previous year. Many more pupils are excluded for a temporary period. Parsons (1996) estimates that this costs £48 million a year in special tuition and social services – more than double the cost of educating these children in school. Managing their own budgets, schools have a clear incentive to exclude their 'problems', rather than manage them, though schools with falling rolls may be forced to accept pupils excluded from other schools.

Background factors are important in exclusion (OFSTED, 1996a). More boys than girls face exclusion, particularly boys from African Caribbean backgrounds (Gillborn and Gipps, 1996). Young people in care are particularly at risk – three quarters of them leave school without qualifications (Action on Aftercare, 1996). Exclusion is associated with poor levels of basic skills, poverty and unemployment, limited aspirations, family difficulties, poor relationships and racism. These pressures should not be seen as causes; many young people face one or more of these problems without resorting to aggressive or disruptive behaviour. But in combination they may form part of a pattern. And the pattern may be stronger in schools, already under pressure and lacking resources, serving neighbourhoods which are themselves facing heavy pressures of poverty, unemployment, family stress and racism. Three out of four pupils permanently excluded at secondary level do not return to mainstream schooling (Gillborn and Gipps, 1996). Some will join the growing group of young people not in school, and later not in work, training schemes or on benefit (Wilkinson, 1995).

The regulatory mechanism, following an OFSTED inspection in England, for schools failing or 'likely to fail' to give their pupils an acceptable standard of education, had by the end of 1995 picked out 105 schools requiring special measures; a further 10 per cent of schools inspected were deemed to have 'serious weaknesses' (OFSTED, 1996b). Yet these failing schools, it turns out, are predominantly located in disadvantaged areas, though it remains unclear how far these are truly weaker institutions, just weighed down by their surroundings, or disproportionately picked out by the criteria used to identify such schools.

THE REAL COSTS OF EDUCATION

Education 'free to all' remains, in theory, a basic principle in the legislation of the 1980s. But what, in practice, do the 'real costs' of 'voluntary contributions' and fund-raising, as well as cuts in clothing grants, the school meals service and eligibility for free school meals, mean to children and parents from low-income families?

School meals are particularly important on health grounds for children from low-income families (Chapter 14), and have long formed part of the education service's 'welfare function'. But with cuts in the school meals service, the removal of local authorities' discretionary powers to provide free meals for low-income families not on income support, and an increasingly 'market' approach with the development of cash cafeterias, free school meals are increasingly stigmatised, and take-up as a percentage of those eligible varies sharply between authorities. The price of a school meal in 1996/97 ranges from 77 pence in the cheapest authority, to £1.61 in the most expensive, a very significant extra cost for low-income families not on income support. In addition, most local authorities have cut back on school clothing grants and many schools instead rely on second-hand schemes and charities for needy families.

Fund-raising and voluntary contributions are increasingly used to subsidise school budgets rather than provide the 'non-essentials'. This is not surprising, when schools are spending on books between a third and a half of what they should for decent library provision (Book Trust, 1996). Figures from OFSTED suggest that 23 per cent of secondary schools and 13 per cent of primary schools suffered from shortages of books that 'adversely affected the standards of lessons' (*TES*, 27 December 1996). According to the National Confederation of Parent Teacher Associations, 92 per cent of primary schools and 75 per cent of secondary schools in 1995 asked Home School Associations for help with the purchase of books and materials, while one in five primary schools and one in three secondary schools asked parents directly for this type of help (NCPTA, 1996). In 1990, schools in county towns and rural areas raised twice as much per pupil as inner city schools (Sumner and Hutchinson, 1990). Parents report constant pressures: 'when I was at school, we never had to pay for anything, whereas now you have to pay for everything ... if they lose a book you have to pay to get another one' (Smith and Noble, 1995).

RESULTS AND OUTCOMES

So far we have examined the impact of educational change since the late 1980s on educational provision. In one sense the results are in line with government policy, to create greater diversity of *institutional* provision, with the national curriculum and its assessment providing the common linking threads. But this diversity can easily be translated into division and inequity.

Yet even this could be justified if educational results and outcomes were improving and more equal chances were provided for children from all social backgrounds. Certainly supporters of these reforms have come close to claiming that the national curriculum, financial devolution to schools and greater parental choice will *by themselves* bring about just this shift towards equal opportunities for all children.

International comparisons of educational performance are one benchmark for standards in the UK. England has consistently performed at or slightly below the average for a set of comparator countries almost since these studies began in the 1960s (Reynolds and Farrell, 1996). This may vary by subject (performance in mathematics at secondary level appears to be falling back, while in science secondary age pupils from England did relatively well, see Keys *et al*, 1996). One consistent finding is that countries such as the UK and the US, which do relatively poorly in these studies, tend to have a long tail of low performance pulling down the overall average score. The recent study on reading performance at age nine in England and Wales (Brooks *et al*, 1996) draws a similar conclusion about the long tail of low performance; the links between educational performance and social disadvantage suggest that this may well be a significant factor in these results.

Following the introduction of the GCSE in 1988 there was a rapid increase in qualifications and staying on rates, though the most recent data show that this is levelling off. However, when these improvements are analysed by different types of area, there appears to be a widening gap between better off and poorer areas. This analysis has to be tentative as only aggregate data are available. As Figure 9.2 shows, staying on rates beyond compulsory level have risen in all areas since 1988. However, in disadvantaged areas (the 25 per cent of local authorities with the highest proportions of families in lower socio-economic groups) the full-time rate at age 17 has risen from about 30 per cent of the age group in 1989 to 48 per cent in 1995, while in the more advantaged areas (the top 25 per cent of local authorities in terms of higher non-manual families) the rate has increased from 39 per cent to 66 per cent. Figure 9.3 shows the pattern for GCSE qualifications. While just under 20 per cent gained Grades A–C in 1988 in the most disadvantaged LEAs, rising to about 32 per cent in 1996, for the advantaged areas the change was from just under 30 per cent to 48 per cent.

Data from individual secondary schools show urban comprehensive schools in the 10 per cent most disadvantaged areas have proportions getting GCSE 5+ Grades A–C at about half the rate of schools in the 10 per cent most advantaged areas (24 per cent as against 49 per cent in 1993). Individual school results suggest that in some areas there are schools with increasing proportions of socially disadvantaged pupils, some of whom have been excluded by other schools. Such schools may find themselves trapped in a vicious circle, with the local authority having limited capacity to help.

CONCLUSION: EXTENDING OPPORTUNITIES AND REAL CHOICES

The conclusion that must be drawn from this analysis is that educational opportunities and results have become *more* unequal in social terms during the 1980s and 1990s. It cannot be the case that 'every child, regardless of background [now has] the chance to progress as far as his or her abilities allow' (*Conservative Manifesto*, 1979). The now much more fractured educational system in part

Figure 9.2: **Percentage of age group aged 17 in full-time education by LEA status: England 1988 to 1995**

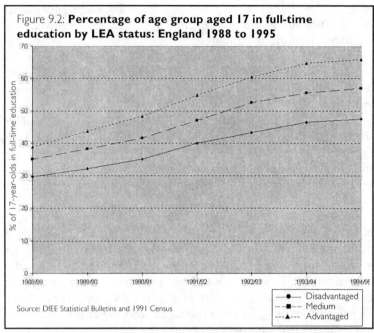

Source: DfEE Statistical Bulletins and 1991 Census

Figure 9.3: **Percentage of age group getting 5+ GCSE Grades A–C, 1988 to 1996 (provisional) by LEA status**

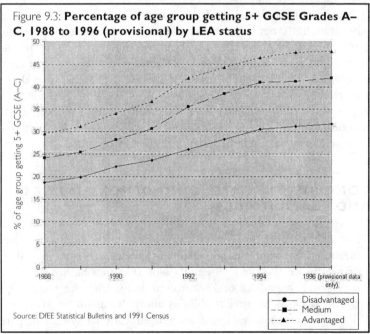

Source: DfEE Statistical Bulletins and 1991 Census

reflects the fragmented wider social and economic structure, where social, economic and spatial factors interact to influence children's 'life chances'. It is too early to say authoritatively how far recent educational policies have contributed to these divisions, but the idea of a 'market' seems likely to lead in this direction, particularly when it is allied with a tough squeeze on overall resources. This ensures there really have to be losers. The continuing top-down nature of the educational changes has also sapped teacher and school morale, as seen in the levels of early retirement. The pressure is likely to be most acute in disadvantaged areas, where the conditions are much more challenging, particularly if central monitoring takes little or no account of these pressures on schools. Schools here have to 'bootstrap' themselves up; some succeed against the odds, but others clearly do not.

WHAT'S TO BE DONE?

There has been too much change simply to turn the clock back to 1979. Questions of choice, access, and educational standards cannot just be pushed back into the bottle. And some of the developments, such as the national curriculum, have been necessary, though not always sufficient, steps towards improvement. In the future, government will have to scrutinise the mass of legislation to identify what has to be abolished, what can be amended, and what safely left alone.

First, effective education for poor areas cannot be separated from a better system for all. It seems most unlikely that this could operate within a competitive market between individual schools. There has to be some intermediate responsibility and power over local schools, including more flexibility in funding and the revival of a better form of partnership between central government, local authority and schools. Centrally directed change may be appropriate at certain stages, but it cannot be the main mode, as it is teachers and schools that ultimately deliver education. As the Audit Commission (1996) recognised, if there is to be a 'market' in education, there has to be effective local intervention and co-ordination to manage it.

Second, a mechanism has to be developed for ensuring that more resources go to schools in disadvantaged areas or that resources nominally allocated by central government on grounds of social need actually reach their target. One way might be clearer identification of the large but obscure AEN component in the central government grant, a proportion of which could be explicitly linked to local authority or school plans for improvement. This would divert far larger resources for improvement programmes.

Third, it is clear that 'choice' on its own is a very blunt weapon for improving schools, tending to produce over-subscribed schools at one end, and rejected schools at the other. At present, enormous resources have been put into assessing schools through league tables and inspection, but rather less into school improvement programmes. Often improvement and certainly 'special measures' are reserved for crisis intervention when a school is already in serious difficulties, by which time it may be too late. As has been wisely observed in the debate on choice in health, a patient's first wish would not be for a *choice* of surgeons but a reasonable guarantee of access to a good surgeon. The same might well apply to parents and schools.

Finally, there is a large number of ways that performance can be raised in disadvantaged areas (Barber and Dann, 1996), but this requires explicit targeting of resources, the raising of morale, and ways of encouraging the best teachers to stay or move to such areas as a positive challenge. American reformers now refer positively to the importance of removing 'barriers to learning' in such areas, with programmes that take us well beyond education and schools.

Thirty years ago the Plowden Report on primary education called for schools in 'deprived areas' to be given priority. 'The first step must be to raise the schools [in these areas] with low standards to the national average; the second quite deliberately to make them better.' But if anything, government policy has moved things in the other direction. Perhaps the next government should take up the challenge again.

REFERENCES

Action on Aftercare Consortium (1996) *Too Much Too Young: the failure of social policy in meeting the needs of care leavers*, Barnardo's.

Audit Commission (1996) *Trading Places: the supply and allocation of school places*, Audit Commission.

Barber, M and Dann, R (1996) *Raising Educational Standards in the Inner Cities*, Cassell.

Book Trust (1996) *School Spending on Books*, Book Trust.

Brooks, G, Pugh, A K and Schagen, I (1996) *Reading Performance at Nine*, NFER/Open University.

Conservative Party (1979) *Election Manifesto*, 1979.

Department for Education (1992) *Choice and Diversity: a new framework for schools*, DfE.

Department for Education and Employment (1996a) *Education and training expenditure since 1979/80*, Statistical Bulletin 5/96, DfEE.

Department for Education and Employment (1996b) *Work and Family: ideas and options for childcare: a consultation paper*, DfEE.

Gillborn, D and Gipps, C (1996) *Recent Research on the Achievements of Ethnic Minority Pupils*, HMSO.

Keys, W, Harris, S and Fernandes, C (1996) *Third International Mathematics and Science Study: first national report Part 1*, NFER.

National Confederation of Parent Teacher Associations (1996) *The State of Schools in England and Wales 1996*, NCPTA.

Organisation for Economic Cooperation and Development (1996) *Education at a Glance – OECD indicators*, OECD, Paris.

Office for Standards in Education (1996a) *Exclusions from Secondary Schools*, HMSO.

Office for Standards in Education (1996b) *The Annual Report of Her Majesty's Chief Inspector of Schools: 1994/95*, HMSO.

Parsons, C (1996) *Exclusions from School: the public cost*, Commission for Racial Equality.

Reynolds, D and Farrell, S (1996) *Worlds Apart*, HMSO.

Smith, G A N (1996) 'Urban education: current position and future possibilities' in Barber, M and Dann, R, *op cit.*

Smith, T, Noble, M and Smith, G (1995) *Education Divides: poverty and schooling in the 1990s*, CPAG.

Sumner, R and Hutchinson, D (1990) *Resources in Primary Schools*, National Foundation for Educational Research.

Walden, G (1996) *We Should Know Better: solving the education crisis*, Fourth Estate.

Wilkinson, C (1995) *The Drop-out Society: young people on the margin*, National Youth Agency.

10 Housing
Norman Ginsburg

In examining changes in housing needs and policies since 1979 it is very difficult to isolate the impact of housing and other social policies on housing needs from the effects of wider socio-economic changes. It might be argued that housing policy itself has been a relatively insignificant factor in the growth of social exclusion compared with, for example, the persistence of mass unemployment, the growth in income inequality and job insecurity, the increase in lone parenthood and the roller-coaster of the housing market. Government policies have certainly played a part in facilitating these latter processes, though perhaps not always explicitly or even intentionally. However, these wider socio-economic changes have had an impact on increasing housing needs and accentuating housing inequalities, in particular with respect to the growth in homelessness and the increased polarisation within the housing market itself. This chapter considers this trend and then examines the role played by housing and associated economic policies on social and economic polarisation in Britain over the past two decades.

HOMELESSNESS

Homelessness is obviously one of the most acute experiences of social exclusion in modern society. The growth in homelessness since 1979 is one indicator of the continued need for social rented housing and yet government policies have limited its supply. The increased incidence of homelessness also has an impact on the access of other groups to social housing. Because of the increased number of families accepted as homeless by local authorities, this group has accounted for a growing proportion of new lettings.

It was only in 1977 that legislation was passed giving households in priority need – a definition which largely excluded 'single homeless' people – reasonably clear rights of access to temporary accommodation and, eventually, to a secure social rented tenancy. Hence, in the period since 1979, the number of households accepted as homeless by local authorities has been taken as the 'headline figure' for homelessness. This figure increased steadily every year from 57,200 in England in 1979, to a peak of 151,720 in 1991, since when it fell gradually to 125,500 in 1995. This fall seems to be accounted for by the increased availability of privately rented accommodation and a substantial increase in the amount of new social housing provision since 1992 (Holmans, 1996). This situation generated some complacency within the Department of the Environment as to future needs for social rented housing, so that it is quite likely that the number of homeless acceptances will start rising again in the late 1990s. The Housing Act 1996 withdrew the right of homeless families to a tenancy in the social rented sector, with the intention of pushing even more homeless families into the private rented sector. There is considerable evidence that for homeless families this sector provides lower quality accommodation, at greater cost to the taxpayer (through housing benefit) and with less security of tenure than do local authority or Housing Association tenancies (Holmans, 1996; Bramley, 1995).

The annual homelessness acceptance figures are, of course, just a measurement of the local authority response over a year, based on a restricted definition of homelessness. A fuller picture based on 1991 census data (Holmans, 1995, Table 4) suggests that on census day there were approximately 110,000 concealed families (such as families having to live with parents), 50,000 would-be couples living apart, 140,000 sharing households, 100,000 single homeless people in hostels, etc, and 10,000 squatters and rough sleepers, as well as the 22,000 families accepted as homeless and living in hostels and bed and breakfast hotels. This gives a total of 430,000 households who could legitimately be described as homeless.

The increase in homelessness during the 1980s was accompanied by a dreadful rise in the number of households in temporary accommodation. Families accepted as homeless usually have to endure a period of weeks, months or even years in temporary accommodation before getting a secure tenancy. At the end of 1980 in England 4,710 households were in temporary accommodation, but by the end of 1992 this had risen to a peak of 63,070 (Wilcox, 1996, Table 84). This accommodation, particularly where it is provided in hostels and bed and breakfast hotels, is often entirely incompatible with normal family life. At the end of 1991 over 12,000 families were in bed and breakfast hotels at an enormous cost to the taxpayer. In 1990, the Government at last made a positive response to the situation by funding local authorities to lease private sector properties on a two or three year basis (Edwards, 1995). This accommodation is more appropriate to the needs of homeless families and is generally less expensive. The numbers in bed and breakfast hotels consequently fell by 1994 to two thirds of the 1991 level, but they started to rise again in 1995 as the private sector leasing 'experiment' withered (Wilcox, 1996, Table 84).

TENURE

The second most obvious parameter of social exclusion in housing is the subordinate status of renting as opposed to owning one's home. One of the simplest ways of indicating this is that in 1994 only 8 per cent of owner-occupied homes in Britain were flats compared with 38 per cent of council homes and 58 per cent of housing association homes. Tenure has been a significant social division in Britain since the first world war, but it has become even more so since 1979. Between 1980 and 1993 the average income of household heads in council housing fell from 48 to 35 per cent of the average income of household heads in mortgaged owner occupation, and from 84 to 59 per cent of the average income of household heads in outright owner occupation (Wilcox, 1996, Table 33). Between 1980 and 1991 the proportion of owner occupiers in the bottom decile of the income distribution fell from 21 to 11 per cent (Malpass and Murie, 1994, Table 6.1). In 1994/95 the average gross weekly household income in council housing was £172.69, compared with £448.64 for owner occupiers; 46.7 per cent of council tenant household income came from social security compared with only 9.3 per cent for owner occupier households (Wilcox, 1996, Table 34). Given the widening of poverty and income inequalities generally since 1979 discussed in Chapters 2 and 3, all these statistics demonstrate a rapidly increasing polarisation between households in owner-occupied and in social rented housing in terms of incomes and labour market status. It may be argued that social rented housing is now more effectively targeted on households with the lowest incomes, but this is at the expense of physical as well as social exclusion on council estates. The process also reinforces the image of social rented housing as a residual and stigmatised provision for poor people, who have little political clout in bidding for adequate housing management and maintenance.

HOUSING POLICY

The two main planks of housing policy since 1979 have been, first, to extend owner occupation as far as possible and, secondly, to retrench severely expenditure on council housing by raising rents, selling off housing and cutting bricks and mortar subsidies and investment. Housing policy has thus played a direct role in the growth of both homelessness and tenure polarisation discussed above because it has marginalised tenants, increased rents and limited the supply of social rented housing. The fall in house prices and hence of confidence in owner occupation in the early 1990s produced a short-term policy reverse which led to increased investment in housing association provision and in the refurbishment of some council estates, but the fundamental principles of Conservative policy remained unchanged. At one stage the Government mooted the possibility of engineering a serious revival of private landlordism, but the cost implications in terms of housing benefit to tenants and possible tax incentives and capital subsidies to landlords made this unattractive to the Treasury.

THE EXTENSION OF HOME OWNERSHIP

From 1979 onwards, particularly in the early years of the Thatcher administrations, the drive to extend home ownership was enthusiastically pursued. Hence between 1979 and 1989 the number of owner occupied dwellings in Britain increased by over 4.5 million, almost half a million a year on average. From 1989 to 1995, however, owner occupation increased only by 1.1 million, around 180,000 a year on average, one third of the earlier rate of increase.

The increase in home ownership followed two key policy changes. The first, introduced in the Housing Act 1980, gave local authority and housing association tenants the right to buy their homes at considerably discounted prices. By the end of 1995, almost 1.7 million social housing properties had been sold in Britain. This sell-off generated receipts of over £26 billion with discounts of a further £24 billion (Wilcox, 1996), making it far and away the biggest of the Government's privatisation programmes. Given that access to and allocation of council housing in the postwar decades favoured white households, inevitably this privatisation was particularly disadvantageous to minority ethnic communities. However, where African Caribbean families have had the opportunity to buy quality council housing they have been more keen to do so than white people (Peach and Byron, 1994).

The second important factor, which stemmed from a number of financial policy changes culminating in the Building Societies Act 1986 (Boddy, 1989), was the deregulation of mortgage finance. Building societies were allowed to increase their borrowing and the mortgage market was opened up to more competition. Mortgage rationing disappeared and lenders were willing to lend an increasing proportion of a property's value, exposing themselves and the borrowers to greater risks. In the run-up to the 1983 election the Government even increased the ceiling on mortgage interest tax relief from £25,000 to £30,000. The cost of mortgage interest tax relief, the most significant 'subsidy' to owner occupiers, jumped from £2.2 billion in 1980/81 to £4.8 billion in 1985/86.

In retrospect the first half of the 1980s was the zenith of pro-home ownership policy. Thereafter the Government gradually accepted that the encouragement of home ownership was fuelling inflation as the increased demand for owner-occupied housing and mortgage finance pushed up house prices and interest rates. These arguments began to take greater precedence over ideological commitment to home ownership, despite Thatcher's tenacious personal commitment to this principle (Lawson, 1992).

WITHDRAWING SUPPORT FOR HOME OWNERS

In response to Treasury concern at the rapid increase in costs associated with this unprecedented rise in home ownership, from 1986 onwards the Conservative Government began to cut back on the financial support given to owner occupiers. The two main areas for action were the payment of mortgage interest to income support claimants (ISMI – income support for mortgage interest) and mortgage interest tax relief (MIRAS). Up until 1986 all claimants of income support (supplementary benefit) had their mortgage interest costs met in full, though the number of such claims was very small until the 1980s. From 1986 ISMI met only half a claimant's mortgage interest costs for the first 16 weeks of a claim; then from October 1995 ISMI was withdrawn completely for the first nine months of a claim. The cost of ISMI quadrupled between 1988/89 and 1993/94 to a peak of over £1.2 billion. The 1995 ISMI cut is a particularly harsh blow against families on low incomes at the margins of owner occupation and will inevitably increase mortgage arrears and repossessions. While 43 per cent of ISMI claimants are unemployed and might possibly have taken out private insurance cover, most ISMI claimants are over 60 or lone parents or disabled and therefore very unlikely to get adequate private cover (Williams, 1995). An investigation into this type of insurance (Ford *et al*, 1995) revealed that private cover did not offer adequate protection against unemployed home owners falling into arrears and that two thirds of mortgage protection policy claims were unsuccessful.

The retrenchment of mortgage tax relief began in 1988 when it was restricted to one allowance per dwelling for new loans, thus ending the double tax relief enjoyed by unmarried couples, which at peak interest rates was worth over £200 a month per household. In an act of remarkable government folly, borrowers were given five months notice of this change, which stoked up house prices fiercely in the summer of 1988. In 1991 the Government restricted mortgage interest tax relief to the basic rate of tax; it had always seemed particularly unjust that higher rate taxpayers benefited more from this tax allowance than poorer taxpayers. Finally, in 1994, MIRAS was cut to 20p in the pound and in 1995 to 15p in the pound. As a result of these measures and the fall in interest rates after 1992, the cost of MIRAS fell to well under £3 billion in 1995/96, compared with a peak of £7.7 billion in 1991/92.

THE CRISIS IN HOME OWNERSHIP

These cutbacks in financial support for home owners, and in particular the withdrawal of double tax relief in 1988, contributed to the fall in house prices and caused the drive for owner occupation in the 1990s to falter. Of course, other factors outside the housing market also served to stifle demand. Probably most significant was the growing insecurity of income and employment in the increasingly flexible labour market. House prices fell most dramatically on large estates and in areas of low-cost owner occupation. The consequences, in the form of negative equity, mortgage arrears and repossessions, have, therefore, been felt most drastically by people on modest or low incomes, who were on the margins of owner occupation. In 1993, 26 per cent of households who had bought their homes between 1988 and 1991 held negative equity (Dorling, 1995, Tables 4.27, 4.28). These households were concentrated in the South of England and were mostly young buyers of cheaper property. Negative equity is less likely to affect more affluent households because they are more likely to have considerable equity in their property and because house price falls were generally far less significant at the upper end of the market. At the peak, in 1992, over 1.75 million households, over 10 per cent of home owners, had negative equity, but this subsequently fell away significantly with the modest recovery in house prices. Nevertheless there remain serious pockets of long-term negative equity, particularly relating to smaller homes 'where demand has been affected by the trend for younger households to rent rather than to buy' (Wilcox, 1996). By the mid-1990s negative equity was no longer concentrated in the South of England, high levels were also recorded in East Anglia and the East Midlands (Wilcox, 1996, Table 45).

The recession of the 1990s produced an explosion in mortgage arrears; at the peak in 1992 there were over 300,000 cases of arrears in excess of six months. In 1995 this had fallen back to around 200,000, compared to only 33,000 in 1982. The impact of such arrears on individual households is vividly portrayed in five case studies presented by Ford (1995). These households lived in the shadow of regular court proceedings threatening repossession and they frequently had to forgo basic necessities in order to keep up payments. In 1995, 49,410 homes were repossessed for mortgage arrears; this was an increase on 1994 figures though certainly far less than the peak of 75,540 in 1991. However, back in 1980, before the Government-led drive to increase the number of low-income home owners, there were only 3,480 repossessions. During the 1990s this most traumatic experience for home owners has become a permanent feature and a mass phenomenon. Between 1990 and 1995 almost 350,000 owner occupier households lost their homes through repossession, on average about 230 every working day, a brutal consequence in part of the pro-home ownership policy.

Given the data on the differential impact of negative equity, unemployment and job insecurity, it is reasonable to suggest that arrears and repossessions are more likely to be experienced by low-income households and therefore by households headed by independent women and by minority ethnic households. The deregulation of mortgage finance in the first half of the 1980s swept away much of the institutionalised conservatism of the lenders which had differentially affected these two groups. Hence, in the 1980s, the growth of mortgaged owner occupation was particularly strong among single women, divorced/separated women and households of African Caribbean and Bangladeshi origin. These groups are likely to have suffered particularly badly in the downturn of the 1990s. There is also some evidence of a return to institutional conservatism among the lenders which disadvantages such groups (Jones, 1995).

SOCIAL RENTED HOUSING

Since 1979, the most consistent aspect of government policy was a panoply of measures to wind down the role of local authorities as managers and providers of rented housing. This was driven by the Government's broad attack on the principle of public service provision – and local government power in particular, by the constant pressure to reduce public spending, by the belief that council estates delivered votes for the Labour Party and by the drive for home ownership. As a result the proportion of local authority dwellings in the housing stock fell from 31.4 per cent in 1979 to 18.9 per cent in 1995. The most significant measures which contributed to this decline were council house sales (discussed above) and the virtual ending of investment in new council house building. In 1994, 1,623 new council homes were completed in Britain compared with 76,997 in 1980. In addition, almost a quarter of a million council dwellings have been transferred to housing association ownership since 1988.

The commitment of Conservative governments to housing associations in preference to local authority housing has never been whole-hearted. Throughout the 1980s the number of housing association starts averaged around 14,000 a year, by no means making up for the decline in new council house building. In the period 1979/94 there was also a 62 per cent decline in the number of house renovations undertaken by housing associations; this had been their main area of activity before 1979. However, in response to the crisis in owner occupation discussed above and rising public concern about homelessness, the number of housing association starts between 1990 and

1995 increased on average to around 30,000 a year. The finance for this increased investment was facilitated by the 1988 Housing Act which deregulated housing association rents and pushed housing associations into seeking private capital finance. In 1992/93 the Government provided £600 million to allow housing associations to purchase 20,000 new houses from private developers to help out the housebuilders. However, since that year gross investment by housing associations (including private finance) has fallen consistently. Following a further big cut in the November 1996 Budget, public capital investment in housing associations in 1997/98 has been set at about one third of its 1991/92 level. All this indicates that government concern about homelessness in the early 1990s was a temporary expedient.

HOUSING BENEFIT AND RISING SOCIAL RENTS

Since the election of the third term Thatcher Government in 1987, government policy for all sectors of rented housing was arguably dominated by one principle above all – raising rents. The rationale was that driving rents towards market levels would generate more private investment in rented housing, thus both facilitating the withdrawal of public funding from the social rented tenures as well as improving quality and supply in the private and housing association sectors; low-income tenants would be protected by housing benefit. Thus between 1988/89 and 1995/96 the cost of housing benefit in cash terms tripled to almost £12 billion, even though the level and scope of the benefit was cut on numerous occasions (see Chapter 6).

The imposition of this regime on social housing – alongside the deregulation of private sector rents in 1989 – inflated private rents, possibly beyond 'market' levels subsidised through housing benefit (Ginsburg, 1995). Hence, over the seven years to 1995/96, the cost of housing benefit for private tenants increased almost threefold (Wilcox, 1996). In attempting to limit these costs, the Government has capped housing benefit for private tenants, thereby pushing some households below the poverty line and even making some households homeless (Bramley, 1995). In January 1996, much tighter limits were introduced on housing benefit for private rented accommodation. Since January 1997 all private tenants have been limited to housing benefit equivalent to the average local rent for a 'suitable size' home. Restrictions on housing benefit for single people under 25 introduced in October 1996 will be extended in October 1997 to all people under 60 living alone. They will be eligible for housing benefit equivalent only to the average rent of a room in a *shared* home.

Local authority rents rose in real terms by 36 per cent between 1988/89 and 1993/94, having remained fairly steady through the mid-1980s after the 51 per cent real rise between 1979/80 and 1982/83. Under the subsidy regime constructed during the 1980s, the Government was able to control closely the level of local authority rents (Ginsburg, 1996). The rise in housing association rents was a direct consequence of rent deregulation and the higher cost of private finance. Hence, housing association fair rents (for pre-1989 tenancies) rose 27 per cent in real terms between 1989/90 and 1993/94 while housing association assured rents (for post-1988 tenancies) rose by 43 per cent in the same period (Newton, 1994, Table 125). In effect the capital subsidies being withdrawn from the social rented sectors are being partially replaced by a revenue subsidy in the form of housing benefit. About 65 per cent of council tenants and 61 per cent of housing association tenants were receiving housing benefit in 1994. So in respect of the social rented sectors, the rise in housing benefit costs is largely a reflection of the reduction of other subsidies.

Increasing numbers of households with incomes just beyond eligibility for housing benefit have found their incomes (net of rent) considerably reduced by higher rents. The rising rent regime has also obviously exacerbated the means-tested poverty trap discussed in Chapter 5.

The Conservative government began to recognise the problems created by its rent raising policy in 1995, when it announced proposals to limit rent increases in local authority properties to the level of inflation with the aim of maintaining affordability by establishing 'a stable and sustainable level of guideline rents in real terms' (DoE, 1995). Councils which raise rents beyond the new guidelines to finance more repairs and maintenance could be penalised by a reduction in their housing benefit subsidy. Having relinquished regulation of housing association rents in 1989, the Government did not have any direct means of holding down rents should it want to do so. Nevertheless, recent policy suggests greater hesitancy in government about the wisdom of moving towards market or capital value rents in the social rented sector.

Single women, divorced/separated women and their children, African Caribbean, African and Bangladeshi households are much more likely to live in social rented housing than other groups (Wilcox, 1996, Table 28b; Mason, 1995, Table 7.3). This is so despite the growth of owner occupation amongst these groups discussed above. Hence the rise in rents, the worsening of the housing benefit poverty trap and the overall decline in investment in the social rented sector since 1979 have differentially affected these groups. In this way, as within owner occupation, policy has contributed to reinforcing gender and ethnic divisions.

CONCLUSION – AGENDAS FOR THE FUTURE

In general Conservative housing policy has become saner in the 1990s than in the 1980s: a welcome development. The 1995 Housing White Paper talked both of the development of 'sustainable home ownership' and of social rented housing continuing to have 'an important role' for people on low incomes as 'the most cost effective way to ensure that they have access to a decent home' (DoE, 1995). Positive measures to further these aims did not emerge.

In relation to owner occupation, the phasing out of MIRAS and its replacement with a mortgage benefit to help low income owner occupiers would concentrate assistance on those most likely to be threatened by arrears and repossession. The Liberal Democrats are the only major party to advocate this change. Both Labour and the Liberal Democrats advocate the phased release of capital receipts from council house sales to increase investment in social rented housing. At least £5 billion is said to be available, but there is serious doubt as to whether a future Labour Chancellor would agree to this. Labour's housing spokesperson has admitted that this measure on its own would not be sufficient to bring investment in social rented housing up to adequate levels (Blake, 1996). The Liberal Democrats and many housing professionals have suggested that more capital investment could be facilitated by changing restrictive rules on what constitutes public sector borrowing, thus giving local authorities the same borrowing powers as their counterparts in other EU countries (Hawksworth and Wilcox, 1995). Labour have promised to restore the rights of homeless households removed under the 1996 Housing Act, while the Liberal Democrats go much further with the notion of a legal 'right to shelter' (Birch, 1996). Finally both Labour and the Liberal Democrats are committed to a reform of housing benefit to ease the poverty trap.

Recent housing policy has been dominated by the dream of setting housing markets free with adverse and sometimes disastrous consequences for inadequately protected consumers and those for whom the market cannot provide. The social and economic costs of the pressures and insecurities created by inadequate or unaffordable housing and homelessness are enormous. The inefficiency of contemporary policy is that it relies on inadequate short-term remedies, such as private renting for homeless families and expensively subsidised rents, while avoiding sufficient long-term investment in bricks and mortar including in the private sector. The measures discussed above would go some way towards mitigating the increasing housing pressures on low-income households, but more wide ranging and positive measures are needed to achieve social justice in housing (such as, for example, in Goodlad and Gibb, 1994). Tougher regulation of mortgage lenders and private landlords to protect consumers, empowerment of tenants in social rented housing and the development of social rented housing as a positive public service would establish a long-term basis for tackling social injustice in housing.

REFERENCES

Blake, J (1996) *Votes for Homes: the 'Roof' guide to British housing politics*, Roof/Coopers and Lybrand.

Boddy, M (1989) 'Financial deregulation and UK housing finance', *Housing Studies*, Vol 4, No 2.

DoE (1995) *Our Future Homes*, White Paper, Department of the Environment, HMSO.

Dorling, D (1995) *A New Social Atlas of Britain*, John Wiley.

Edwards, R (1995) 'Making temporary accommodation permanent', *Critical Social Policy*, No 43.

Ford, J (1995) *Which Way Out? Borrowers with long-term mortgage arrears*, Shelter.

Ford, J and Wilcox, S (1994) *Affordable Housing, Low Incomes and the Flexible Labour Market*, National Federation of Housing Associations.

Ford, J, Kempson, E and Wilson, M (1995) *Mortgage Arrears and Possessions*, Department of the Environment, HMSO.

Ginsburg, N (1995) 'The impact of rising rents on housing benefit and rented housing', *Benefits*, No 14.

Ginsburg, N (1996) 'Recent changes in social housing' in May, M, Brunsdon, E and Craig, G (eds) *Social Policy Review 8*, Social Policy Association.

Goodlad, R and Gibb, K (1994) *Housing and Social Justice*, London, the Commission on Social Justice/Institute of Public Policy Research.

Holmans, A (1995) *Housing Demand and Need in England 1991-2011*, Joseph Rowntree Foundation.

Hawksworth, J and Wilcox, S (1995) 'The PSBR handicap' in Wilcox, S, *Housing Finance Review 1995/96*, Joseph Rowntree Foundation.

Holmans, A (1996) 'Meeting housing needs in the private rented sector' in Wilcox, S, *Housing Review 1996/97*, Joseph Rowntree Foundation.

Jones, C (1995) 'Now houses of ill repute are in red line districts', *Guardian*, 25 October, p33.

Lawson, N (1992) *The View From No.11*, Bantam.

Malpass, P and Murie, A (1994) *Housing Policy and Practice*, Macmillan.

Mason, D (1995) *Race and Ethnicity in Modern Britain*, Oxford University Press.

Newton, J (1994) *All in One Place: The British Housing Story 1973-1993*, Catholic Housing Aid Society (CHAS),

Peach, C and Byron, M (1994) 'Council house sales, residualisation and Afro Caribbean tenants', *Journal of Social Policy*, Vol 23, No 3.

Wilcox, S (1996) Housing Review 1996/97, Joseph Rowntree Foundation.

Williams, P (1995) 'A shrinking safety net for a shrinking market' in Wilcox, S, *Housing Finance Review 1995/96*, Joseph Rowntree Foundation.

11

Health
Michaela Benzeval

INTRODUCTION

One major feature of the growing social divisions in Britain is that the health gap between rich and poor has widened. Although the relationship between disadvantage and poor health is far from unique to this country, as was shown in Chapters 2 and 3, the massive increases in income inequality during the 1980s were much greater in the UK than in other developed countries except New Zealand. These trends highlight the need for radical new policies to reduce premature deaths and avoidable illness.

Since the influential Black Report was published in 1980, the international evidence has grown to such an extent that it is now indisputable that social and economic circumstances dominate the distribution and overall standards of health in modern populations. People who live in disadvantaged circumstances have more illnesses, greater distress, more disability and shorter lives than those who are more affluent. Such injustice could be prevented but this requires political will. So far British policy makers have failed to rise to this challenge. The question is will the next government have the courage to tackle this unnecessary suffering and waste of lives?

The purpose of this chapter is threefold. First, to review the latest evidence about the health divide in Britain and how it has changed since 1979. Secondly, to review the policy response by successive Conservative governments to the existence and consequences of social inequalities in health. Finally, to set out a new agenda that would reduce social variations in health, if the political will could be found to implement it.

EVIDENCE

Socio-economic differences in health have been recorded in Britain for over a century. However, by far the most significant event in recent history was the publication of the Black Report in 1980. Relying heavily on data from the 1970-72 Decennial Supplement on occupational mortality, the Working Party concluded that: 'class differences in mortality are a constant feature of the entire human life-span … At *any* age people in occupational class V have a higher rate of death than their better-off counterparts' (Townsend and Davidson, 1982).

Such inequalities still existed at the beginning of the 1980s. Figure 11.1 uses data from the Decennial Supplement for the 1980s, which again shows a marked social class gradient in mortality for children and for adults of working age. For children (aged 1-15), men (aged 20-64) and women (aged 20-59) there was a rise in the age and sex standardised mortality ratios (SMRs) from occupational classes I to V. People in unskilled occupations and their children had twice the chance of dying prematurely as their professional counterparts.

Throughout the 1980s and 1990s a considerable body of evidence accumulated that showed the poor health experience in terms of premature mortality and excess morbidity of people living in disadvantaged circumstances. (For more detailed reviews see Whitehead, 1992; Benzeval *et al*, 1995a). For example, between 1985 and 1993, over 400 empirical studies were published in Britain documenting the extent and nature of the health divide (Mackenbach, 1994).

In many ways there is nothing especially remarkable about these social variations in health in Britain. They are found in most if not all countries (Kunst and Mackenbach, 1994). A number of reasons have been put forward to explain health inequalities including people's living and working conditions, their resources and social relationships and their behaviours (Townsend and Davidson, 1982; Blaxter, 1990). However, the weight of evidence seems to suggest that it is people's material circumstances across the life course that are most important (Davey Smith *et al*, 1994 Vågerö and Illsley, 1995).

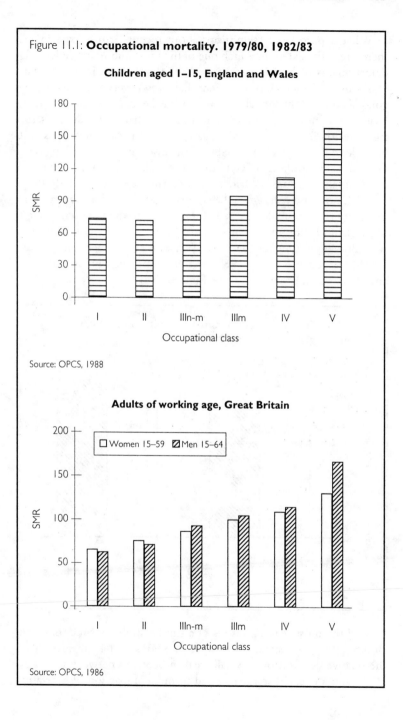

Figure 11.1: **Occupational mortality. 1979/80, 1982/83**

Children aged 1–15, England and Wales

Source: OPCS, 1988

Adults of working age, Great Britain

☐ Women 15–59 ▨ Men 15–64

Source: OPCS, 1986

What is particularly significant about recent British experience, therefore, is the extent to which one of the most important underlying determinants of health has changed for the worse. Since the mid-1980s income inequality in Britain has grown very substantially by comparison with historical and international experience (Hills, 1995). Evidence is now beginning to accumulate that at about the same time health inequalities also began to widen. Although it is not possible to demonstrate a causal link, the association is a striking one. Four recent studies suggest that the relative health status of disadvantaged groups in Britain did deteriorate during the 1980s.

Phillimore and colleagues (1994) investigated trends in age-specific mortality rates in small areas (electoral wards) in the northern region of England. In the most deprived areas, in 1981/83, mortality rates were 36 per cent higher for 15–44 year olds and 65 per cent greater for those aged 45–54. By 1989/91 these ratios had increased to 66 and 95 per cent respectively (see Figure 11.2).

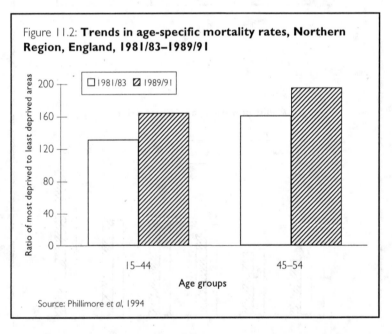

Figure 11.2: **Trends in age-specific mortality rates, Northern Region, England, 1981/83–1989/91**

Source: Phillimore et al, 1994

One of the most striking results of a similar study by McLoone and Boddy (1994) investigating changes in SMRs (0–64) in relation to the relative deprivation of small areas in Scotland between the early 1980s and a decade later, emanated from a comparison of mortality ratios in the most deprived areas of Glasgow relative to the least deprived. Between the early 1980s and the early 1990s the ratios had risen from 96 per cent to 124 per cent higher in the most disadvantaged areas.

The two final pieces of evidence are provided by the *OPCS Longitudinal Study* (LS), which links vital statistics to successive decennial censuses for a 1 per cent sample of the population. Figure 11.3 shows differences in SMRs (15–64) between 1976/81, 1982/85 and 1986/89 for a cohort of men aged 15 years or over at the 1971 Census by their social class at the time of that census (Harding, 1995). Deaths in the first five years of follow-up were excluded to reduce the impact of selection effects. Three main findings are of interest. First, there is a marked social class gradient for each of the three time periods. Second, the relative SMRs for social classes I–IV are broadly stable over time. Finally, however, the SMR for social class V – the most disadvantaged occupational group – sharply deteriorated from being 80 per cent higher than social class I in 1976/81 to 128 per cent higher in 1986/89.

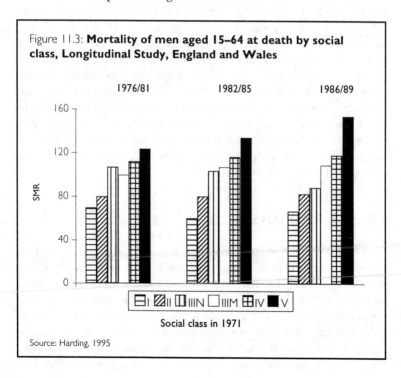

Figure 11.3: **Mortality of men aged 15–64 at death by social class, Longitudinal Study, England and Wales**

Social class in 1971

Source: Harding, 1995

More recently Filakti and Fox (1995, p28) have used the LS to confirm the general thrust of these results for women as well as men across a broader age range and using different measures of socio-economic status. They concluded that:

> comparisons of the 1970s and 1980s suggest a widening of relative differences in mortality by housing tenure and by car access. In particular, the relative positions of local authority tenants compared with owner occupiers and males without car access worsened in the 1980s.

All of these studies appear to show a widening of the health divide. However, there are considerable methodological problems in conducting time trend analysis, so the results must be treated with caution. Nevertheless, the wealth of evidence about the extent and nature of the health divide that has accumulated across the developed world during the 1980s means that no one can doubt that health inequalities are a real social problem. Evidence from the early 1990s shows that considerable variations in health still exist between different social groups. For example, the latest Decennial Supplement for 1991/93 shows a progressive increase in SMRs for men from occupational class I through to occupational class V, with the death rate for unskilled workers being about three times higher than that for professionals (Drever *et al*, 1996). Similarly analysis based on the *General Household Survey* for 1992/94, shows that inequalities in morbidity continue to be a prominent feature of the health divide (see Figure 11.4). Both adults and children in the bottom two-fifths of the income distribution are much more likely to report a limiting longstanding illness, after standardising for age and sex, than those at the top of the income distribution.

POLICY RESPONSES

Despite such a mountain of evidence, government action in Britain to tackle inequalities in health has been conspicuous mainly by its absence. The Black Report, commissioned by the Labour Government in 1977, not only amply demonstrated the existence of health inequalities but also put forward a broad social policy strategy to reduce them. However, when it was delivered to the incoming Conservative Government in 1980, it was eventually published on the August bank holiday with a foreword by the then Secretary of

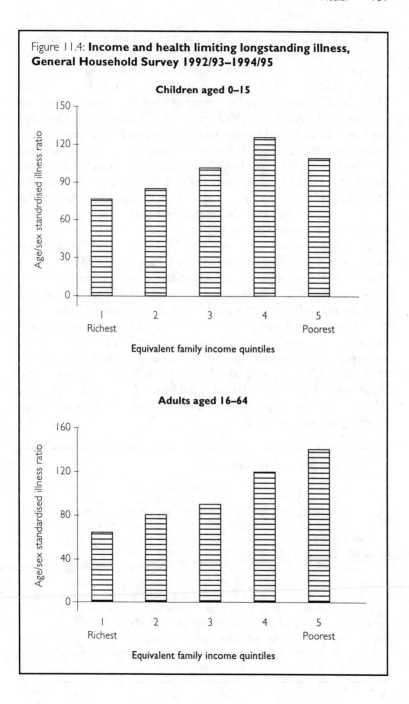

Figure 11.4: **Income and health limiting longstanding illness, General Household Survey 1992/93–1994/95**

State for Health, Patrick Jenkin, disclaiming its recommendations.

During the 1980s health policy was preoccupied with managerial concerns about value for money in the NHS rather than the health of the population. Despite signing the World Health Organisation's *Health for All* strategy in 1985, it was not until the 1990s that policies to improve the nation's health began to be formulated in Britain. Yet even then discussions by government on inequalities in health were largely evaded. The Green Paper on the *Health of the Nation* published in 1991 (DH, 1991) only briefly alluded to health inequalities and the resulting White Paper published in 1992 (DH, 1992), made the briefest of references to 'variations in health status between different socio-economic groups'. Neither document made any policy recommendations about how to reduce the health divide.

Substantial criticism of both the Green and White Papers for failing to pay serious attention to health inequalities led in 1994 to the establishment of a sub-group of the Chief Medical Officer's Health of the Nation working group to review variations in health. This group produced a strategy document at the end of 1995 which recommended 'what steps the Department of Health and the NHS should be taking to tackle variations' (DH, 1995). The publication of the report represented a fundamental change in the Government's approach to health inequalities. Finally, the existence of social variations in health was acknowledged by the Department of Health and a policy response put forward. Some of the key recommendations of the report are set out in Box 1.

Box 1: **Variations in Health report**

First, that the Department of Health must take the lead across all government departments in arguing for *social* policies that promote health. In particular the report identifies the need for national alliances between government departments to tackle the causes of variations that are outside of the scope of the Department of Health's responsibilities, and for other departments to take account of the health impact of their policies, including addressing the issue of health variations.

Secondly, that purchasers must build into their mainstream business plans and activities policies to tackle inequalities in health. This should include the identification and targeting of particularly vulnerable groups, the introduction and evaluation of specific interventions to promote health among disadvantaged groups and the forging of strategic local alliances to improve the health of communities.

Finally, that despite a universal health care system, the NHS needs to work much harder to promote equitable access to health care, through better resource allocation mechanisms and removing barriers of access to care.

While all the recommendations were welcome, and many of them long overdue, the report alone was not sufficient to put equity on the agenda in any real sense. As the Working Group acknowledged:

> there already exist vehicles for taking the work forward and many of the tools needed are also available … what is needed now is … a much more explicit targeting of the issue within existing policies and activities (DH, 1995).

Unfortunately, it is this explicit targeting that has failed to materialise. For example, the cross-government Cabinet Committee on health and the guidance for policy appraisal and health, introduced by the Health of the Nation White Paper (DH, 1992) have had little visibility and there is no evidence that either has been paying any attention to the problem of health inequalities. Similarly, although many purchasers may have made small initiatives to promote the health of vulnerable groups at the margins of their activities, they have not put equity at the centre of their policy agendas.

What is now required is a strategic commitment to reducing social variations in health. A clear leader needs to be identified at Cabinet level to make equity and health a central focus of the next government's health policy. Equally importantly, mechanisms that already exist, such as the cross-government Cabinet Committee, health impact assessments and national targets for health, need to be given an equity focus. Only when reducing health inequalities is truly seen as a priority across government departments will the injustice of the preventable health burden of poverty be redressed.

What is required is the political will to make equity in health a priority in the UK in the same way as it is in other European countries. For example, The Netherlands has promoted a national consensus between all political parties, trade unions, employer organisations, the business and medical communities, to make equity a generally accepted goal for health policy (Gunning-Schepers, 1989). The second five-year programme on health inequalities that began in 1995 places a high priority on stimulating local initiatives to promote the health of disadvantaged groups. Even more recently, the Swedish Government has established a parliamentary committee and a high-powered ministerial group to review public health issues: 'Both the committee and the ministerial group will be particularly concerned with reducing the class- and gender-related differences now existing in matters of health' (Swedish Ministry of Health and Social Affairs, 1995).

Serious efforts to tackle the causes of inequalities in health are long overdue in Britain. Some of the factors that cause health inequalities and the kinds of policy responses that are required to reduce them are discussed in the next section.

AN AGENDA FOR ACTION

In drawing up its agenda for action the King's Fund worked with leading experts to develop policies in a small number of key areas for priority action (Benzeval *et al*, 1995a). Four different types of factor that affect people's health, either directly or indirectly, were selected for investigation. These include:

- factors in the physical environment, such as the adequacy of housing, working conditions and pollution;
- social and economic influences such as income and wealth, levels of unemployment, and the quality of social relationships and social support;
- behavioural factors and barriers to adopting a healthier personal lifestyle; and
- access to appropriate and effective health and social services.

Policy initiatives were developed for one example of each factor: housing, poverty, smoking and access to health care. Set out below is a brief description of the health problems and policy recommendations in each of these four areas.

HOUSING

In Britain, housing has long been an issue of public health concern. Despite dramatic improvements in the housing stock over the last hundred years the UK still has some of the coldest, dampest houses in Europe as well as a large number of people who are homeless. As outlined in Chapter 10, the 1980s saw a rapid rise in homelessness, mortgage arrears and repossessions (Best, 1995). Despite these problems, government expenditure on housing sharply declined (Best, 1994), dramatically reducing the building of new social housing and local authorities' ability to improve and repair existing properties.

These trends are particularly significant because inadequate housing can have adverse effects on people's health. For example:

- people sleeping rough are three times as likely to have chronic chest conditions as the general population (Bines, 1994);
- homeless families, temporarily housed in bed-and-breakfast accommodation, have high rates of infections, gastroenteritis, child accidents, parental stress, poor child development and nutritionally unsatisfactory diets (BMA, 1987);
- inadequate or unaffordable heating almost certainly contributes to hypothermia and excess winter mortality among older people;
- stress among adults (Platt *et al*, 1989).

As Ginsburg indicates in the previous chapter, a range of policies is needed to tackle these housing problems in ways that reduce inequalities in health (see also Best, 1995). Investment in extra new public housing and improving the existing housing stock should be promoted as a matter of urgency. Similarly, community regeneration schemes should be introduced in areas of high deprivation to improve the environmental, economic and social structures of disadvantaged neighbourhoods. Help is also needed for owner occupiers on low incomes, many of whom experience difficulties with their mortgage payments: 'mortgage benefits', similar to housing benefits, should be established.

The King's Fund report suggested a number of ways in which such policies could be financed. For example, public housing could be transferred out of the public sector to local housing companies, which would enable capital to be raised to finance improvements to properties and estates without being a strain on public expenditure. Considerable savings could also be made by removing the remaining tax relief on mortgage interest payments. These could be used to provide capital subsidies for housing associations and local authorities, enabling them both to build more houses and to charge lower rents that would in turn reduce the cost of housing benefits to the social security system.

FAMILY POVERTY

Reducing poverty is vital to any strategy to tackle inequalities in health. Poverty can affect health in a number of different ways.

- Living in poverty may have a physical effect on health because it results in a lack of the basic necessities such as food, shelter and warmth (Graham, 1984).
- In addition, poverty affects people's behaviour, by restricting the

choices available to them. A healthy diet is more expensive than an 'unhealthy' one (see Chapter 14) (NCH, 1991) and many older people in Britain do not heat their homes for fear of excessive fuel bills (Kempson, 1996).

- Finally, trying to live on a low income can be stressful and health damaging in itself. For example, a divorced woman on income support explained:

> Every time you buy something you count it up in your head just to make sure when you get to the checkout you've got enough ... People like me – we do this every single day of our lives, the strain must tell somehow (Kempson, 1996, p44).

The best way of reducing family poverty is to tackle one of its main causes by developing employment opportunities for all. Benzeval and colleagues (1995b) recommend that policies in this area should include:

- expanding pre-school education, particularly for children living in disadvantaged circumstances ;
- increasing resources for education in disadvantaged areas;
- improving education and training programmes for people experiencing long-term unemployment;
- improving the quality and quantity of childcare services in Britain.

However, given that it is unlikely that all families will be able to escape from a reliance on benefits in the foreseeable future, the social security system also needs to be reformed (Chapter 17). One way of reducing family poverty would be to increase the value of means-tested benefits such as income support and family credit (Benzeval and Webb, 1995). Alternatively, CPAG argues that substantially increasing child benefit should be a central part of a wide-ranging anti-poverty strategy (Oppenheim and Harker, 1996).

Possible ways of financing such improvements include abolishing the upper earnings limit on employee's contributions to national insurance, increasing marginal rates of income tax on the better-off and restricting personal tax allowances. Such policies would create a fairer tax system and help to reverse the recent increases in economic inequality (Benzeval and Webb, 1995). However, a political con-stituency – persuaded of the case for tax and benefit changes that promote equity – is needed to achieve radical change.

SMOKING

Although the number of people who smoke has fallen substantially over the last three decades, this reduction has occurred mainly among more affluent social groups so that smoking is now predominantly a habit of people in disadvantaged circumstances. Particularly high smoking rates are found among people who are unemployed and young adults with children, especially lone parents (Townsend, 1995).

Smoking increases the risks of most major killers such as lung cancer and heart disease. However, it should be not be assumed that the health divide has a single cause. Substantial socio-economic gradients in mortality and morbidity exist among non-smokers (Marmot et al, 1984). Moreover, behaviours are determined by the social environment in which people live. For example, there is considerable variation among social groups regarding the extent of choice they have over their behaviours. Studies suggest that high smoking rates among people with low incomes are a 'way of meeting rather than shirking responsibility ... [providing] a way of coping with the constant and unremitting demands of caring' (Graham, 1993, p182).

Policies to reduce smoking may include improving health education and cessation advice in ways that are sensitive to the pressures of people's lives and supported by wider policies to create a supportive environment, restricting the availability of cigarettes and creating smoke-free environments. Two policies, however, are a priority (Townsend, 1995): controlling tobacco advertising and increasing taxation on tobacco-related products.

It is estimated that banning the advertisement and promotion of cigarettes and tobacco-related products would reduce smoking by approximately 7.5 per cent (Townsend, 1993). In particular, given that young people are thought to be more influenced by advertising and that it is more prevalent in tabloid papers and on posters in disadvantaged areas, a ban would have most effect on teenagers and those with low incomes. In addition, increasing the real price of cigarettes would reduce both the number of people who smoke and the number of cigarettes smoked by those who continue (Townsend, 1995). However, the cost would fall disproportionately on people with low incomes and should not be lightly contemplated in isolation from a broadly based anti-poverty strategy.

THE NHS

The health service must take the lead in encouraging a wider and more strategic approach to developing healthy public policies. At both the national and local level the health service must be assertive in developing alliances that put equity in health at the centre of the policy agenda. In addition, it must put its own house in order by:

- ensuring that resources are distributed more equitably between areas in proportion to their relative needs; and
- responding appropriately to the health care needs of different social groups.

Existing resource allocation mechanisms in the NHS have done much to address some of the historical inequities in health care provision, but further reforms are needed. The distribution of GPs between areas is not adequately related to the relative need for them (Benzeval and Judge, 1996), and the equity principle of recent reforms of the resource allocation mechanism for the hospital sector has been watered down (Benzeval *et al,* 1995c).

In addition, as purchasing decisions are devolved to more local areas, two responses are required as a matter of urgency:

- substantial resources need to be top sliced to enable local health authorities to take a broad population approach – to assessing needs, monitoring access to care and providing community-based services – that is required to deliver equitable services; and
- a fairer system of allocating resources to GP fundholders needs to be established.

The equitable allocation of resources is a necessary but not sufficient condition for equitable access to health care on the basis of need. Perhaps what is most worrying is how little is known about whether this principle is actually being achieved. The NHS needs to make much greater efforts to assess whether it is achieving equal access for equal need for all social groups. Local health authorities need to develop equity audits as a matter of urgency.

Where there is evidence that people with poor socio-economic circumstances are inadequately served in relation to their needs, a new approach that empowers communities and individuals needs to be adopted. Some studies suggest that barriers blocking access to health care can be reduced through the introduction of more sensitive and appropriate community-based services.

CONCLUSION

Inequalities in health remain a significant problem in Britain, as in the rest of the developed world. What is particularly worrying in this country, however, is that the growth in economic inequalities during the 1980s is leading to even wider health inequalities. Radical changes to economic and social policies are required to promote social justice for all in Britain. Winning support for such policies will not be easy but it must be done if health inequalities are to be reduced. The next government must put equity at the centre of its health policy. The appalling waste associated with unnecessary death, disease and disability is both an economic loss and a social injustice. The question is: will the next government have the political will to make a serious start?

REFERENCES

Benzeval, M and Judge, K (1996) 'Access to health care in England: continuing inequalities in the distribution of GPs', *Journal of Public Health Medicine,* vol 18, no 1, pp33–40.

Benzeval, M, Judge, K and Whitehead, M (eds) (1995a) *Tackling Inequalities in Health: an agenda for action,* King's Fund.

Benzeval, M, Judge, K and Whitehead, M (1995b) 'Unfinished business' in Benzeval *et al* (1995a), pp122–40.

Benzeval, M, Judge, K and Whitehead, M (1995c) 'The role of the NHS' in Benzeval *et al* (1995a), pp95–121.

Benzeval, M and Webb, S (1995) 'Family poverty and poor health' in Benzeval *et al* (1995a) pp69–81.

Best, R (1994) 'The Duke of Edinburgh's Inquiry into British Housing: Three years on', in Wilcox, S (ed) *Housing Finance Review 1994/95,* Joseph Rowntree Foundation, pp7–17.

Best, R (1995) 'The housing dimension' in Benzeval *et al* (1995a), pp53–68.

Bines, W (1994) *The Health of Single Homeless People,* Housing Research Finding no 128, Joseph Rowntree Foundation.

Blaxter, M (1990) *Health and Lifestyles,* Tavistock/Routledge.

BMA (British Medical Association) (1987) *Deprivation and ill-health,* British Medical Association Board of Science and Education Discussion Paper, BMA.

Davey Smith, G, Blane, D and Bartley, M (1994) 'Explanations for socioeconomic differences in mortality', *European Journal of Public Health,* vol 4, no 2. pp131–44.

DH (1991) *The Health of the Nation: A consultative document for health in*

England Cm 1523, HMSO.

DH (1992) *The Health of the Nation: A strategy for health in England* Cm 1986, HMSO.

DH (1995) *Variations in Health: what can the Department of Health and the NHS do?*, Variations Sub-Group of the Chief Medical Officer's Health of the Nation Working Group, Chaired by Jeremy Metters, Department of Health.

Drever, F, Whitehead, M and Roden, M (1996) 'Current patterns and trends in male mortality by social class (based on occupation) *Population Trends,* vol 86, pp15-20.

Filakti, H and Fox, J (1995) 'Differences in mortality by housing tenure and by car access from the OPCS Longitudinal Study', *Population Trends,* vol 81, pp27-30.

Graham, H (1984) *Women, Health and the Family,* Wheatsheaf Books/ Harvester Press.

Graham, H (1993) *Hardship and Health in Women's Lives,* Harvester/ Wheatsheaf.

Gunning-Schepers, L (1989) 'How to put equity in health on the political agenda', *Health Promotion,* vol 4, pp149-50.

Harding, S (1995) 'Social class differences in mortality of men: recent evidence from the OPCS Longitudinal Study', *Population Trends,* vol 80, pp31-37.

JRF (Joseph Rowntree Foundation) (1995) *Inquiry into Income and Wealth, Chaired by Sir Peter Barclay,* vol 1, Joseph Rowntree Foundation.

Kempson, E (1996) *Life on a Low Income,* Joseph Rowntree Foundation.

Kunst, A E and Mackenbach, J P (1994) 'The size of mortality differences associated with educational level in nine industrialised countries', *American Journal of Public Health,* vol 84, no 6, pp932-37.

Mackenbach, J P (1994) 'Socioeconomic inequalities in The Netherlands: impact of a five year research programme', *British Medical Journal,* vol 309, pp1487-91.

Marmot, M, Shipley, M and Rose, G (1984) 'Inequalities in death-specific explanations of a general pattern?', *The Lancet,* 5 May, pp1003-6.

McLoone, P and Boddy, F (1994) 'Deprivation and mortality in Scotland, 1981 and 1991', *British Medical Journal,* vol 309, pp1465-70.

NCH (National Children's Home) (1991) *Poverty and Nutrition Survey, 1991,* National Children's Home.

OPCS (Office of Population Censuses and Surveys) (1986) *Occupational Mortality 1979-80, 1982-83, Decennial Supplement, Part 1 Commentary,* OPCS series DS no 6, HMSO.

OPCS (1988) *Occupational Mortality 1979-80, 1982-83, Childhood Supplement,* OPCS series DS no 8, HMSO.

Oppenheim, C and Harker, L (1996) *Poverty: the facts* (revised and updated third edition), CPAG,.

Phillimore, P, Beattie, A and Townsend, P (1994) 'Widening inequality of health in Northern England', *British Medical Journal*, vol 308, pp1125-28.

Platt, P, Martin, C, Hunt, S and Lewis, C (1989) 'Damp housing, mould growth and symptomatic health state', *British Medical Journal*, vol 298, pp1673-78.

Swedish Ministry of Health and Social Affairs (1995) *Press Release*, 138/95, 14 December.

Townsend, J (1993) 'Policies to halve smoking deaths', *Addition*, vol 88, pp43-52.

Townsend, J (1995) 'The burden of smoking' in Benzeval *et al* (1995a), pp82-94.

Townsend, P and Davidson, N (eds) (1982) 'The Black Report' in Townsend, P *et al* (eds) (1992) pp33-213.

Townsend, P, Whitehead, M and Davidson, N (eds) (1992) *Inequalities in Health: The Black Report and the Health Divide*, new edition, Penguin Books.

Vågerö, D and Illsley, R (1995) 'Explaining health inequalities: beyond Black and Barker', *European Sociology Review*, vol 11, no 3.

Whitehead, M (1992) 'The health divide' in Townsend, P *et al* (eds) (1992), pp219-437.

ACKNOWLEDGEMENT

Material from the *General Household Survey*, made available through the Office of National Statistics and ESRC Data Archive, has been used by permission of the Controller of H.M. Stationery Office.

12 Unemployment

Paul Convery

The 1980s and 1990s were the decades when mass unemployment became a political and economic reality for millions of people. It has been presented as an unfortunate but unavoidable feature of the new global economic order and, over the spans of two savage recessions, described by Norman Lamont as a 'price worth paying' (Hansard) to enable the British economy to emerge leaner and more competitive. But until the mid 1970s unemployment was rarely higher than about 2.5 per cent of the workforce. In the South East, even in 1974, the unemployment rate was just 1.4 per cent while in the regions of Britain, which subsequently became blighted by mass layoffs, unemployment rates remained low. In Scotland, Wales and the North West, less than 4 per cent of the workforce were unemployed.

Since the mid-1970s unemployment has consistently risen during periods of recession, and the jobless rate has never fully recovered to its pre-recession level even during spells of subsequent growth. Each post-recession trough has remained higher with the number of claimants at half a million in 1975, one million in 1979, 1.6 million in 1990 and 1.9 million by late 1996 (Figure 12.1). During each of the major recessions of 1980/82 and 1990/92 unemployment rose to just over 3 million claimants. The first recession caused unemployment rates of 17 per cent in Northern Ireland, 15 per cent in the North of England, 13 per cent in the West Midlands and 14 per cent in Scotland and Wales.

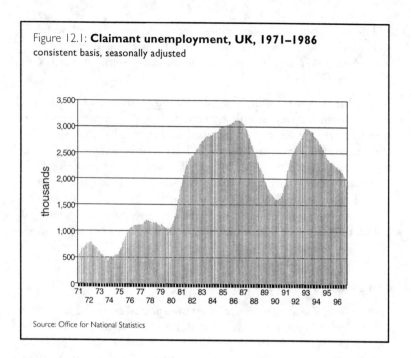

Figure 12.1: **Claimant unemployment, UK, 1971–1986**
consistent basis, seasonally adjusted

Source: Office for National Statistics

THE CAUSES OF UNEMPLOYMENT

There is no single cause of unemployment and no single cure. If there was, debate would simply focus upon whether it was good or bad to move the one policy instrument that might resolve it. Unemployment is the result of at least five major factors, most of which are within the grasp of political and economic intervention: poor international competitiveness, deliberate actions by Government, the effect of external shocks, the effects of technological change and the effects of growing inequality which underpins the tendency for fewer people to do work.

COMPETITIVENESS

The British economy has suffered from poor international competitiveness – a problem summarised nearly 20 years ago by the National Economic Development Office (NEDO, 1977):

> The relatively slow growth and low level of real income in the UK economy compared with other industrial countries, the faster rate of

UK price inflation, the relentless decline in our share of world exports ... and a persistent succession of balance of payments crises have long been recognised to be fundamental problems in the UK economy.

While Britain's malaise might now be thought of as a 1970s phenomenon, competitiveness still remains low. UK competitiveness in manufacturing trade was 65 per cent higher in 1994 than in 1984. But France and Germany are both 70 per cent higher while Japan is 90 per cent higher than in 1984 – with most of that growth taking place since 1990. Britain's overall balance of trade has remained in consistent deficit since 1985 with a particularly serious imbalance between goods and services: the deficit in goods has averaged £10 billion per year since 1990 while the surplus in services only averages £4 billion per year.

EXTERNAL SHOCKS

Structural problems are worsened by unexpected events or the effect of political interventions. For example, the reunification of Germany following the events of 1989 placed huge stresses on the public expenditure and capital formation capacity of the former West German economy. The combination of Germany's fiscal and monetary prudence and its central role driving the western European economy caused recession throughout the continent.

Similarly, a world recession was precipitated in 1974 by the oil exporting countries of the OPEC who raised the price of oil by 400 per cent. Although many commentators regard this event as having sparked the first significant hike in post-war unemployment in the UK, the employed workforce still grew by half a million between 1973 and 1979 – when the jobless totals rose by three-quarters of a million.

GOVERNMENT ACTION

Despite the impact of these external events, the 'shocks' affecting the British economy in both cycles were less significant than the effects of political decisions which caused Britain to enter deep recession in both the 1980s and 1990s. For example, during the first recession, UK unemployment rose from 7 per cent to 13 per cent (between 1979 and 1983) yet the top 15 countries of the OECD experienced a rise from only 5 per cent to 8 per cent in the same period. The 1990s recession was similar with unemployment in the UK rising from 6 per cent to 10 per cent between 1990 and 1993 while the OECD unemployment rates rose from 6.5 per cent to 8.5 per cent (OECD, 1996).

One aspect of both the British recessions was 'home grown': a combination of high interest rates and an overvalued currency.

	1979/81	1990/92	1996
Interest rates peak (3 mth IBR)	18%	15%	6%
Sterling	$2.00 to $2.30	$1.65 to $1.90	$1.50

In both recessions, an overvalued currency made British export goods excessively expensive and encouraged cheap imports quickly causing losses, bankruptcies and redundancies. Between 1979 and 1981, the output of manufacturing industry fell by 15 per cent and it took another six years before output recovered to the 1979 level. Similarly, between 1990 and 1992, manufacturing output fell by 7 per cent and did not recover to the 1990 level until the middle of 1995. Even service industries lost output for a full two years between 1980 and 1982 – a pattern repeated between 1990 and 1992 when service industry output declined by about 2 per cent.

In 1983, the House of Commons Treasury and Civil Service Committee described government policy between 1979 and 1981 as:

> by far the most excessive overvaluation which any major currency has experienced in recent monetary history … (and) was probably the most important single element in its effects on domestic inflation as well as on British trade, production and unemployment.

This verdict on interest rate policy and exchange rates was repeated in the 1990s following the UK Government's conscious decision to 'shadow' the Deutschmark and to subsequently peg the value of Sterling at an unrealistically high rate within the European Exchange Rate Mechanism (ERM). In September 1992, the financial markets traded heavily against Sterling's overvaluation and the currency was ejected from the ERM when it became unsustainable. Ironically, this involuntary devaluation forced a complete reversal of policy and dramatically improved Britain's export performance leading to growth in output, earning and, eventually, employment.

THE EFFECT ON REGIONS

Superficially, the 1980s and 1990s recessions had quite different effects. The first recession hit the North of Britain, Wales, Scotland and the Midlands leaving the South East, South West and East Anglia relatively unscathed. In 1984, the rate of unemployment in East Anglia was half that of Northern Ireland, the North of England and Scotland. By contrast, the second recession affected all regions with unemployment rates tending to converge. According to the orthodox definition of unemployment from the Labour Force Survey, in 1993, unemployment in London was significantly worse while the South East and East Anglia had marginally higher rates than in 1984. By the worst point of the 1990s recession (Spring 1993), UK unemployment was 1.5 percentage points lower than it had been in 1984 (see Figure 12.2). London's unemployment rate was 13.2 per cent compared with 10.4 per cent nearly a decade earlier. However, the rate for the North of England fell by 5 percentage points (from 16.3 per cent to 11.3 per cent) while the rate in Scotland declined from 15 per cent in 1984 to 10.2 per cent (the UK national average).

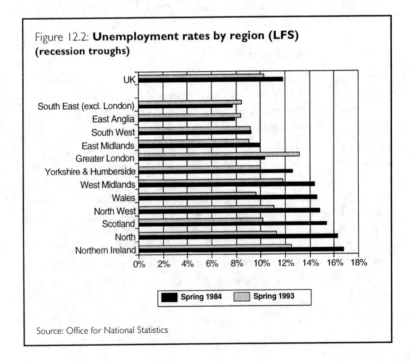

Figure 12.2: **Unemployment rates by region (LFS) (recession troughs)**

Source: Office for National Statistics

Data for employment also shows a particularly marked loss of jobs in London. However, some of the regions which appeared to have been spared the worst of the recession, according to the regional unemployment figures, are shown to have experienced job losses equal to or worse than the UK average. Table 12.1 shows the decline in jobs between 1990 and 1993 (employees and self-employed combined).

TABLE 12.1: **Change in number of jobs 1990/93**

	Total Spring 1990	Total Spring 1993	Change: totals	Change: %
South East (excl London)	5,354,000	5,002,000	−352,000	−7
Greater London	3,329,000	2,996,000	−333,000	−10
East Anglia	1,017,000	956,000	−61,000	−6
South West	2,191,000	2,085,000	−106,000	−5
West Midlands	2,433,000	2,233,000	−200,000	−8
East Midlands	1,878,000	1,831,000	−47,000	−3
Yorkshire & Humberside	2,194,000	2,148,000	−46,000	−2
North West	2,787,000	2,620,000	−167,000	−6
North	1,258,000	1,244,000	−14,000	−1
Wales	1,201,000	1,129,000	−72,000	−6
Scotland	2,229,000	2,177,000	−52,000	−2
Northern Ireland	588,000	575,000	−13,000	−2
GB	25,871,000	24,421,000	−1,450,000	−6
UK	26,459,000	24,996,000	−1,463,000	−6

Source: Office for National Statistics

THE EFFECT ON INDUSTRIES

The collapse of employment in both recessions did not affect all industries and regions equally. Between 1979 and 1983, there were 1,705,000 jobs lost in manufacturing industries while the service sector suffered a net loss of 247,000 jobs. Retail distribution shed 276,000 employees, hotels and catering 84,000 and the construction industry 203,000. Few sectors escaped unscathed, though banking, insurance, financial and business services gained 122,000 new employees.

By contrast, the 1990s recession saw fewer manufacturing jobs go.

The conventional perception of this period was that unemployment was mainly hitting the service industries and occupational groups like managers and professionals. If the media are to be believed, the early 1990s was characterised by redundancy among the middle classes and white collar workers. In reality, more than two-thirds of all net job losses incurred in manufacture and in construction (see Table 12.2).

TABLE 12.2: **Changes in employment by industrial sector**

	Total Spring 1990	Total Spring 1993	Change: totals	Change: %
Agriculture & fisheries	505,000	437,000	−68,000	−13
Energy & water	465,000	370,000	−95,000	−20
Manufacture	5,452,000	4,870,000	−582,000	−11
Construction	2,131,000	1,721,000	−410,000	−19
Hotels, distribution, catering	5,239,000	4,863,000	−376,000	−7
Transport & communication	1,586,000	1,516,000	−70,000	−4
Banking, finance & insurance	3,428,000	3,302,000	−126,000	−4
Public administration, education & health	5,510,000	5,859,000	+349,000	+6
Other services	1,463,000	1,400,000	−63,000	−4
Not specified/other	91,000	83,000	−8,000	−9
All	**25,870,000**	**24,421,000**	**−1,449,000**	**−6**

Source: Office for National Statistics

Over the recession, the net loss of jobs among non-manual workers remained steady. Figures are not available for 1990 but between 1991 and 1993:

- the number of employees and self employed in non manual occupations declined from 14,572,000 to 14,417,000 – a decline of just 1 per cent;
- the number of manual workers fell from 10,744,000 to 10,024,000 – a loss of 7 per cent;
- the number of managers and administrators increased by 175,000;
- the number of professional occupations increased by 87,000.

This trend has continued so that, by 1996, the number of manual workers had fallen to barely 10 million while the number of non-manuals had risen to just over 15 million.

THE NEW JOBS

Even at times of rising unemployment and high levels of redundancies, new employment replaces lost jobs and many people made redundant will enter new jobs quite rapidly. For example, during the worst period for job losses, between Spring 1992 and Spring 1993, over 1.2 million people were made redundant. Of these about 27 per cent were back in work within three months and nearly half were re-employed within six months. The data for the period underlines this: although 1.2 million jobs were lost, the net decrease in overall employment was 243,000. Of these, 166,000 people were added to the unemployment total (LFS definition) with the remainder becoming economically inactive.

However, as employment has recovered following both recessions, most jobs growth has been concentrated in part-time work and the bulk of new jobs have been taken by women. Thus, although the employed labour force grew by nearly two and a half million between 1984 and 1986, male full-time work fell by 2 per cent while male part-time work grew fivefold. The number of women working full-time has increased by 16 per cent and the number working part-time by 19 per cent, as Figure 12.3 and Table 12.3 show.

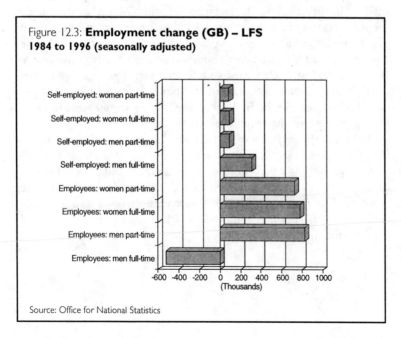

Figure 12.3: **Employment change (GB) – LFS 1984 to 1996 (seasonally adjusted)**

Source: Office for National Statistics

TABLE 12.3: **Number of men and women working, 1984 and 1996: full-time and part-time**

Seasonally adjusted (GB)	Spring 1984	Spring 1996	Change	% of all net change in employment
All men, full-time	13,066,000	12,856,000	–210,000	–9
All women, full-time	5,380,000	6,256,000	+876,000	36
All men, part-time	184,000	1,107,000	+923,000	38
All women, part-time	4,264,000	5,081,000	+817,000	34
All in employment	22,894,000	25,300,000	+2,406,000	100

Source: Office for National Statistics

What's wrong with part-time employment or more women working? First, unemployed people want full-time work – indeed the jobseeker's allowance rules require them to accept work of up to 40 hours per week. So the majority of net additional jobs are unsatisfactory from the perspective of unemployed people.

Secondly, wage rates are significantly lower for women employees and for part-timers. Data from the Labour Force Survey shows that median hourly earnings for women are only 74 per cent of male median earnings. Hourly earnings for part-timers are even lower: at £4.00 per hour, median earnings are just 59 per cent of the full-time equivalent. And for part-timers, hourly rates are actually going down. Between 1995 and 1996, median full-time earnings grew by 3.2 per cent while part-time earnings fell by 4 per cent for men and by 1 per cent for women. So, by mid-1996, the *average (mean)* weekly wage for a part-time woman employee was just £80.

Although the majority of part-timers choose to work fewer hours than full-timers, a significant minority do not. In 1984, about 420,000 people were doing a part-time job because they could not get a full-time one. By 1996, this had risen to 800,000 'involuntary' part-time workers. This underemployment is the equivalent of 490,000 full-time jobs – the number required to satisfy their potential demand for full-time hours.

WHO IS HIT BY UNEMPLOYMENT?

The main risks of unemployment fall disproportionately on those who are poorly qualified and unskilled, those who are young and inexperienced, older people in the final 10 to 15 years before statutory pension age, workers with poor health or who have a disability and people from ethnic minorities. In addition, long term unemployment itself becomes a barrier to employment as it erodes work-related skills and repeated unsuccessful job-search and rejection can undermine self confidence and motivation.

As the total number of unemployed people increases so does the average length of time they spend out of work. Between 1979 and 1986 the average claimant unemployment spell rose from five months to eight months, falling to seven months in 1990. For 90 per cent of claimants (ie, excluding the small number of very long-term unemployed) the average duration rose again to ten months in 1993, falling back to nine months by 1996.

The number of long term unemployed (greater than one year) as measured by the Labour Force Survey rose sharply in the early 1980s, peaking in January 1986, falling until 1990 and then rising again as shown in Table 12.4.

TABLE 12.4: **Long-term unemployed**

	Long-term unemployed	Per cent of all unemployed
Spring 1984 (peak)	1,475,000	47
Spring 1990 (trough)	607,000	32
Autumn 1993 (next peak)	1,243,000	44
Autumn 1996 (most recent)	843,000	38

Source: Office for National Statistics

YOUTH UNEMPLOYMENT

Young people *and* older workers disproportionately face the worst unemployment. For young people, unemployment worsened when the 1980s recession coincided with a sharp rise in the youth population:

- 1984 – 1 in 7 16–17-year-olds were unemployed
- 1993 – 1 in 8 16–17 year olds were unemployed
- 1996 – 1 in 10 16–17 year olds were unemployed

Although in 1996 the absolute number of unemployed 16 to 24 year olds was half a million lower than in 1984, the total population group was 1.75 million smaller too. So, as Figure 12.4 shows, unemployment rates for this age group are only slightly lower than a decade earlier (15 per cent compared with 19 per cent in 1984).

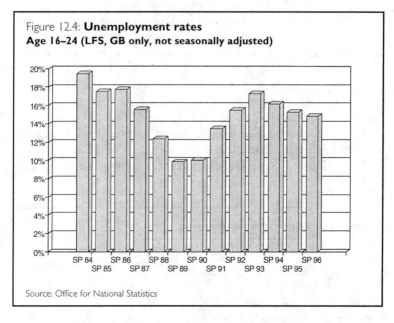

Figure 12.4: **Unemployment rates Age 16–24 (LFS, GB only, not seasonally adjusted)**

Source: Office for National Statistics

For immediate school leavers (those aged 16 and 17) the unemployment rate was as bad in 1996 as it was in the 1980s. Then, 13 per cent of the entire age group was unemployed; by Spring 1993 it was nearly 9 per cent and, alarmingly, unemployment for this age group continued to rise so that, by Spring 1996, just over 10 per cent (142,000) were jobless, despite the promise of a guaranteed place on Youth Training (YT). This total is 21,000 higher than Spring in the previous year – an increase of nearly a sixth at a time when general unemployment (based on the LFS) fell by about 5 per cent. The highest figure for a Spring quarter since the 1980s, this represents a percentage unemployment rate of 18.6 per cent (almost one in five of all economically active 16 and 17-year-olds) (Chatrik and Convery,

1997). The main reason for this growth is that there are simply more young people. The population in this age group grew by about 78,000 between Spring 1995 and 1996 – about a quarter of this growth has been among young people who have failed to find jobs. However, the bulk of the population growth (about two-thirds) has ended up either in work or in training.

Eighty-five per cent of unemployed 16 and 17-year-olds have no form of income despite the Government's 'YT Guarantee'. Young people were first denied an automatic right to income support in September 1988. In place of a benefit safety net, the Government promised a guaranteed YT place but made arrangements for selected groups not on a scheme either to receive income support or a temporary bridging allowance. Only 21,500 young people received any state income in the second quarter of 1996. This is just 15 per cent of the 142,000 young people who were registered unemployed.

UNEMPLOYMENT AMONG OLDER PEOPLE

The decline in economic activity among older people (particularly men) has been evident between the early 1980s and mid 1990s. In 1984, just over 77 per cent of men aged 50-64 were economically active; by 1996 this had fallen to 72 per cent. However, over the same period the proportion of women aged 50-59 who were economically active rose from 59 per cent to 63 per cent (Table 12.5).

TABLE 12.5: **Long-term unemployment: by age, UK, Summer 1996**

	Long-term unemployed	All unemployed	Long-term as % of all unemployed in age group
Aged 16-24	168,000	797,000	21
Aged 25-34	259,000	631,000	41
Aged 35-44	196,000	428,000	46
Aged 45-54	163,000	329,000	50
Aged 55-65	123,000	213,000	58
Aged 16-34	427,000	1,429,000	30
Aged 35-65	482,000	969,000	50
All ages	909,000	2,398,000	38

Source: Office for National Statistics

ETHNICITY

According to the LFS standard definition, 17 per cent of Black people aged 16 and over were unemployed compared with 7.8 per cent for white people. But the numbers of Black people who want work (disregarding the jobsearch and availability criteria in the orthodox definition – see below) shows that 30 per cent of Black adults are unemployed. Over half (53 per cent) of Bangladeshi and Pakistani women want work. In total nearly half a million Black people are unemployed. This is reflected in the numbers who are *employed*. Only about half of Black working-age adults (53 per cent) are in employment compared with 73 per cent of white people, with only 33 per cent of Pakistani and Bangladeshi people in employment (Shire, 1997).

Among Black young people unemployment rates are even higher: 27 per cent for men and 22 per cent for women, according to the standard LFS definition. This reflects a process of inequality which starts once Black people leave school. A third of white youngsters who do not go into further education get jobs on leaving school, only 15 per cent of a similar age group of Black young people do so.

QUALIFICATIONS AND PREVIOUS OCCUPATIONS

The lowest rates of unemployment are recorded among those holding a degree or a higher level vocational qualification. Of the 3.66 million people who are economically active, only 143,000 (or 3.9 per cent) were unemployed according to the Spring LFS. Of the population whose highest level of qualification is in nursing, just 1 per cent are unemployed while, for those with a teaching qualification, only 2.8 per cent are jobless. The unemployment rate for people who have only a Youth Training leavers certificate, is 21 per cent while for those with no qualifications at all, the unemployment rate is 13 per cent. Indeed, this latter group accounts for more than a quarter of the entire unemployed population.

Just as possession of higher level qualifications reduces the chances of unemployment, so too does occupational background. According to the most recent LFS, the unemployment rate for Great Britain was 8.3 per cent, with the following variations between occupations:

- managers and administrators 4 per cent
- professional occupations 2.4 per cent
- associate and technical and professional 4.3 per cent
- manual 8.5–11.6 per cent.

There is a similar variation when measuring unemployment against industry sectors:

- public administration, education and health 3.5 per cent
- the financial sector 4.7 per cent
- construction workers 11.4 per cent.

By contrast, the disparity between manual and non-manual occupations has begun to close among the long term unemployed – reflecting that long-term unemployment itself erodes any comparative advantage that non-manual long-term unemployed jobhunters may have. Non-manual workers comprise 60 per cent of the employed workforce. In 1991, 11 per cent of the long-term unemployed were from non-manual occupational backgrounds, but when long-term unemployment peaked in 1993, this section of the workforce accounted for nearly a quarter of all those unemployed for a year or more – a proportion which has remained constant ever since.

RECURRENT UNEMPLOYMENT

Data from the Benefit Claimant Count reveal how many people experience recurrent spells of unemployment. Of the 800,000 people starting a claim for benefit during the three months to July 1996, 26 per cent had not received an unemployment related benefit in the preceding 10 years. However, 32 per cent had made a claim on either one or two previous occasions and 24 per cent had made claims five or more times previously.

INACTIVITY AND 'NON-EMPLOYMENT'

Not everybody *wants* to work or *has* to work but a significant feature of the modern labour market is growth of economic inactivity. This is partly attributable to increased participation in education. Among 16 to 24-year-olds, only 71 per cent are economically active compared with 76 per cent in 1984, despite a 1.7 million decline in the population group. Similarly, many women withdraw from the labour market if they have children – only 48 per cent of women with a child aged under five are in employment compared with 67 per cent of all working-age women. Employed men still outnumber women in employment by 13.9 million to 11.3 million. Most of this gap is made up by self-employment, where men exceed women by three to one. However, among employees the gap is closing: in 1979, 59 per cent of all employees were men; by 1996 the gap had narrowed to barely one million and men made up only 52 per cent of employees.

With male participation in the employed workforce declining, where are they going? Obviously, many are unemployed, but as significantly, there is a growing proportion who have become economically inactive. As Figure 12.5 and the Table 12.6 show, the number of men who are of working age and economically inactive remained fairly steady during the 1980s but rose sharply after 1990. It increased by 706,000 between Spring 1990 and Spring 1996. There are now 2,689,000 men of working age who are economically inactive. Expressed as a percentage of all men of working age, this inactivity rate has risen from 11.1 per cent to 14.9 per cent between 1990 and 1996.

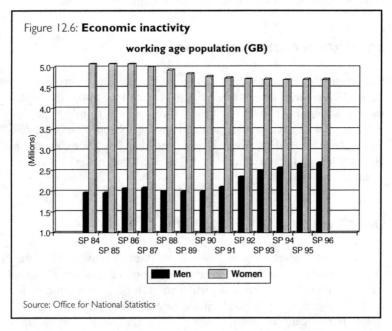

Figure 12.6: **Economic inactivity**

working age population (GB)

Source: Office for National Statistics

By contrast, female inactivity is about half a million higher than in 1984 and about 120,000 higher than Spring 1990 but as a proportion of the working age female population, the inactivity rate fell from 33 per cent in 1984 and has remained steady (at about 28 per cent) since 1990.

TABLE 12.6: **Economic activity**

	Spring 1984	Spring 1990	Spring 1996
Men of working age (16-64)			
Inactive	1,954,000	1,983,000	2,689,000
as % of all working age men	11.2%	11.1%	14.9%
Women of working age (16-59)			
Inactive	5,229,000	4,568,000	4,686,000
as % of all working age women	33.1%	28.1%	28.4%

Source: Office for National Statistics

Thus male inactivity seems to be disguising unemployment, and this is particularly evident in regional and subregional inactivity rates for men. Male inactivity averages 15 per cent for the UK, yet it varies from 24 per cent on Merseyside to just 11 per cent in the South East, excluding Greater London (see Table 12.7 and Figure 12.7). This means that one in four men of working age in Merseyside are completely outside the 'active' labour market (neither employed nor unemployed according to the standard definitions). What makes this picture even starker is to express the numbers and proportions for *non-employment*. In other words, those men of working age who are either unemployed or inactive. Then we see that in Merseyside 37 per cent of all working age men are *not employed*.

For the UK as a whole in Spring 1996 there were 18,579,000 men of working age, of whom:

- 2,864,000 were inactive;
- 1,534,000 were unemployed (according to the LFS conventions);
- a total of 4,398,000 or 24 per cent of the whole male working age population non-employed.

This is the rate of *non-employment* and is shown for regions/sub regions in Figure 12.7 and Table 12.7.

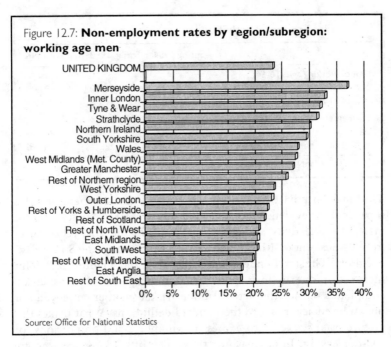

Figure 12.7: **Non-employment rates by region/subregion: working age men**

Source: Office for National Statistics

After Denmark, Britain has the highest female labour force participation rates in Europe. Nonetheless, there has been a sharp rise in the number of households where no adult is earning at all. The LFS shows that almost one in five of all non-pensioner and non-student households have non-earning adults. So in 1996 more than four and a half million individuals of working age lived in workless households (53 per cent of the total workless population of 8.6 million) compared to 1.2 million individuals (or 18.5 per cent of the 6.7 million non-working population) in 1997 (Table 12.8).

TABLE 12.7: **Non-employment by region**

	Inactivity rate %	Non-employed rate %
Merseyside	24	37
South Yorkshire	21	33
Tyne & Wear	21	32
Northern Ireland	20	32
Strathclyde	20	30
Wales	20	30
Inner London	19	28
Greater Manchester	19	28
Rest of Northern region	17	27
West Midlands (Met. County)	16	26
West Yorkshire	16	24
Rest of Scotland	15	23
Rest of North West	15	23
Rest of Yorks & Humberside	14	22
South West	14	21
Outer London	14	21
East Midlands	13	21
Rest of West Midlands	13	20
East Anglia	12	18
Rest of South East	11	18
United Kingdom	**15**	**24**

Source: Office for National Statistics

Note: inactivity rate expresses those inactive as a percentage of all working age men; non-employed rate expresses the inactive and the unemployed as a percentage of all working age men. The difference between the two is less than the normally described 'unemployment rate' which expresses the number unemployed as a percentage of the economically active population only – not the whole population of working age.

TABLE 12.8: **Percentage of households without a working adult**

1977	6.5%
1979	8.3%
1983	15.1%
1987	16.7%
1991	15.3%
1994	19.1%

Source: Office for National Statistics

THE ECONOMIC COST OF UNEMPLOYMENT

The cost of unemployment to the Exchequer in 1995/96 has been estimated to be £23.4 billion – equivalent to 4.6 per cent of gross domestic product. The 'Exchequer cost' – which rose from £16.5 billion in 1990/91 – measures direct central government expenditure on benefits to unemployed people, lost revenue from PAYE and national insurance contributions, and indirect taxes which the unemployed would have paid when in work.

The estimated cost of benefits paid to unemployed people during 1995/96 was £9,020 million. This includes unemployment benefit, income support, housing benefit, council tax rebates and payments from the social fund. In addition, an estimated £1,828 million was paid in sickness and incapacity benefits to approximately 180,000 people who wanted work and were available for work but were not required to be available for work on health grounds. The cost of administering these benefits in the DSS and Employment Service added a further £840 million while payments from the redundancy fund (plus its administration) added a further £210 million. In total, direct public expenditure on unemployment is likely to be £11.9 billion in 1995/96.

However, benefit-related costs account for just under half the overall Exchequer cost because foregone income tax and national insurance contributions together average some £4,390 per claimant. Claimants are not the only unemployed people who are not earning and, therefore, not contributing to revenues. The LFS data for 1995/96 showed a total of 1,607,300 men and 846,900 women unemployed in addition to whom, there were a further 353,900 men and 636,500 women who, while not having actively sought a job within the previous four weeks, stated that they wanted jobs and were free to start work if one was offered.

Based on these figures, lost revenue from earnings is estimated to be £4.6 billion for income tax and £5.3 billion for national insurance contributions. Furthermore, if all these unemployed people were in work they would have more disposable income and through their increased spending would pay approximately £1.6 billion more in indirect taxes.

As Figure 12.8 and Table 12.9 show, the cost per unemployed claimant has risen from nearly £6,000 in 1990/91 to nearly £8,000 in 1995/96. The total cost, however, has declined slightly having peaked in 1993/94 at £24.8 billion.

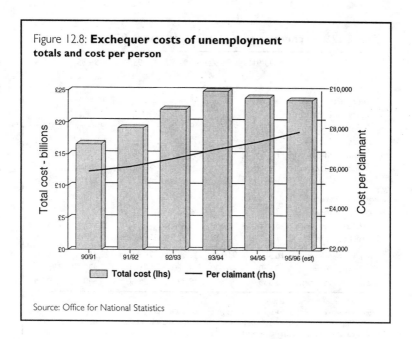

Figure 12.8: **Exchequer costs of unemployment totals and cost per person**

Total cost (lhs)   —— Per claimant (rhs)

Source: Office for National Statistics

HIDDEN UNEMPLOYMENT

With 28 per cent of the working age population *not employed* the conventional measures of joblessness do not adequately reflect the real demand for work. Since November 1982, the main unemployment indicator has been the monthly claimant count – a measure now widely discredited as a result of numerous changes to benefit rules which directly impact on the published figures (Atkinson, 1989). Although Britain has implemented an annual Labour Force Survey (LFS) since 1984 and a quarterly Survey since 1992, its results are not given the prominence of the benefit claimant count. The claimant count is a poor indicator of unemployment because it only measures those actually receiving benefits and is very susceptible to administrative action. Even the Government has called it 'a by-product of the administrative system used for paying unemployment related benefits'.

TABLE 12.9: **Exchequer cost of unemployment (GB)**

	90/91 £	91/92 £	92/93 £	93/94 £	94/95 £	95/96 £
Direct costs						
Benefits for claimant unemployed (a)	5,320m	7,690m	9,040m	9,750m	9,100m	9,020m
Benefits for 'non'-claimants (b)	1,605m	1,427m	1,306m	1,802m	1,839m	1,828m
Administration costs (c)	455m	565m	646m	769m	803m	840m
Redundancy Fund	141m	298m	318m	277m	231m	210m
Foregone revenue						
Income tax total (net)	3,612m	3,878m	4,402m	4,911m	4,804m	4,643m
NI contributions total	3,692m	4,086m	4,846m	5,678m	5,521m	5,334m
Indirect taxes total	1,727m	1,152m	1,423m	1,650m	1,613m	1,559m
Total Exchequer cost	16,552m	19,096m	21,981m	24,836m	23,911m	23,433m
Cost per claimant	5,940	6,160	6,580	7,070	7,420	7,960
Cost per 'non'-claimant	3,330	3,080	3,320	3,660	3,840	4,000

Source: Office for National Statistics
Notes: 1995/96 estimated on part-year data and government expenditure plans.
    (a) Claimant benefit costs include unemployment benefit, income support, housing benefit, council tax/
        community charge rebates, payments from the social fund.
    (b) Estimate of sickness and invalidity/incapacity benefits paid to those people who are classed by the
        Labour Force Survey as short-term and long-term sick and disabled but who want work and could
        start a job.
    (c) Administration costs exclude the local authority borne costs of housing benefits and council tax/
        community charge rebates (global cost 1994/95 respectively £279m and £196m).

In 1995, the report of a Royal Statistical Society enquiry argued that the measurement of unemployment is problematic because the concept is no longer as simple as when the social and economic norm was for one full-time 'principal breadwinner' per household. As discussed earlier, over a very long period, the British labour market has seen a significant growth of other models: part-time work, self employment, early retirement, female participation, increased working hours and the end to many forms of regulation.

The monthly claimant count records how many people meet the entitlement conditions for jobseeker's allowance or national insurance credits and receive benefit but, as a measure of the under-use of labour in the economy and the unmet demand for work or the social distress caused by unemployment, the claimant count is of little help as it fails to record three broad groups of jobless people.

First, unemployed people who fail to qualify for, or have exhausted their entitlement to six months of non-means-tested jobseeker's allowance (previously unemployment benefit) and subsequently fail to qualify for income-related jobseeker's allowance (previously income support). A typical example is someone who has a working partner and/or savings (possibly from a redundancy payment) which exceed the upper end of the savings 'taper' of £8,000. This mainly explains why so few women are included in the claimant count – according to which the unemployment rate for women is 4.1 per cent compared with 10.2 per cent for men.

Secondly, benefit recipients who are actively looking for work yet receive income support without having to be available for work (eg, lone parents or men aged over 60 are also not included).

Thirdly, unemployed people who are temporarily disqualified from receiving an unemployment related benefit, for example those who are deemed to be unemployed for reasons of misconduct or voluntarily leaving a job are also excluded. This number has grown considerably in recent years (see Chapter 6). For example, in the six months to June 1996, 64,700 people were disqualified for up to 26 weeks on these grounds. Over the last three years, a larger group of disqualified claimants are those penalised for failing to meet the increasingly stringent requirements of actively seeking and availability for work. In the year to April 1996, there were 237,500 decisions to sanction claimants on these grounds along with a further 80,000 claimants penalised for declining to attend a compulsory government programme.

LABOUR FORCE SURVEY

The LFS is a sample survey of 60,000 households which ignores benefit status and simply identifies those people who say they want work. For reasons of international comparability, the LFS uses a 'standard' unemployment definition of the International Labour Organisation which counts as unemployed all those who have not undertaken any work for pay or profit in the survey reference week, who want work, are available to start within two weeks and have looked for work within the previous four weeks.

Despite its different measure, the LFS tends to return totals which are roughly similar to the claimant count. However, the two counts measure different groups of people. The claimant count over-records unemployed men but under-records unemployed women (see Table 12.10). The picture is further complicated because there is only limited overlap between the two measures: of the 2.2 million LFS unemployed, only 1.14 million are benefit claimants while the remainder (49 per cent) receive no benefits.

TABLE 12.10: **Number of unemployed according to LFS and claimant count, Autumn 1996**

	LFS	Claimants	Difference
All	2,226,000	1,902,000	+324,000
Men	1,415,000	1,434,000	−19,000
Women	811,000	469,000	+342,000

Source: GB.

Conversely, of the 1.9 million in the claimant count, the LFS recognises only 1.1 million as being unemployed with the remainder being:

- 472,000 claimants who are economically *inactive* because they do not conform to the criteria of being available to start work and having sought work in the LFS reference period;
- 313,000 claimants who are em*ployed* according to LFS concepts – these are claimants who are probably undertaking part-time work (within the rules), although the survey evidence is unreliable.

BROADER MEASURES

The LFS also shows how many *other* people want work – even though they may not fully meet the criteria of the 'standard' test. At Summer 1996, 2.4 million additional people said they wanted work. Of these, 922,000 said they were available to start a job within two weeks. These people would conform to the 'standard' definition if they had also looked for work within the survey reference period. However, many are women, older men or otherwise 'discouraged' workers who for a variety of reasons did not look for work (see Table 12.11).

TABLE 12.11: **Reasons why men and women work part-time**

	Men	Women	All
Awaiting result of job application	2,900	2,700	5,700
Student	67,200	53,900	121,100
Looking after family/home	21,400	264,700	286,200
Temporary sick/injured	19,700	18,500	38,200
Long-term sick/disabled	72,100	44,400	116,500
Believes no job available	80,100	50,700	130,900
Not yet started looking	27,700	43,600	71,300
Other inactive	70,700	81,800	152,600
Total	**362,000**	**560,400**	**922,500**

Source: Office for National Statistics

The definitions of the Labour Force Survey class the 230,000 people who are in 'work-related government employment and training programmes' as part of the labour force but they are not counted as unemployed. However, they are plainly not *in* employment and yet are temporarily excluded from work. If they were not participating in a programme, virtually all would be recognised as unemployed by the Survey. It should be remembered that a proportion of those on Youth Training are already classed as 'employees' because they receive a wage and will have 'employee status' within YT – or they are classed as being on a 'Modern Apprenticeship'.

The LFS also reveals how many part-time workers in the labour force are working fewer hours than they want: the part-time 'under-employed'. According to the LFS, there are 6.4 million part-time workers, while the majority said they did not want full-time work, a significant minority, 800,000 people, said they did. It should be noted that, the LFS definition of employment is extremely broad – it counts as employed everyone who is engaged in work for pay or profit for one hour or more during the week before interview. Although these 800,000 involuntary part-timers represent just 13 per cent of all in part-time work, they work an average of just 14.7 hours per week compared with the average of 38 hours worked by full-timers.

Not all these groups of people are unemployed in the sense that they would enter employment at 24 hours notice, but the 'spectrum' of unemployed people – from those who are immediately job-ready through to those who need childcare or might only take part-time work – more effectively reflects the total potential workforce and the people whose incomes are reduced through lack of work. The spectrum shows a 'slack capacity' of nearly five and a half million – which is equivalent to almost one in six of the working age population (Summer 1996):

'Standard' LFS unemployed	2,327,000
plus 'inactive' who want work	2,444,000
plus government schemes	209,000
plus f/t equivalent under-employed	490,000
Total	**5,470,000**

This unmet demand for work has not abated over the period of growth in employment (see Table 12.12 and Figure 12.9). Although the jobless number has fallen, this has been compensated by a rise in the number of economically 'inactive' who want work. Compared with Spring 1992, the 'standard' definition of unemployment was 357,000 lower but, although the 'slack' total fell from a peak of six million in Winter 1993/94, the Spring 1996 figure was identical to that of Spring 1992. So, increasingly, the number of unemployed, as defined by the orthodox LFS measure, forms a shrinking proportion of the total number in the 'slack' labour force. As the final column in Table 12.12 shows, the orthodox unemployment measure accounted for 62 per cent of the whole 'slack' labour force in Spring 1985. Although this proportion rose slightly between 1990 and 1992, it has steadily diminished and now represents just 42 per cent of the 'slack' labour force.

The strongest growth component within the 'slack' labour force is people who are economically 'inactive' but want work. Between Spring 1992 and Summer 1996 this total grew by 454,000 from 1,976,000 to 2,430,000. Within this population are three categories of people:

- those available to start work but who have not looked for work (the 'Broad' LFS) – 198,000 more in Summer 1996 than in Spring 1992;
- those not available to start, but who have looked for work – 96,000 smaller;
- those not available to start and who have not looked for work – 352,000 more.

TABLE 12.12: **Labour market slack, GB (all ages) LFS – not seasonally adjusted: Spring of each year**

	Standard LFS unemployed	Inactive who want work: available, not looked	Other inactive who want work	Government work-related employment & training	Full-time equivalent of involuntary part-time workers	Total 'slack' labour force	'Slack' labour force as % of all working age population
1985	2,990,000	1,204,000	1,015,000	390,000	261,000	4,845,000	14.1%
1986	2,996,000	1,316,000	1,003,000	400,000	273,000	4,985,000	14.5%
1987	2,912,000	1,178,000	796,000	498,000	271,000	4,859,000	14.1%
1988	2,392,000	1,130,000	848,000	527,000	247,000	4,296,000	12.4%
1989	1,989,000	1,087,000	1,003,000	478,000	245,000	3,799,000	10.8%
1990	1,894,000	1,138,000	1,104,000	448,000	213,000	3,693,000	10.5%
1991	2,329,000	1,111,000	1,028,000	412,000	276,000	4,128,000	11.7%
1992	2,684,000	742,000	1,235,000	364,000	380,000	5,405,000	15.3%
1993	2,849,000	897,000	1,330,000	341,000	482,000	5,899,000	16.7%
1994	2,656,000	967,000	1,398,000	322,000	497,000	5,840,000	16.5%
1995	2,376,000	963,000	1,404,000	273,000	491,000	5,507,000	15.5%
1996	2,265,000	939,000	1,491,000	230,000	481,000	5,406,000	15.2%

Note: in 1995, the results of LFS were re-weighted and rebased to take account of data from the 1991 Census. In this table, the categories of 'economically inactive' have not been re-weighted, so minor discontinuities arise between Spring 1991 and Spring 1992. The errors should not exceed -0.4 per cent and +1.3 per cent (these being the revision factors for the Spring 1992 totals respectively for the Standard LFS definition unemployed and the total economically inactive).

Source: Office for National Statistics

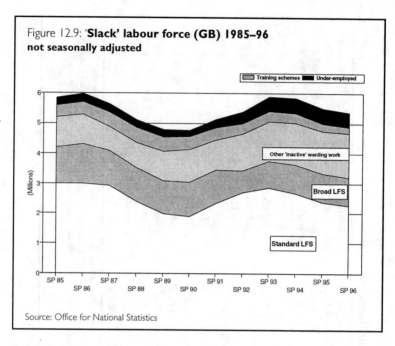

Figure 12.9: **'Slack' labour force (GB) 1985–96** not seasonally adjusted

Source: Office for National Statistics

Behind this growth are two general trends: people who have been 'discouraged' from the mainstream workforce, having become unemployed and then moving into 'inactivity'; secondly, those previously completely 'inactive' who have become more 'encouraged' by the prospect of finding work and – although not necessarily engaging in jobsearch – now aspire to work.

The omission of so many other people from the official unemployment count partly explains why the 2.7 million new jobs created between 1984 and 1990 had such a limited impact on the claimant count. Many new vacancies were filled by the 'hidden unemployed' and by new entrants to the labour market. This occurred on a smaller scale between 1992 and 1996 when, as the number of jobs grew by one million, unemployment measured by the orthodox LFS definition fell by only 670,000.

REFERENCES

Atkinson, A B with Micklewright, J (1989) 'Turning the screw: benefits for the unemployed, 1979-1988', in Atkinson, A B, *Poverty and Social Security*, Harvester Wheatsheaf.

Chatrik, B and Convery, P (1997) 'Nine out of ten unemployed young people have no income', *Working Brief*, Issue 81, Unemployment Unit.

NEDO (1977) *International price competitiveness, non-price factors and export performance*, NEDO.

OECD (1996) 'Employment Outlook', *Eurostat standardised unemployment rates 1996*, OECD.

Second Special Report from the Treasury and Civil Service Committee Session 1982-93 – International Monetary Arrangements, HMSO, May 1983.

Shire, D (1997) *Half Truths, Half Measures*, Black Employment Institute.

All other data from the following Office for National Statistics publications and online source: LFS Quarterly Bulletin; LFS Historical Supplement; LFS online data (Quantime Ltd); Labour Market Trends; online claimant count data including JUVOS cohort (NOMIS), Social Trends 1996, Economic Trends Annual Supplement 1996/96. Other sources: government departmental expenditure plans for relevant years.

13 Privatisation of utilities
Elaine Kempson

Successive Conservative governments have been committed to a programme of deregulation and privatisation. While this commitment to free markets has been generally controversial, the privatisation of the utilities has been especially so. Proponents of privatisation have argued that it leads directly to increased efficiency and paves the way for competition, so lowering prices and improving the quality of service for consumers. However, there were other government motives behind this programme. First, there was a strongly held belief that public services are inherently inefficient. Secondly, competition was seen as the best way of ensuring high service quality for consumers. Thirdly, the desire to generate a stream of revenue was an important part of government fiscal policy. And finally, there was a commitment to creating a 'share-owning democracy'.

In practice, these aims were often in conflict. Without exception, the sale of these public assets has attracted criticism because they were undervalued at the time of privatisation, because the shares became concentrated in a small number of hands and because of the size of the Chief Executives' pay increases immediately following privatisation. Opponents of privatisation maintain that the utilities (and fuel and water in particular) are essential services and, as such, should be kept within the public sector. Concerns, typically, focused on how low-income consumers would fare in a more commercial regime.

THE CHRONOLOGY OF PRIVATISATION

Privatisation of the utilities began in 1984, with the sale of British Telecom. British Gas was sold in 1986 and the ten statutory water companies in England and Wales in 1989. (Water supply has, so far, remained in the public sector in Scotland.) The most recent privatisations have been the 12 regional electricity supply companies and the National Grid in 1990 and the electricity generating companies in 1991. Since 1984, only two of the four utilities have been opened to competition – telecommunication services (in 1986) and gas (in 1995). Competition in the supply of electricity is expected in 1998.

Transfer of these companies to the private sector was accompanied by the setting up of independent regulators – Oftel (for telephones); Ofgas (gas); Offer (electricity) and Ofwat (water). The role of these regulators is to ensure that companies are run efficiently and to protect the interests of consumers. Where these two objectives are in conflict, shareholders' interests take precedence. In general, regulators have adopted an economic model of regulation, focusing on the control of monopoly profits (through price caps) and the promotion of competition. Moreover, in setting tariffs, the regulators are not allowed to show 'undue discrimination' or 'undue preference' to particular classes of consumers.

It is now 12 years since this programme of privatisation began and almost six years since its completion – time enough to gauge the impact that it has had on the lives of households who live on low incomes. There were three main concerns about the impact of utility privatisation on low-income households: that it would lead to rising charges; that companies would take a more commercial approach to arrears recovery; and the possible loss of access to utility services. Each of these concerns is considered in detail below.

CHARGES

Price cuts were one of the main claims made by the Government to 'sell' privatisation to taxpayers and, generally speaking, these claims have proved to be right. Except for water charges, consumers have seen falls in utility bills. But it would seem that consumers, as a whole, have not always benefited as much as they might have done. At the same time, there has been an increase in price differences between different parts of the country. Moreover, some groups of consumers have benefited more than others – with the poorest consumers sometimes paying the highest charges for their utilities.

PRICE CHANGES

Telephone charges have fallen by more than 40 per cent, in real terms, since privatisation. But these falls have been of greatest benefit to businesses and high spending individuals as this is where BT has faced the greatest competition. Over the first seven years following privatisation (to 1991), line rental charges for domestic users rose in real terms and charges for local and cheap rate calls decreased by a smaller amount than long-distance peak rate calls. As a consequence, most domestic phone users have only really benefited from price cuts since 1990/91.

Gas prices, too, have fallen since privatisation and were 31 per cent cheaper in real terms in 1992 than they were in 1985, but these price falls were caused primarily by a fall in gas purchase costs and not by efficiency gains. Indeed, it has been argued (Ernst, 1994) that consumers benefited too little from this fall in costs and British Gas could have cut prices by far more over that period. In real terms, British Gas was paying 27 per cent less for gas in 1991 compared with 1987, while price cuts for consumers were just 12 per cent. The regulator, Ofgas, has since imposed tighter price controls. Moreover, the phased introduction of competition seems also to be bringing some further price cuts for consumers living in areas where British Gas now has competitors. In the South West, where competition was first introduced, about 12 per cent of consumers have changed supplier, typically saving around 25 per cent on their bills (Offer, 1996a).

The situation with electricity prices was more complex. Over the early 1980s when the electricity supply companies were in public ownership, charges for domestic consumers were falling in real terms, largely because coal was cheaper. But immediately prior to privatisation, prices rose considerably – to make the sale of the supply companies more attractive to investors and to enable the newly privatised companies to hold prices down. Indeed, since privatisation, charges have fallen by around 10 per cent in real terms. Even so, it is only since 1993/94 that charges have fallen below their pre-privatisation level (Offer, 1996b).

Of all the four utilities, charges for water have proved to be the most controversial – with very large increases in domestic water and sewerage bills since privatisation. In 1989/90 the average consumer paid £118.91 (£155.65 at 1996 prices); average bills for water and sewerage in 1996/97 will be £218 – an increase of 40 per cent, or £62.35 a year, in real terms.

In general, though, income support claimants will not have greatly benefited from these price changes. Benefit levels are uprated in line with prices and the falls in gas and electricity prices taken into account when setting benefit rates. Water charges were introduced into the Rossi uprating index only in 1992, so the large increases that occurred over the first three years after water privatisation were not reflected in social security benefit increases. It has been claimed that, in 1993, the sum for water included in weekly benefit was £2.25 (McNeish, 1993), while the average water bill was £3.56 (Ofwat, 1993).

DIFFERING CHARGES BY LOCALITY

Water and electricity charges vary between local supply companies and, although this was the case even before they were privatised, local variations are now much greater.

Pre-privatisation, there was a 41 per cent difference between the charges made by water companies with the lowest and highest average domestic charges – a figure that had been constant for at least three years. This gap has widened and currently (1996/97) stands at 82 per cent, a slight fall from a peak of 88 per cent in 1994/95. Put another way, people living in Devon and Cornwall pay £329 a year, on average, which is £148 a year more than the £181 paid by Thames Water's customers.

There is a similar, but slightly smaller, variation in electricity charges. A customer of SWALEC, the Welsh supplier, who uses 3,300 units of electricity a year pays £311.64, which is £49.55 or 19 per cent more than a similar customer of Yorkshire Electricity. Once again these differentials have widened. Before privatisation the difference between the highest and the lowest charging companies was just 12 per cent. Moreover, electricity companies also differ in the extent to which they charge extra for customers with pre-payment meters, so that the difference between the highest and lowest pre-payment meter charges is 22 per cent or £59.32 a year (Offer, 1994; Offer, 1996b).

Following privatisation, British Gas *reduced* local price differentials and moved towards the development of uniform standing charges across the country. As a result, people living in the North of England and the Midlands faced increases that were almost twice the national average between 1987 and 1991 (National Consumer Council, 1993). However, British Gas is currently indicating that, in future, it wants to be able to set charges to reflect the costs of supply. This will mean that gas charges, too, will vary from one part of the country to another.

This trend towards regional charges is a matter of some concern, since people in similar circumstances with similar levels of consumption will be paying differing amounts. And while an amount for fuel and water charges is included in social security payments, this is based on national average figures. So, while someone living in Cornwall would be paying £624 a year for water and electricity a similar person in Kent would pay just £447. An extra £3.40 a week is a large sum for someone living on a state pension or income support.

DIFFERING CHARGES BY PAYMENT METHOD

Customers with pre-payment meters have always paid more than those with quarterly accounts. In the case of electricity, a customer using 3,300 units a year can typically expect to pay between £17 and £20 a year more if they have a pre-payment meter. Price variations between companies mean that customers of four companies pay more than £20 a year extra – the highest being Northern at £24.72, while those of a further four companies pay less than £17 – the lowest being Hydro Electric in Scotland, which actually charges pre-payment meter customers £4.62 a year *less* than those with quarterly bills (Offer, 1996b). Gas customers, too, pay more for gas if they use a pre-payment meter and the Gas Consumers Council notes that the differentials between pre-payment and other tariffs have been widening in recent years.

More recently, utility suppliers have been developing other forms of differential pricing, which are said to reflect the relative costs incurred in supplying different groups of customer. British Gas has gone furthest down this route and began by introducing their DirectPay tariff in early 1995. This offered a 5 per cent discount to customers who paid their gas bills by monthly direct debit from their bank account. Concerns were immediately expressed that this discriminated against other prompt payers and that people without bank accounts (most of whom have very low incomes) were excluded.

Following a referral by the Gas Consumers Council, Ofgas decided that such discounts were both a fair reflection of relative costs and within the terms of the licence, provided similar discounts were introduced to other customers who paid promptly. As a result, British Gas introduced OptionPay in July 1995, which gives a quarterly £2 discount (equivalent to 2.4 per cent reduction on average) to prompt payers. This includes customers who settle quarterly accounts promptly, pay by monthly standing order or have a quarterly variable direct debit. At the same time a further discount was offered to DirectPay customers, bringing it to 6.6 per cent. As a consequence, British Gas now has four separate tariffs. The cheapest is DirectPay, followed by OptionPay, the basic tariff for quarterly billing, with pre-payment meter charges being the highest.

ARREARS MANAGEMENT AND DISCONNECTIONS

Excluding those who deliberately pay on the red demand, most people who fall behind with their utility bills do so because they can't rather than won't pay (Rowlingson and Kempson, 1993). In some cases, financial difficulties are caused by loss of earned income through redundancy, failed self-employment or long-term sickness or disability. In others, they result from a relationship breakdown. But the group who face the greatest difficulty paying utility bills are people who have been living on social security for any length of time (Berthoud and Kempson, 1992; Field, 1989; Herbert and Kempson, 1995; Rowlingson and Kempson, 1993)

Levels of default are affected both by changes in charges and by general economic conditions, being at their highest in times of recession. Unfortunately, statistics on levels of default are not generally available, although we do have information, from two household surveys, on levels of water debt. In 1989, before privatisation and the most recent recession, fewer than one per cent of households had fallen into arrears with water charges. Five years later, after substantial increases in water charges and a severe recession, the figure stood at 9 per cent of all households. Both factors had undoubtedly played a part in the increase in water debt, along with the separate collection of water charges from council tenants who had previously paid them with their rent (Herbert and Kempson, 1995).

DISCONNECTION AND DISCONNECTION POLICY

Levels of disconnection for non-payment of bills are often used as a proxy for levels of debt. In fact, it is a far better indicator of companies' arrears management policies than of the difficulties faced by customers. A study of water debt showed that levels of arrears across the country varied far less than the level of disconnections – indeed some water companies virtually had a policy of non-disconnection (Herbert and Kempson, 1995). Generally, speaking, levels of disconnection in all four utilities rose around the time of privatisation but have fallen since. Again, just as with price changes, there are some significant differences among the four utilities.

Figures on telephone disconnections have (unlike the other utilities) only recently been published – on the insistence of the regulator Oftel. The first statistics became available in May 1995 and showed that a staggering 765,000 people had been disconnected during the previous 12 months. The most recent figures show an increase to 820,126. The regulator has said that this is unacceptably high and steps should be taken to reduce the level of disconnection (Oftel 1996).

Gas disconnections had been fairly stable over the early 1980s but rose dramatically following privatisation – from 35,626 in 1985 to a high of 60,778 in 1987. The regulator, Ofgas, the Gas Consumers' Council and other consumer groups (through PUAF – the Public Utilities Access Forum) expressed concern about the high level of disconnections, which had levelled out at around 19,000 a year by the early 1990s. This prompted British Gas to commission an independent study of the circumstances of people they were disconnecting, the reasons for their non-payment and why 90 per cent of them had no contact with the company prior to disconnection. The resulting report (Rowlingson and Kempson, 1993) must have been uncomfortable reading for British Gas but, to their credit, they called a public seminar to discuss the findings and set up a review of their debt recovery procedures. This resulted in a revised debt and disconnection code of practice, which was implemented in 1995. More importantly, the level of disconnections has fallen, with 14,511 domestic customers disconnected during 1995 (Table 13.1).

TABLE 13.1: **Gas disconnections for non-payment (domestic customers)**

Year	Number of disconnections
1979	35,166
1980	41,846
1981	28,725
1982	28,813
1983	30,971
1984	33,768
1985	35,626
1986 (privatisation)	45,255
1987	60,778
1988	40,037
1989	19,379
1990	19,013
1991	18,636
1992	15,707
1993	16,068
1994	16,308
1995	14,511

Source: Gas Consumers Council

Disconnections by the electricity supply companies had fluctuated between 90–100,000 for most of the early 1980s, but had fallen to 80,557 in 1988/89 – just before privatisation. Since that date, the number of disconnections has fallen rapidly, to the point where only 838 domestic customers were disconnected for non-payment in 1995 (Table 13.2).

Just as with charges, water companies' levels of disconnection have given rise to the greatest level of concern. Fears that the level of disconnection might rise following privatisation led to intensive lobbying for the Water Bill to end English and Welsh companies' right to disconnect for non-payment of charges. When it became clear that this was unlikely to be successful, lobbyists changed tactics and pressed, instead, for a requirement that companies obtain a court order before they could disconnect domestic customers. This requirement was included in the Act that was passed by the Government.

TABLE 13.2: **Electricity disconnections for non-payment (domestic customers)**

Year	Number of disconnections
1979/80	98,894
1980/81	118,221
1981/82	108,266
1982/83	91,334
1983/84	90,722
1984/85	91,039
1985/86	102,714
1986/87	98,823
1987/88	88,910
1988/89	75,230
1989/90	80,557
1990 (privatisation)	69,739
1991	48,000
1992	18,080
1993	3,769
1994	1,228
1995	838

Sources: Electricity Consumers Council; Offer.

Despite this safeguard, levels of water disconnection in England and Wales were not restrained following privatisation. In 1989/90, the year of privatisation, 8,426 households were disconnected for non-payment of water charges – a figure that had jumped to 21,282 in 1991/92. This caused an uproar among consumer groups who discovered that their safeguard of a court hearing had not only failed to protect vulnerable households from disconnection, but had actually added court charges to their debt. Moreover, an independent study of water debt and disconnection (Herbert and Kempson 1995) found wide disparities in arrears recovery practices and the use of disconnection by individual water companies. At one end of the spectrum, the attitude of some companies was fairly relaxed, investing a good deal of resources in negotiating payment plans with customers who were unable to pay. In these cases, summonses and disconnections were seen as a last resort. At the other extreme, companies adopted a 'short, sharp, shock' approach. In these cases, the debt recovery timetable was deliberately short and summonsing, or even disconnection, was viewed as an effective way of making customers pay (Herbert and Kempson, 1995). Again, pressure from consumer groups and the regulator has led to a big drop in the level of disconnection, which in 1995/96 had fallen back to 5,826 – the first year that it was below the level at privatisation (Table 13.3).

TABLE 13.3: **Water disconnections for non-payment (domestic customers)**

Year	Disconnections
1988/89	15,255*
1989/90 (privatisation)	8,426
1990/91	7,673
1991/92	21,282
1992/93	18,636
1993/94	12,452
1994/95	10,047
1995/96	5,826

*includes non-domestic disconnections, which totalled 1,587 in 1989/90 and 2,391 in 1991/92
Source: Ofwat

In general, then, privatisation seems to have encouraged most utility companies to take a more commercial stance on arrears, with the level of gas and water disconnection increasing shortly after the sale. However, pressure from consumer groups and regulators' debt and disconnection codes of practice have clearly reduced the numbers to levels that are lower than they had been pre-privatisation. Telephone disconnections remain very high, although pressure from the regulator and the publication of the figures will almost certainly lead to a decline. The electricity supply companies are the exception to the general pattern, with disconnections falling steadily since just before privatisation. It is, however, important to acknowledge that other changes have also played a part in reducing the level of disconnections – notably the wider installation of pre-payment meters and the greater use of direct deductions from social security payments.

PRE-PAYMENT METERS

Traditionally, fuel bills were spread by using coin in the slot meters, but as crime levels rose they were phased out and replaced by quarterly credit accounts. This undoubtedly caused difficulties for many low-income households. However, advances in information technology have led to the development of new pay-as-you-go options, which the privatised utility companies are using widely as an alternative to disconnection.

The electricity companies led the way even before they were privatised, but the number of households with pre-payment electricity meters has risen substantially since and now stands at 3.5 million. The introduction of pre-payment gas meters was slower, largely because there were greater technical difficulties to be overcome. The new Quantum meters began to be introduced during 1993 and, by the end of 1995, 566,000 households paid for their gas in this way. There can be little doubt that there is an inverse link between the numbers of meters and disconnections, as the number of households disconnected from their gas supply peaked when meters were in short supply.

The introduction of pay-as-you-go options for water charges has been slower still. Pre-payment devices were tested by two water companies in 1994 and are now being used by 14 companies in England and Wales, who, between them, have installed pre-payment devices in 15,076 homes. These devices have an important difference from gas and electricity pre-payment meters – they are a way of spreading fixed annual charges and do not measure the use of water.

It must be acknowledged that pay-as-you-go options are liked by many customers on low incomes, who find it much easier to budget in this way (Herbert and Kempson, 1995; Kempson *et al*, 1994; Rowlingson and Kempson, 1993), but they are not without their disadvantages. First, as we have already seen, households with pre-payment gas and electricity meters generally face additional charges for their fuel supply. (The one exception is Hydro-Electric, which actually charges its pre-payment meter customers less). Secondly, there are frequent complaints of limited access to facilities where keys for pre-payment meters and devices can be re-charged – often involving costly bus fares (Birmingham Settlement, 1993; Herbert and Kempson, 1995). Thirdly, there is widespread concern about *self disconnections* – that is, customers rationing supply or cutting themselves off because they do not have the money to pay for their supply of gas, electricity or water. In all cases, customers are not cut off immediately – fuel meters have an emergency button that can be pressed for limited additional supply and water devices do not shut down for a week or so after the last payment has been made. Even so, there is good reason to be concerned if all that has been achieved by the introduction of pre-payment options is the replacement of disconnection (the level of which is reported) by self-disconnection (which is not). Studies of households with pre-payment gas and electricity meters (Birmingham Settlement, 1993) and pre-payment water devices (reported in Herbert and Kempson, 1995) both found that rationing and self-disconnections were a problem. Companies can monitor which households regularly self-disconnect and there may well be a case for regulators to require regular reporting of self-disconnections and for these statistics to be made available alongside company disconnections.

DIRECT PAYMENTS

Since privatisation, both British Gas and the water companies have increased the number of applications made to the Benefits Agency for customers' arrears to be repaid by direct deduction from social security payments. This is in contrast to the electricity companies whose use of direct payments has fallen considerably over the past ten years (Table 13.4).

TABLE 13.4: **Direct deductions from benefit for electricity, gas and water charges**

| Year | | Number of direct deductions | |
	Electricity	Gas	Water
1986	179,000	132,000	n.a.
1987	163,000	138,000	n.a.
1988	152,000	152,000	n.a.
1989	131,000	134,000	n.a.
1990	100,000	123,000	n.a.
1991	96,000	146,000	n.a.
1992	95,000	192,000	n.a.
1993	76,000	204,000	161,000
1994	74,000	231,000	218,000
1995	71,000	214,000	235,000

Source: Social Security Statistics, 1986-1996

In 1995, direct payments were made for:

• 71,000 households with electricity bill arrears, which averaged £10.72 a week;

- 214,000 with gas bill arrears, averaging £10.10 a week; and
- 235,000 with arrears on water and/or sewerage, averaging £5.72 a week (Social Security Statistics, 1996)

Again, some people welcome having this arrangement as it enables them to get their finances straight (Kempson *et al*, 1994; Mannion *et al*, 1994). Although, set against this, there are very real concerns that social security claimants have money deducted from what is, already, a basic minimum to live on. The Benefits Agency cannot, in fact, deduct more than 25 per cent of the benefit due to a claimant without his or her permission. In practice, claimants are not aware of this and some agree to levels of deductions that cause real financial hardship (Rowlingson and Kempson, 1993).

A study of direct payments concluded that they have both advantages and disadvantages (Mannion *et al*,1994). They protected people from disconnection, were cheaper than pre-payment meters and, for many, made budgeting a lot easier. On the other hand, they reduced the money people had available and limited their opportunities for juggling bills. In some cases, therefore, they had made it harder for people to make ends meet. Lack of information also left people unsure of whether their arrears were being repaid and how much they still owed. Some also found that, when they had to come off direct payments, they had much greater difficulty budgeting and, again, fell behind with fuel or water bills. In February 1997 the Conservative Government mooted the idea of ending the Fuel Direct facility for benefit claimants. Given its widespread use, its abolition would almost certainly cause real problems for substantial numbers of claimants.

ACCESS

There is growing concern, generally, about access to utility supplies. Both BT and some electricity companies use credit scoring techniques to assess the risk that a new customer will default. Those found to be a high risk are required to pay a security deposit before the supply is connected. Of course, it will be those who can least afford to pay a deposit who are most likely to have to pay one. Oftel has calculated that around 20 per cent of domestic phone customers face this condition of supply – involving charges of up to £150. The regulator, in his latest annual report, encourages BT to replace 'security deposits' with agreements with customers to set a financial ceiling on call charges (Oftel, 1996).

In fact, Oftel has been more active in promoting the cause of universal access than the other three regulators and has defined it as *affordable access to basic telecomms services for all those reasonably requesting it, regardless of where they live.* In a fully competitive market there needs to be a supplier of last resort and Oftel has proposed that a Universal Service Fund should be set up. This would be managed by a third party, with contributions made by all telephony companies in proportion to their basic telephone revenues. Companies could then 'pay or play'. Initially, the universal service obligation would be offered to BT. If they decline, the company needing the lowest subsidy would get the franchise for a set period. If there were no bids, then BT would have to take on the obligation.

THE OVERALL IMPACT OF PRIVATISATION ON LOW-INCOME HOUSEHOLDS

To date, the long-term impact of utility privatisation on low-income households has been rather better than was feared at the outset. Fuel prices and telephone charges have fallen and fewer people are now being disconnected from essential fuel and water supplies. But whether the companies would have delivered these benefits of their own accord must be in doubt. There can be no question that the utility regulators (except Ofwat) have driven charges down by their price controls. Likewise, pressure from consumer groups and the regulators has curbed the tendency of most companies to take a tougher approach to the non-payment of bills.

There are, however, worrying signs that the future may not be quite as rosy. Falls in disconnection have largely been achieved by the introduction of pre-payment meters – which seems almost certainly to have been accompanied by a growth in rationed use and self-disconnection from fuel and water supplies. There are also trends towards offering different tariffs linked to payment method, which have benefited better-off households who are able to set up direct debits from bank accounts, at the expense of poor households who use pre-payment meters. The requirement for households judged to have a high risk of arrears to make security deposits also has a disproportionate effect on low-income households.

As we move towards competitive markets, at least for fuel and telephony, there will be a continuing need for tough regulation to protect poor households. Yet there is pressure, from the companies and others, for a relaxation of controls, in the belief that free markets will ensure that all consumers get the best possible deal. Experience with financial services must question that belief, since about one in five households are effectively excluded from all mainstream financial institutions (Kempson, 1994; Leyshon and Thrift, 1995). Where they *can* gain access, it is generally to very expensive niche suppliers who specialise in meeting the needs of poor people.

The challenge for the next ten years will be to provide a system of regulation that ensures poor households can gain access to essential utility services at a price they can afford.

REFERENCES

Berthoud, R and Kempson, E (1992) *Credit and Debt: The PSI Report*, Policy Studies Institute.

Birmingham Settlement (1993) *The Hidden Disconnected: an investigation of consumer, fuel company and agency responses to pre-payment meters and Fuel Direct*, Birmingham Settlement.

Ernst, J (1994) *Whose Utility? The social impact of public utility privatisation and regulation in Britain*, Open University Press.

Field, J (1989) *Electricity Council and Electricity Consumers' Council Survey of Code of Practice Arrangements*, SCPR (unpublished).

Herbert, A and Kempson, E (1995) *Water Debt and Disconnection*, Policy Studies Institute.

Kempson, E (1994) *Outside the Banking System: a review of households without a current account*, HMSO.

Kempson, E, Bryson, A and Rowlingson, K (1994) *Hard Times? How poor families make ends meet*, Policy Studies Institute.

Leyshon, A and Thrift, N (1995) 'The restructuring of UK financial services industry in the 1990s: a reversal of fortune?', *Journal of Rural Studies*, Vol 9, No 3, pp223–41.

McNeish, D (1993) *Liquid Gold: the cost of water in the '90s*, Barnardos.

Mannion, R, Hutton, S and Sainsbury, R (1994) *Direct Payments from Income Support*, HMSO.

National Consumer Council (1993) *Paying the Price. A consumer view of water, gas, electricity and telephone regulation*, HMSO.

Offer (1996a) *Annual Report 1995*, HMSO.

Offer (1996b) *The Competitive Electricity Market from 1998: price restraints*, Offer.

Offer (1994) *Annual Report 1993*, HMSO.

Oftel (1996) *Annual Report 1995*, HMSO.

Ofwat (1993) *Annual Report 1992*, HMSO.

Rowlingson, K and Kempson, E (1993) *Gas Debt and Disconnection*, Policy Studies Institute.

14

Dividing up the cake: food as social exclusion

Tim Lang

THE SITUATION AT THE END OF THE 1970s

The food situation before the election of the Conservatives in 1979 was by no means rosy. The Black Report on Inequalities in Health in 1980 drew attention to under-nutrition among the young and called for an extension of school meals to reduce the effect on the children of the poor (Townsend and Davidson, 1982). The scandal that followed the attempted suppression of the findings (Townsend, 1987) in some respects obliterated the fact that the report was an indictment of divisions which existed *before* the Conservative Government was elected. A review by one of the Black Committee members had already suggested that health problems stemmed from inequality in general (Morris, 1979).

Two studies had highlighted food poverty in particular. The first, conducted in 1977, reviewed the (in)adequacy of benefits and showed that supplementary benefit was inadequate to cover the nutritional needs of the largest 8 to 10 year old children, however efficient their mothers' food purchasing behaviour (Walker and Church, 1978). This study of 50 families on supplementary benefit, revealed that they spent around 40 per cent of their income on food, compared with the national average of 22 per cent.

The second study of 231 at-risk children in poor areas of London between 1973 and 1976, published in 1979, showed a connection between the amount of money spent on diet per person per week and growth rates in children (Nelson and Naismith, 1979). The study revealed a close relationship between restriction of income, poor diet and small size of child. Its authors concluded that 'at least 11 per cent of the children in this study are mildly to moderately malnourished' and needed dietary intervention (Nelson and Naismith, 1979). In a later study, Nelson showed that school meals were the most important nutritional support outside the home for low income families even though many failed to meet the nutritional targets set for them by government at that time (Nelson and Paul, 1983).

This rediscovery of food poverty raised fundamental questions about British social justice. Had the absolute numbers of food poor declined only to leave some stranded? Were the mechanisms for alleviating food poverty too blunt to work? Did food require new attention? Almost as soon as these questions were posed, the 1979 general election made them obsolete. The newly elected Government determined that welfare itself was the problem and that salvation for the nation as a whole lay in revitalising a market economy. Since then the Government has persistently denied food poverty and, faced with this intransigence, critics have had to prove it all over again. In 1997, the case has been made that, first, food poverty both exists and affects health and choice and, secondly, changes in food retailing have created new mechanisms for the social exclusion of the poor.

CUTTING BACK ON FOOD CASH

In 1899, Rowntree found that 9.91 per cent of the people surveyed in York lived in a state of 'primary poverty' in that they could not afford to purchase a diet which contained the basic nutrients in the cheapest form. Revisiting Rowntree a century later, Stitt and Grant (1997) calculated that 21 per cent of the British population were living in such a state in the mid 1990s. How had this state of affairs come about?

The welfare state had two strands to its food safety net. If the 'warp' was direct food provision such as school meals, the 'weft' was the benefits system. Since 1979, both have been systematically 'unpicked' (Leather, 1996). Other chapters in this volume amplify cuts in benefits, but one additional point is worthy of mention. Since the 1930s there has been pressure to persuade the state to set optimum standards for nutrition which could be factored into benefits and used to calculate needs and deficits (Advisory Committee on Nutrition, 1937). Sixty years on, we are no clearer. For decades food policy observers have tried to get official figures on how much cash is estimated to be spent on food within the benefits rates. This has become a senseless saga.

In 1948, the National Assistance Board set assistance scales which, though secret, were assumed to include some element for food. In 1979 the Department of Health and Social Security produced its new system based upon minimum levels of nutrients, recommended daily amounts (RDAs), below which deficiency might be expected. However, the small opportunity to get higher benefits to take account of extra food needs, under the Diet Addition scheme, was abolished when income support was set up in 1988. Next the RDA system was itself replaced by the dietary reference value (DRV) system in 1991 (Department of Health, 1991; Killeen, 1994).

In the midst of this change, the Ministry of Agriculture, Fisheries and Foods (MAFF), stung by its consumer panel, began the sisyphean task of trying to create a theoretical nutritionally adequate diet that cost £10 per week. It managed to produce one (MAFF Food Science Division 1, 1992), where the nutrients met DRV targets but the result failed the reality test. Consumers in Strathclyde, for instance, found it wholly unacceptable on grounds of taste, cost and choice (Killeen, 1994; Leather, 1992). Local retailers did not even sell some of the products. In the words of one of the panel (Leather, 1992):

> To follow [MAFF's low cost diet], low-income households would have to cut out meat entirely, more than double their consumption of tinned fruit and frozen vegetables (an implicit assumption that they cannot afford enough fresh fruit and vegetables), double their consumption of breakfast cereals (in order, presumably, to achieve sufficient levels of fibre and fortified vitamins), eat five times more wholemeal bread than at present, and eat more white bread. Of the eight slices of bread to be eaten each day, only three would have even a thin spread of margarine and butter; the rest would be eaten dry. Yoghurts and other dairy products are completely excluded. Expecting poor consumers to eat a totally different diet from the rest of the population is discriminatory. And as one commentator said, they had better not watch any television, especially if they have kids.

In the 1980s, the independent Family Budget Unit began the task of creating a 'modest but adequate' diet which could be used to estimate need and want (Bradshaw, 1993). Its work has been respected but unrecognised where it matters, within the state machinery. So the net effect is that by the 1990s we are no clearer than in the 1930s about how the state calculates benefits with regard to food. This is needless secrecy.

CUTTING BACK ON SERVICES

With regard to food benefits in kind, the 'weave' of the welfare safety net, most attention has focused on children. The Black Working Party report had expressed uncertainty as to the effectiveness of school milk and meals in preventing a dietary class divide, but nonetheless saw them as important preventive social measures. The incoming Conservative Government dismissed such thinking. Propelled by the argument that standards were not needed, the 1980 Education Act abolished nutrition standards for school meals. Yet, in subsequent years, between 1979 and 1986, the proportion of poor school children taking free school meals rose from 12 per cent to 18 per cent (Whitehead, 1989). Faced with this growing need, the Government drastically reduced eligibility for free school meals in the 1986 Social Security Act.

A government survey of 10–15-year-old children conducted in 1983 found that three quarters were obtaining excessive amounts of energy from fats and that young women had worryingly low intakes of iron (DHSS, 1986). This was the first official survey to suggest that diet was being affected by changes in the food economy and in society, although early warning had been given in 1980 by a study of 65 families living on supplementary benefit (Burghes, 1980). This suvey, the first of the Thatcher era to do so, found food intake being reduced to make ends meet: parents fed children first, and lack of money was cited as the reason for a lack of fresh fruit and vegetables in the diet.

In 1984, the Maternity Alliance, a coalition of groups concerned about mothers and children, found that pregnant women on supplementary benefit could not afford a nutritionally adequate diet (Durward, 1984). A study of 107 women and children in Milton Keynes in 1984 reported 51 per cent of lone parents and 30 per cent of mothers in low-income two-parent families cut down on food for financial reasons (Graham, 1986). Another study found this process of self-denial penalised women especially hard: because they generally held responsibility for food purchases and cooking, mothers would feed their children and husbands before themselves (Charles and Kerr, 1985).

Although children and state support for their diet were particularly poignant features of 1980s social policy research, in the early 1980s studies began to question whether children were the only victims of the new poverty and whether Rowntree-style absolute insufficiency of diet should be the sole criterion for concern. The *Breadline Britain* study in 1983 for London Weekend Television asked people to define what they considered to be a decent standard of living and then applied those criteria to the country. It estimated that 7 million people had had to go without food at some time in recent months due to lack of money (Mack and Lansley, 1985).

In 1982/84, a study of 1,000 people on low incomes in the north of England analysed four groups: employed, unemployed, retired and people on government youth schemes (Lang *et al*, 1984). It found that people missed meals when they were short of cash. Food was the flexible item in the domestic budget and with fixed costs being deducted at source, people were forced to cut back on eating to make ends meet. Thirty-nine per cent of unemployed people in the sample had gone without food for lack of money in the previous year; 20 per cent of the people on government youth training schemes had cut back. A quarter of the unemployed said they did not have enough money for food all week. The picture painted by the study was of people tightening belts, making do, trading down in food quality, not eating three meals a day. Only 14 per cent of the unemployed ate one piece of fresh fruit a day – this at a time when epidemiological evidence about the need to increase intake of anti-oxidants was mounting (World Health Organisation, 1990; Chen Junshi *et al*, 1990; Cannon, 1992). Across all four low-income groups studied, large numbers said they were only just about managing – 49 per cent of the unemployed, 35 per cent of the employed, 46 per cent of the retired and 25 per cent of those on a government youth training scheme (Lang *et al*, 1984).

These high figures were exceeded elsewhere. In Renfrewshire, a study of 440 people found highly localised and extensive food poverty. Forty-five per cent had 'just about' enough money for food all week; 13 per cent did not. Twenty per cent had had to go without a meal in the last year due to lack of cash, twice the North of England study's figure (Milburn *et al*, 1987). The unemployed suffered disproportionately hard. Forty per cent of the total sample reported they cut back on food and 41 per cent said they either only just had enough money to eat or did not have enough. Fruit was infrequently eaten and most people would have liked to eat more meat if they could afford it.

In 1991 a study conducted by the National Children's Home found that not one of the 354 low-income families surveyed was eating a diet which met current nutrition guidelines (NCH Action for Children, 1991). Two thirds of the children and over half the parents were eating a nutritionally poor diet. Additionally, one in five parents missed food in the previous month because they did not have enough money; nearly half had gone short in the previous year; and one in ten children under the age of five years had gone without food in the previous month. Parents knew the diet was inadequate but could do little about it.

EATING HEALTHILY?

A consistent research finding has been that people on low incomes share the rest of the population's desire to eat healthily. People on low incomes might eat a poorer diet than others but this is due to cost not to lack of concern or information (Sheiham *et al,* 1987; Sheiham *et al,* 1990). In the words of a review of a number of research projects, 'making ends meet on a low income means going without ... It leads to poor diets, with choices between eating healthy foods or having sufficient to eat ...' (Kempson, 1966).

Back in 1985, alarmed by the rising evidence of people cutting back on eating and about the impact of the 1986 Social Security Act, a working party drawn from professionals, the voluntary sector and academics was formed under the auspices of the London Food Commission to review the evidence on food poverty. Analysis of National Food Survey data showed that between 1980 and 1983 the gap in spending on food widened between low-income families (earning less than £80 per week in 1983) and high-income families (earning more than £250 per week) (Cole-Hamilton and Lang, 1986). People in classes IV and V were at risk of under-nutrition, failure to thrive, vitamin and mineral deficiencies and poor dental health. An estimated 7 per cent of older people suffered some form of malnutrition. A study of older people in institutional care found half the sample had vitamin C levels equivalent to those found in people with scurvy (Cole-Hamilton and Lang, 1986). The new poor may not be an homogeneous group, but they are united in having restricted diets.

The working party also tackled the argument, then current in health education circles, that the poor ought to receive specially targeted health advice. A costing exercise based on the National Food Survey data showed that to eat a healthy diet, following government advice, would cost 35 per cent more than the average cost of the food intake of a low-income household (Cole-Hamilton and Lang, 1986).This finding was flatly rejected by the Government in its Review of Social Security, 1985/86, and by the supermarkets. In a letter to the Director of the London Food Commission in January 1986, John Major, then Minister for Social Security, said rather ingenuously that 'the Review of Social Security did not pursue questions of adequacy [of benefit to meet healthy eating criteria] as it was felt this would not be fruitful.' He continued: 'there is no agreement on what constitutes adequacy' and concluded that '... each claimant is free to decide how to budget their income according to their individual requirements'.

In fact, for the three previous years, a bitter battle had raged over health education following the suppression of a NACNE report, which had argued that the nation as a whole needed to alter its diet to reduce the incidence of coronary heart disease (CHD) and other diet-related ill-health almost all of which are affected by socio-economic status (see Chapter 11). To do this, the British *en bloc* needed to cut back on their intake of fat, particularly saturated fats, and sugars and to increase consumption of fibre. This evidence-based policy proposal was deeply threatening to certain food industry interests and led to a further battle over whose responsibility it was to alter diet – the individual, the food industry or the state?

Although the NACNE report was eventually published (NACNE, 1983), it helped lead to the demise of the semi-independent Health Education Council and its replacement by the Health Education Authority (HEA) which is anchored more firmly within Whitehall control. Despite this, and as a result of the London Food Commission's work, the HEA commissioned a nutritional review of food poverty. This documented all the relevant studies of the post-war period and amounted to an indictment of government inaction. It was never published (Isobel Cole-Hamilton, 1988).

Individualism was in the driving seat. The 'Look After Your Health' (LAYH) campaign, exuberantly led by the then junior Minister, Mrs Edwina Currie, *de facto* asserted that it was now the responsibility of the poor if they ate badly. Responding to a study based in the Northern Health Region which indicated a link between ill-health and material deprivation (Townsend *et al*, 1987), she stated that the key issue was 'ignorance ... and failing to realise they [the poor] do have some control over their lives' (quoted in Townsend *et al*, 1988). The LAYH campaign represented the nadir of food policy in the post War period, ignoring research and denying policy experience and influence. It was victim blaming and deeply resented by people on low incomes (see, for example, the statement by a lone mother in Malseed, 1990). Yet its confident assertion tapped years of criticism and stigmatisation of the poor. One is reminded of George Orwell in *The Road to Wigan Pier*, in which he concluded that only the rich have the opportunity to enjoy healthy, wholesome food; the poor are forced to seek instant, tasty food (Orwell, 1962). Sixty years later the point was still having to be made.

In a recent study it was found that if lone parents tried to shop for healthy, fresh food, their families could eat more healthily but still less healthily than better-off families (Dowler and Calvert, 1995). In another study of 200 lone parent households in London, this time for MAFF, Dowler found clear evidence that households living on income support were less likely to be eating brown bread, pasta, chicken, semi-skimmed milk, cheese, some vegetables, fruit, fruit juices or to be using oil for cooking – ie, most indicators of a 'healthy' diet – than those not on benefits (Dowler, 1995). In 1991, the Scottish Heart Health Survey showed that both men and women in manual occupations had a poorer quality diet than those in non-manual occupations. Different intakes of fruit and vegetables were marked (Bolton-Smith *et al*, 1991). How much evidence of the class-diet-health connection did the Government need?

THE IMPACT OF MODERN FOOD RETAILING

If much of the 1980s debate was a reinvention of the social policy wheel, one feature was genuinely new. This was the argument that changes in the food economy, particularly the arrival of supermarkets, had altered the shopping and dietary options of the poor. This was first articulated in a study of London (Lewis, 1985). London was then experiencing what other towns and regions had already gone through – the arrival of giant supermarkets. The research found that new and planned stores were away from high streets, limiting local competition and leading to the closure of small stores. To retailers, size is everything because, per square foot of sales area, there is more turnover and profit. Lewis checked prices for 84 key food items representative of foods bought by low, middle and high income households and found a variation of up to 21 per cent between stores. This amounted to a loss of potential savings for low income consumers of up to £4.50 per week (1985 prices). She also found a narrower range of foods in smaller, more local stores.

This created a new avenue of research (Raven *et al*, 1995; Piachaud and Webb, 1996). In a study of Hampstead, Mooney, a community dietitian, found that it was better to be poor in a rich area than poor in a poor area (Mooney, 1987). She created two hypothetical shopping baskets of food. One was 'healthy' and contained, for instance, wholemeal bread and skimmed milk. The other contained less healthy alternatives. Purchasing these baskets in her health authority area, she found that the lowest availability of healthy food was in the most deprived area, where the healthier basket of food cost between 63 per cent and 73 per cent more. Mooney's conclusions reinforced concerns about supermarkets, particularly on pricing policy, and she called for healthier options to be sold as loss leaders. A subsequent study in Lancashire echoed these criticisms of stores: no shop stocked all the foods in the 'healthy' basket (Chief Environmental Health Officer, 1988).

In 1988, the Welsh Consumer Council – already concerned about the impact of the loss of corner shops on local life (Welsh Consumer Council, 1982) – commissioned a study to explore these issues in the principality. From a survey of 57 food items in 111 shops, prices for a standard basket of goods varied from £17.11 to £21.94, with multiple retailers by far the cheapest (Welsh Consumer Council, 1990). The report echoed Lewis' and Mooney's findings: 'healthy' foods generally cost more and were less widely available than their standard equivalent, were less available in small shops and were more available in urban areas close to large shops (Welsh Consumer Council, 1990). Across the UK, the NCH 1991 study found the greatest difference in costs in rural areas and Scotland (NCH Action for Children, 1991).

By the mid-1990s, there were few who doubted the existence of price variations first identified by Lewis. Piachaud and Webb (1996), for example, found price differences of up to 60 per cent between supermarkets and corner stores for the same goods. They calculated that the worst-off pensioner couples, mainly dependent on state benefits, could be out of pocket by up to £8.40 per week, over 10 per cent of total income, depending on whether they had access to the cheapest goods in hypermarkets or only to the most expensive provided by small shops.

The key issue which such research has uncovered is not just the price advantage which the large multiples have through their superior buying power, but the fact that for people on low incomes, travelling to the shops has now become an additional cost in itself. In economic terms, the cost of transport is externalised by the retailers and born, disproportionately by the poor. An 80p bus journey either way mounts up (Speak *et al*, 1995), and may be debited from money that otherwise would have gone on food. In 1994, the Ferguslie Women's Poverty Group estimated that each shopping trip added £2 in transport (Leather and Lobstein, 1994).

Five studies funded by the Joseph Rowntree Foundation in the early 1990s produced a collective picture of people juggling competing interests, 'shopping around for bargains and value-for-money', having to shop at the end of the day to get the pre-closing prices, and all the countless tactics of surviving on a low income (Kempson, 1996). As one person surveyed said, 'If I know we ain't got no food, and the gas man's waiting, I'm sorry, I'm going to buy my shopping. They're OK. The gas will survive' (Kempson, 1995). All the families in another study managed to get enough to eat, but such 'success' was achieved at a price, such as self-denial, family stress and unwelcome changes in diet and shopping habits (Dobson , 1994). People vary in their responses to low income. Some cut back all round, some 'trade down' by buying cheaper, lower quality foods and others feed the children and (male) partners before themselves.

As discussed earlier, this juggling act is mainly performed by women: 'Let's face it, we'd all steal to feed our children' as one mother of three children put it (Leather, 1996). The general pattern is to do a weekly shop on benefit day. When money runs low, shopping is done daily for that day's food. Diet, therefore, deteriorates as the week goes on. A fifth of the Rowntree sample of lone parents had to 'make do' with whatever they had edible in the house, rather than choosing what they wanted (Dowler and Calvert, 1995). This restriction of time and geographical horizons is a consistent feature of modern food poverty. Yet for the more affluent, the reverse is the case. Shopping generally within Britain has become more infrequent and more long-distant (Raven *et al*, 1995).

GOVERNMENT POLICY: FROM DENIAL TO COPING

In 1992, the Government signalled a change of policy. Having for 13 years denied the poverty/ill-health connection, the 1992 *Health of the Nation* White Paper, steered by the Department of Health, but signed by all government departments, tacitly acknowledged it (as noted in Chapter 11).

From now on, accommodation was to be reached with critics of its health policy. Evidence that from the mid 1980s the health gap between rich and poor was widening again after decades of narrowing worried the Department of Health. This led to a shift in policy from the denial of food poverty to an exploration of coping strategies. The voluntary sector was funded by the Department of Health to support a network of food poverty projects. This uncovered an awesome array of projects in local authorities, health trusts, churches and community groups (Leather and Lobstein, 1994): groups were opening shops and cafes, running coupon and transport schemes, Local Exchange Trading Schemes (LETS), working with special interest and needs groups and running cookery classes (National Food Alliance, 1994). Such positive action is a testament to the grit and energy of local activists and communities, but they are at best curative rather than preventative. Databases, such as that launched in 1996 by the Health Education Authority and National Food Alliance, help projects learn from others' experience but do not transfer any resources to the poor. Projects teaching cooking skills are needed not just for the poor but for everyone, since the national curriculum removed practical skills from the classroom. (On the class divide in cooking, see Lang *et al*, 1996.)

In 1994, the Department of Health set up the Low Income Project Team (LIPT), as part of the Nutrition Taskforce established in the wake of the *Health of the Nation*. This reported in 1996, having been prevented from talking about money (Department of Health, 1996). Despite this handcuff the LIPT report made useful inroads on government complacency. First, it acknowledged that there was a problem of poverty-related ill-health. Secondly, it mapped out a number of strategies for tackling the problem. Most importantly, it recognised that the food retailing revolution had by-passed and excluded the poor and that this situation had to be reversed.

THE INSULT: THERE IS PLENTY OF FOOD

We should not be surprised by this picture of the relationship between food and poverty. In its way food poverty in the UK echoes findings elsewhere in both rich and poor countries. There are of course important differences between our own and, say, African experiences of food poverty. The differences are both absolute – we have no *kwashiorkor* – and relative, but at both global and European levels, circumstances and policies echo our own in an eerie fashion. This is due to neither *zeitgeist* nor accident but to the dominance of a particular view of political economy which argues that economic progress will come only from reducing the state's role, placing responsibility on individuals for their own fate and emphasising competitive trade as the motor force of economic growth. Undoubtedly, this recipe yields huge bonuses for its winners, but for the losers the outcome is both humiliation and exclusion.

The United Nation's Children's Fund estimates that one person in five in the developing world suffers from chronic hunger – 800 million people in Africa, Asia and Latin America and that:

> over two billion people subsist on diets deficient in the vitamins and minerals essential for normal growth and development, and for preventing premature death and such disabilities as blindness and mental retardation. (UNICEF, 1993).

Even in the rich world, the possibility of feeding people well and producing food in a socially just and an environmentally sustainable manner is fracturing before our eyes. Under the 'set-aside' system, a feature of the reforms of the Common Agricultural Policy introduced in 1992 which were modelled on schemes in the USA, European farmers are paid handsomely *not* to produce food on up to 15 per cent of their land. In 1991, the Common Agricultural Policy cost European consumers £24.9 billion (MAFF, 1992). Worse, 80 per cent of this direct support to farmers goes to the largest 20 per cent of farms (House of Lords, 1992).

Poverty amidst plenty is an old, old story. Since the Irish Famine a century and a half ago, it has become commonplace that food may be exported under the noses of the malnourished. Food will go to where prices are best for the trader. And if people lack purchasing power, they starve. In his study of Africa, Raikes (1988) argues that European attempts, in the name of aid, to modernise African agriculture have merely 'modernised hunger', allowing wealthier farmers and more fertile areas to gain at the expense of others. As the British supermarket shopper browses along rows of produce, flown thousands of miles from Kenya and Tanzania to grace our dinner tables, we should remember that relatively close by – in Zaire and Mozambique, for instance – there is rank malnutrition. Social exclusion has an international dimension. The last 20 years should teach us that tackling food poverty requires complex solutions from simple truths, at home and abroad.

REFERENCES

Advisory Committee on Nutrition (1937) *First Report*, Ministry of Health, HMSO, 27-29.

Bolton-Smith, C, Woodward, A L and Tunstall-Pedoe, H (1991) 'Nutrient intakes of different social classes: results from the Scottish Heart Health Study', *British Journal of Nutrition*, vol 6, no 55, p321-35.

Bradshaw, J (1993) *Household Budgets and Living Standards*, Joseph Rowntree Foundation.

British Medical Association (1939) *Nutrition and Public Health*, Proceedings of a National Conference on the Wider Aspects of Nutrition, 27-9 April.

Burghes, L (1980) *Living from Hand to Mouth: a study of 65 families living on supplementary benefit*, Child Poverty Action Group/Family Services Unit.

Cannon, G (1992) *Food and Health: The Experts Agree.*

Charles, N and Kerr, N (1985) *Attitudes towards the Feeding and Nutrition of Young Children*, Health Education Council, Research Report 4.

Chen Junshi, T, Campbell, C, Junyao, Li and Peto, R (1990) *Diet, Lifestyle and Mortality in China*, Oxford.

Chief Environmental Health Officer, Lancashire County Council (1988) *Report to Committee*, Lancashire County Council.

Cole-Hamilton, I (1988) report to Health Education Authority, unpublished.

Cole-Hamilton, I and Lang, T (1986) *Tightening Belts*, London Food Commission.

Department of Health (1996) *Low income, food, nutrition and health: strategies for improvement. Report by the Low Income Project Team for the Nutrition Taskforce*, Department of Health.

Department of Health (1991) *Dietary Reference Values for Food Energy and Nutrients for the United Kingdom*, HMSO, pp54-69.

DHSS (1986) *The Diets of British Schoolchildren*, Department of Health and Social Security.

Dobson, B, Beardsworth, A, Keil, T and Walker, R (1994) *Diet, Choice and Poverty*, Family Policy Studies Centre.

Dowler, E (1995) *Factors Affecting Nutrient Intake and Dietary Adequacy in*

Lone-Parent Households, MAFF Project no 2B043, Human Nutrition Unit, London School of Hygiene and Tropical Medicine, March.

Dowler, E and Calvert, C (1995) *Nutrition and Diet in Lone-Parent Families in London*, Family Policy Studies Centre.

Durward, L (1984) *Poverty in Pregnancy*, Maternity Alliance.

Graham, H (1986) *Caring for the Family*, Health Education Council, Research Report 1.

HM Government (1992) *Health of the Nation*, HMSO.

House of Lords (1992) *Development and Future of the Common Agricultural Policy*, HL Paper 79-1, HMSO.

Kempson, E (1996) *Life on a Low Income*, Joseph Rowntree Foundation.

Killeen, D (1994) 'Food and nutrition', in Fyfe, G (ed) *Poor and Paying for It*, Scottish Consumer Council/HMSO.

Lang, T, Caraher, M, Dixon, P and Carr-Hill, R (1996) *Class, income and gender in cooking: results from an English survey*, paper to the International Conference on Culinary Arts and Sciences, Bournemouth, 25-28 June.

Lang, T, Hannon, E, Andrews, H, Bedale, C and Hulme, J (1984) *Jam Tomorrow?*, Manchester Polytechnic Food Policy Unit.

Leather, S (1992) *By Bread Alone? Poverty and diet in Britain today*, MAFF Consumer Panel, CP (92) 9/8, January.

Leather, S (1992) paper to Look After Your Heart Network Day on Food and Low Income Initiatives, 2 October.

Leather, S (1996), *The Making of Modern Malnutrition*, Caroline Walker Trust.

Leather, S and Lobstein, T (1994) *Food and Low Income: A practical guide for advisors and supporters working with families and young people on low incomes*, National Food Alliance.

Lewis, J (1985) *Food Retailing in London*, London Food Commission.

Mack, J and Lansley, S (1985) *Poor Britain*, Allen and Unwin.

MAFF Food Science Division 1 (1992) *The cost of alternative diets*, Consumer Panel, CP (92) 9/3, January.

Malseed, J (1990) *Bread without Dough: understanding food poverty*, Horton Publishing.

Milburn, J, Clarke, A and Smith, F (1987) *Nae Bread*, Health Education Department, Argyll and Clyde Health Board.

Ministry of Agriculture, Fisheries and Food (1992) *Agriculture in the UK: 1991*, HMSO.

Mooney, C (1987) *Cost, Availability and Choice of Healthy Foods in Some Camden Supermarkets*, Hampstead Health Authority Department of Nutrition and Dietetics.

Morris, J N (1979) 'Social inequalities undiminished', *Lancet*, i, pp87-90.

National Advisory Committee on Nutrition Education (NACNE) (1983) *A Discussion Paper on Proposals for Nutritional Guidelines for Health Education in Britain*.

National Food Alliance (1994) *Get Cooking!* Newsletter.

NCH Action for Children (1991) *Poverty and Nutrition*, NCH Action for Children.

Nelson, M and Naismith, D (1979) 'The nutritional status of poor children', *Journal of Human Nutrition*, 33, pp33-45.

Nelson, M and Paul, A (1983) 'The nutritive contribution of school dinners and other mid-day meals to the diets of schoolchildren', *Human Nutrition: Applied Nutrition*, 37A, pp128-35.

Orwell, G (1962) *The Road to Wigan Pier.*

Piachaud, D and Webb, J (1996) *The Price of Food: missing out on mass consumption*, STICERD, London School of Economics.

Raikes, P (1988) *Modernising Hunger*, Catholic Institute for International Relations/James Currey.

Raven, H and Lang, T with Dumonteil, C (1995) *Off our Trolleys? Food retailing and the hypermarket economy*, Institute for Public Policy Research.

Sheiham, A, Marmot, M, Rawson, D and Ruck, N (1987) 'Food values: health and diet', in Jowell, R, Witherspoon, S and Brook, L (eds) *British Social Attitudes – the 1987 Report*, Gower Publishing.

Sheiham, A, Marmot, M, Taylor, B and Brown, A (1990) 'Recipes for health', in Jowell, R, Witherspoon, S and Brook, L (eds) *British Social Attitudes – the 7th Report*, Gower Publishing.

Smith, D (1994) 'The Social Construction of Dietary Standards: The British Medical Association – Ministry of Health Advisory Committee on Nutrition Report of 1934', in Maurer, D and Sobal, J, *Eating Agendas: food and nutrition as social problems*, New York, pp279-303.

Speak, S, Cameron, S, Woods, R and Gilroy, R (1995) *Young Single Mothers: barriers to independent living*, Family Policy Studies Centre.

Stitt, S and Grant, D (1997) *Poverty in Britain in the 1990s: Rowntree revisited*, Polity Press.

Townsend, P and Davidson, N (1982) *Inequalities in Health*, Penguin.

Townsend, P, Davidson, N and Whitehead, M (1988) *Inequalities in Health*, Penguin.

Townsend, P, Phillimore, P and Beattie, A (1987) *Inequalities in Health in the Northern Region*, Northern Regional Health Authority/Bristol University.

UNICEF (1993) *Food, Health and Care: the UNICEF vision and strategy for a world free from hunger and malnutrition*, United Nations Children's Fund.

Walker, C and Church, M (1978) 'Poverty by administration: a review of supplementary benefits, nutrition and scale rates', *Journal of Human Nutrition*, 32, pp5-18.

Welsh Consumer Council (1982) *From Corner Shop to Superstore*, WCC.

Welsh Consumer Council (1990) *Shopping for Food: a study of food prices and availability in Wales*, WCC.

Whitehead, M (1988) 'The health divide', in Townsend, P, Davidson, N and Whitehead, M, *Inequalities in Health*, Penguin.

World Health Organisation (1990) Diet, *Nutrition and the Prevention of Chronic Disease*, Technical Series, no 797, Geneva.

Section Three

COMBATING POVERTY AND SOCIAL EXCLUSION

15 How will the scissors close? Options for UK social spending
John Hills

Looking to the future of UK social spending, policy-makers – and those who would influence them – face two blades of a pair of scissors. The top blade, pointing upwards, represents the upward pressures on social spending. Public demand or needs for provision of the kinds of welfare services which are generally provided through the state in Britain are rising. The lower blade, pointing downwards, represents the political – and possibly economic – pressures to restrain or cut tax, and so limit the funds available for public welfare spending.

As time goes by the scissors must close. Spending must be financed. The question is how this will occur – by the lower blade rising to meet the other as increasing demands for welfare provision are accommodated through higher tax-financed spending, by the upper blade falling to allow low taxes through cuts in services, or by something in between? The rest of this chapter discusses the pressures driving these choices, and some of their potential consequences.

RISING WELFARE DEMAND

There are three key reasons why one would expect demand for the core welfare services – health, education, and social security – to increase over coming years and decades:

- demographic change;
- the effects of rising inequality and international competition; and

- rising affluence and people's preferences.

The first two of these are discussed below. As far as the third is concerned, it seems clear from international comparisons, from cross-sections across different income groups within the population, and from trends over time, that higher incomes are associated with increased demands for education and especially health care provision (see Chapters 9 and 11). Education and health care appear to be 'luxuries' as economists define them – as we become richer we want more of them and are prepared to devote greater fractions of our incomes to them. Even if nothing else changes, if average incomes continue to rise, so, one would expect, will the pressure for greater provision – public or private – in these areas.

DEMOGRAPHIC CHANGE

Demography is a problem for two reasons. First, much of what the welfare state does is about smoothing out people's living standards over the life cycle and meeting needs which are concentrated at particular ages. While education is concentrated on the young, health care and social security spending, like pensions, are concentrated on those over 65, and health spending is highest for the very elderly (Hills, 1993, figure 5). Recent official population forecasts are that the share of the population aged 65 or over will rise from 16 per cent in 1996 to 24 per cent in 2041. At the same time the share of the very elderly, 85 or over, will rise from under 2 per cent to over 4 per cent (OPCS, 1993). More recent projections have revised these numbers downwards, particularly for the very elderly.

This combination is, of course, the source of the so-called 'demographic time-bomb' facing welfare spending in the next century, a problem discussed as much in other countries as in the UK. The fact that other countries face significant problems does not, however, mean that the UK faces similar ones, as Figure 15.1 illustrates. This shows recent forecasts made by the Organisation for Economic Co-operation and Development (OECD, 1995) for the future costs of public pensions as a share of national income (GDP), comparing their costs in 1995 with those in the year when spending is forecast to reach its peak. The projections are based on current pension policies and population forecasts for each of the 'G7' countries.

The picture is in many ways remarkable. In Germany, Italy and

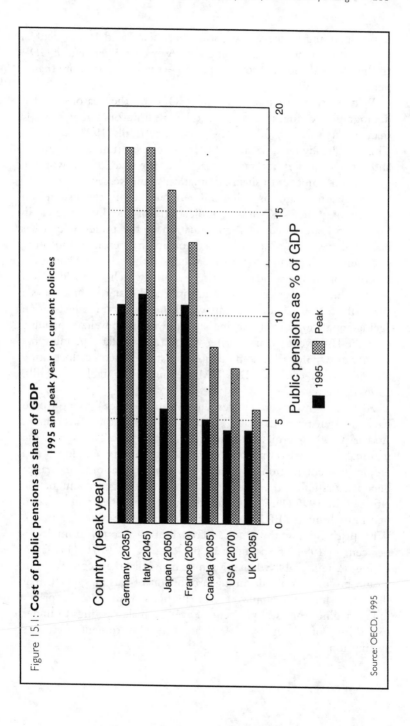

Figure 15.1: **Cost of public pensions as share of GDP**
1995 and peak year on current policies

Source: OECD, 1995

Japan, spending is forecast to rise by between 7 and 10 per cent of GDP, and in France, Canada and the USA by over 3 per cent of GDP. In the UK – already the lowest spender – the rise is no more than 1 per cent of GDP.

Why is there such a difference? One of the reasons is that demographic changes are forecast to be less unfavourable in the UK than in virtually any other OECD country (Hills, 1993, figure 6). The UK already has a sizeable elderly population (unlike, say, Japan), and its recent fertility rates mean that the size of its working population is not set to shrink dramatically (unlike, say, Italy).

The second reason is rather different, and lies in the assumption of current policies. Crucially, projections of the kind shown in Figure 15.1 are based on a continuation of the policy which has been followed since the early 1980s of linking pensions and other state benefits to prices rather than earnings. If the economy continues to grow and living standards to rise, benefits which are fixed in real terms – linked to prices – become easier and easier to finance as a share of other incomes. It is this which has offset the effects of an ageing population and of growing unemployment on welfare spending over the last twenty years, during which total welfare spending has neither grown nor shrunk in relation to national income, fluctuating around 25 per cent of GDP (HM Treasury, 1996, table 1.3; Hills, 1995, figure 6).

As far as pensions are concerned, continued price-linking would have an even more dramatic effect according to the Government Actuary's (1995) projections shown in Table 15.1. This shows the national insurance contribution rates (combining employer and employee contributions) required to pay for national insurance benefits, including the basic state pension, taking account of the effect of the 1995 Pensions Act on the future cost of earnings-related pensions through SERPS and raising women's pension age to 65. With price-linking, the required contribution rate *falls* from 18.25 per cent in 1994/95 to under 16 per cent by 2040/41. This fall is even more remarkable when it is remembered that these contributions would be levied on a declining proportion of earnings, given that the upper limit for employee contributions would also be price-linked, falling from 120 per cent of average male earnings to under two-thirds of them by 2030 on the Government Actuary's assumptions.

TABLE 15.1: **Government Actuary forecasts**[1]

	Benefits price-linked	Benefits earnings-linked
1994/95	18.25	18.25
2000/01	17.7	19.0
2010/11	17.4	20.9
2020/21	16.8	22.2
2030/31	17.2	25.4
2040/41	15.8	25.9
2050/51	14.0	25.3

Notes: 1. Combined employer and employee NIC contributions rates required to finance National Insurance benefits. Figures include effects of 1995 Pensions Act. They represent gross costs. Effects on public finances may result in different net costs.

Source: Government Actuary, 1995.

The corollary of this 'solution' to the fiscal crisis is, however, that state pensions and other benefits would become progressively less and less valuable in relation to other incomes, and less and less effective in smoothing life cycle incomes – eventually becoming 'nugatory' in Michael Portillo's famous phrase. If we had followed a policy of price-linking the basic pension for the last 50 years, it would currently be worth £25 per week for a single pensioner, rather than the £62.45 it will actually be in 1997/98. Whether or not the equivalent of £25 was a reasonable amount to ask someone to live on in 1948, few people would think it so today, given contemporary general living standards. Yet unless something changes, that is the kind of relative income which current policies imply for many of tomorrow's pensioners.

As the table shows, a return to earnings-linking national insurance benefits would mean that contribution rates would have to rise – reflecting the growth in the pensioner population as well as the maturing of SERPS and more married women being entitled to pensions in their own right. By 2040/41, combined contribution rates would have to be more than 7.5 percentage points higher than in 1994/95.

As a measure of the impact of ageing on spending if the relative value of benefits was preserved, this kind of calculation has some short-comings, however. On the one hand it only looks at one aspect of the demographic problem for spending, leaving out its effects on other kinds of social security and, in particular, on health spending. On the other, it looks only at *gross* costs, ignoring, for instance, the beneficial effects on other parts of the public finances of rising taxes and reduced means-tested benefits as incomes from sources like SERPS become more important.

In an earlier exercise (Hills, 1993), I examined what the combined impact on public spending on the 'big ticket' items of health, education, and social security, would be simply as a result of the ageing of the population between 1991 and 2041, assuming that spending for people of any given age would be maintained *relative to current incomes* – ie, linking benefits to GDP per capita, and assuming that education and health spending would reflect both the numbers of relevant ages, but also the need to keep salaries up with incomes elsewhere in the economy. Allowing for maturing pensions as forecast by the Government Actuary and the effect of the 1995 Pensions Act, the effect would be to increase spending by the equivalent of 4.5 per cent of GDP.[1]

Calculations of this kind tend to be met with two different responses, largely reflecting political stance. For some, 4.5 per cent of GDP quickly translates into the equivalent of over £30 billion at today's prices, and from there to a need to increase income tax rates by around 12 pence in the pound. In the current political climate this is seen as self-evidently absurd and unthinkable.[2]

The second response is to point out that this increase would accumulate over a period of nearly 50 years, revenues having to rise by the equivalent of a mere 0.1 per cent of GDP each year – £700 million at today's prices, the kind of amount dwarfed by Treasury errors in forecasting next year's tax revenues. Even the 50 year total would represent less than a third of the increase in welfare spending's share of GDP over the shorter period between 1946 and 1976, and would not take UK welfare spending even up to today's European

---

1. To this one could add an expected increase in the cost of social care for the very elderly. These are, however, very hard to predict. One recent estimate by the Department of Health suggested that public spending on social care would be *lower* as a percentage of GDP in 2030 than now (Joseph Rowntree Foundation, 1996, Table 24). Other estimates have suggested substantial potential increases, but with a wide range between plausible 'high' and 'low' figures (Nuttall *et al*, 1995).

2. It is convenient to ignore in such calculations that income tax only raises a quarter of tax revenues. If the same amount was raised by increasing all taxes in proportion – by about an eighth – the increase in, say, the basic rate of income tax would be about 3 pence in the pound, which has a much less dramatic sound.

average (while other countries cope with far more serious demographic pressures). Looked at in this way, the 'time-bomb' seems a damp squib.

My own conclusion is that ageing populations do cause rising demand for welfare services. There is, however, nothing in the UK situation as far as demography is concerned which will make the welfare state in its current form 'unaffordable' – if as a country we *choose* to maintain its relative generosity. Whether as a nation we *will* make this choice is a different matter, explored below.

At the bottom of this is the following. As a nation we are living longer, but are expecting to spend nearly all of that extra life expectancy in retirement. Much, if not most, of what the welfare state achieves is about transfers across the life cycle – particularly from people of working age to those in retirement (Falkingham and Hills, 1995). This leaves us with a choice. We can pay more during our working lives to maintain relative standards during an increasing period of retirement. Alternatively, we can carry on paying the same during our working lives, but spread the jam out more thinly during retirement, accepting lower relative provision – which is, in effect, what the policy of price-linking social security benefits implies. The only way out of this choice would be to spend at least part of our increased life expectancy at work. This may happen in part as a result of the raising of women's pension age from 60 to 65 between 2010 and 2020. However, official pension ages do not necessarily determine actual working lives, as recent trends towards much earlier male effective retirement ages show (Hills, 1993, figure 25).

Crucially, the same dilemma exists whether transfers are made through taxation and the social security system or through private pension contributions and savings and the private sector. The timing of transfers and the effects on different generations may vary, but the form of the transfer does not change the fundamental problem of a rising need to transfer resources across the life cycle. Demography of itself does not imply a conclusion either way for the balance between public and private sectors.

RISING INEQUALITY AND INTERNATIONAL COMPETITION

The rapid growth of inequality in the UK between the late-1970s and the start of the 1990s has been well documented earlier (see

Chapters 2 and 3). Although the causes of this are varied (Barclay, 1995; Oppenheim and Harker, 1996), some of them affect other countries as well, albeit not to the same degree as the UK, and some reflect the effects of increasing global economic competition. Without discussing this in detail, there are several features of this which are important in thinking about the future of social policy and spending, particularly if policy is to be aimed at ensuring that everyone does have a stake in society and the well-being of the economy.

First, the increasing importance of education and training is so widely accepted as to have become a platitude. In both international terms and in the domestic labour market, education and training matter more than they did before, and those without skills or qualifications are in an increasingly weak position. Britain's relatively poor long-term performance in non-elite education is one reason why it was worse hit than, say, Germany in terms of the effects on wage inequality in the 1980s as the bottom dropped out of the market for unskilled labour.

Longer periods in higher quality education and training imply, however, two kinds of costs: the direct costs of the teaching involved, and the 'opportunity cost' of the time spent being educated or trained. Again, whether it is paid for publicly or privately, *someone* is going to have to pay more for these costs than in the past.

Second, the policy of linking pensions and other social security benefits to prices rather than earnings or any other measure of contemporary living standards was part of the reason why inequality grew so rapidly. The growing inequality within the pensioner population is an example of this (Hancock and Weir, 1994). During the 1980s an increasing divide opened up between those pensioners dependent on state benefits and those with occupational pensions. With each successive cohort retiring, a greater number have reasonable incomes from occupational pensions or from savings, and so are, in aggregate, better off than their predecessors. However, the proportion of the working population covered by occupational pensions ceased to rise 30 years ago (Dilnot *et al*, 1994, figure 2.2). Allowing for the low value of the 'personal pensions' which some without occupational pensions have taken out, for the low entitlements of those with interrupted careers, long periods of unemployment, low pay, or part-time work, and the effects of higher divorce rates than in the past, a substantial minority of pensioners will continue to retire with their living standards largely dependent on the level of state benefits. Counteracting the recent trends for such groups to fall behind the rest of the population implies the kinds of increased costs for the public sector discussed above as general benefit levels are maintained in *relative* terms – unless the overall structure of the system is changed in some way.

The obvious form of such restructuring of social security to maintain living standards at the bottom while controlling overall costs is, however, means-testing. Other features of the growth of inequality during the 1980s suggest that this may not offer the neat solution which is sometimes claimed for it. For instance, for the working population one of the reasons for growing inequality was the polarisation between so-called 'work rich' two earner couples and 'work poor' couples without an earner. The main factor driving this was a sharp deterioration in the speed with which couples, where neither had earnings, got back into employment (Gregg and Wadsworth, 1996). In this the effects of ending up on means-tested income support are strongly implicated.

In reaction to the growth in the numbers of people of working age receiving benefits and problems of this kind, both the Government and the Labour Party have concentrated on actual or proposed initiatives which fall under the general heading of 'welfare to work' strategies (Department of Social Security, 1996; Labour Party, 1996). Many of these are essentially about softening the effects of means-testing, for instance for a limited period allowing benefits or other support to continue while people return to work (see, for instance, Commission on Social Justice, 1994 or Barclay, 1995 for discussion of some of the issues involved). It is often argued that such strategies may save public spending in the long run, as the numbers receiving benefits are reduced and as tax revenues come in. However, whether they do so – and whether they even 'pay for themselves' over the long run – it seems inevitable, unless they work through penalties on those remaining on benefit, that they involve increased costs in the short term.

A final aspect of the growth of inequality with strong implications for social policy is the rapid growth in polarisation between housing tenures, discussed by Ginsburg earlier, and linked to this a growth in the social and economic differences between different areas or neighbourhoods (Giles *et al*, 1996; Philo, 1995; Green, 1996). Such area polarisation raises fears of areas spiralling downwards as low expectations and lack of contact with the labour market feed in on themselves. Countering such pressures with regeneration programmes requires long term support and at least reallocation of resources from elsewhere in the system towards areas which are otherwise becoming marginalised.

INCREASING CONSTRAINTS ON RESOURCES?

The pressures for welfare provision are thus clearly, and perhaps inexorably, upwards, even if they are not growing as fast as alarmist discussions would imply. At the same time, the conventional political wisdom is that the constraints on acceptable tax revenues are becoming tighter and tighter: the bottom blade of the scissors is pointing firmly downwards. The unpopularity of the 1992/97 Government for much of its period of office was clearly linked to the fact that taxes increased, when people thought they had been promised tax cuts. At the same time, many commentators believe that the Labour Party lost the 1992 election on the tax issue.

Whatever the strength of the political argument, it is hard to find convincing evidence that the pressure of international economic competition demands a reduction in the British tax ratio. In terms of competitiveness it is the total price charged for our exports which matters to foreigners thinking of buying, not how we decide as a nation to split the proceeds between individual and collective consumption. To be sure, the mobility of financial capital and of certain kinds of labour imply problems for countries which try to impose tax rates at the top of the international range. But the UK is not a high tax country. Over the last twenty years the UK has moved from being slightly above the mid-point of the international range of tax as a share of national income to being clearly well below the international average. This is a result of a British tax ratio which has, in fact, varied little over time, while the ratios in both high tax and low tax countries have risen steadily (Hills, 1996a, figures 4.2 and 4.3).

The constraints on tax — at least in ranges around current British levels — arise from political preferences, but here there is a paradox. Despite the deep-seated conventional wisdom described above, when asked the public gives a rather different view, as can be seen from Figure 15.2. This gives the responses to the question which the *British Social Attitudes Survey* has been asking since 1983 about views on the balance between public spending and taxation. Back in 1983, 9 per cent wanted the two to be lower, 32 per cent wanted both increased, while the majority opted for the status quo. Over time opinion has shifted — in favour of higher taxation. Even after the tax

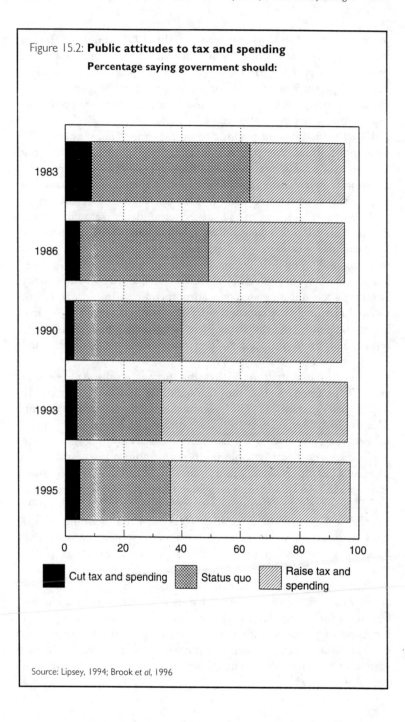

Figure 15.2: **Public attitudes to tax and spending**

Percentage saying government should:

Source: Lipsey, 1994; Brook et al, 1996

increases since 1993, 61 per cent of the 1995 sample said they wanted higher taxes and spending, and only 5 per cent wanted the two cut (Lipsey, 1994; Brook *et al*, 1996). If one is to believe these data, the pressure is actually for *higher* tax-financed spending, and there seems no way the figures could be interpreted to support cuts in spending as a way of allowing lower tax.

How is this apparent paradox to be explained? There seem to be three possibilities. The first is that for some reason people are not expressing their true preferences to the surveys. When answering the question they may have in mind the kind of spending they want, but assume that the increased taxes will fall on *someone else*. However, in the most recent version of the survey respondents were confronted with the question of whether they would still want higher spending on particular services even if it meant specified increases in their own tax bill. While the overwhelming majority wanting greater health spending fell somewhat, it remained a majority, and a majority continued to want increased education spending (Brook *et al*, 1996). Other individual programmes – defence and arts spending – fared less well. Spelling out tax consequences thus has some effect on the results, but does not lead to preferences for higher health and education spending to melt away.

A second explanation is that the survey results *do* represent people's preferences for the tax/spending trade-off, while the unpopularity of the 1992/97 Government reflects something different. The rise in tax levels since 1992 has not been accompanied by a rise in spending and services – it has been necessary to fill a hole in the public finances. Taxes have gone up with nothing to show for the increase. The unpopularity of this is unsurprising, but tells us nothing about the long-term decision on where tax-financed public spending should be set. At the same time it is easily forgotten that at the 1992 election a majority voted for higher tax-financed spending of one kind or another, while academic analysis disputes the idea that Labour lost the election on its actual tax policies (Heath *et al*, 1994).

Finally, however, it is one thing to want higher spending of a particular kind even if it means higher taxes on oneself, but quite another to trust politicians with what may be seen as a blank cheque by voting for parties perceived as high tax. People may *want* greater provision of public services, but do not trust politicians to deliver them. If true, this may support arguments for a widening of the earmarking or hypothecation of taxes to particular ends (Mulgan and Murray, 1993).

BRINGING THE SCISSORS TOGETHER

So where does this leave us? Overall there are three broad choices. The first is to look the demographic and other pressures squarely in the face, decide that the costs are not really so great, and that resources can be found to meet them – either from taxation or transferred from reduced public spending in some other part of the third of public spending outside the main welfare areas. At the same time some would argue not just for maintenance of the current relative *status quo*, but for improvements or restoration of cuts (for instance Townsend and Walker, 1995; Castle and Townsend, 1996).

It seems clear that this route will be followed for parts of public spending. The place of health care within the public sector is largely uncontested. Even the Thatcher Government of the late-1980s recoiled from the cost and inefficiency of US-style private medical insurance, and public opinion still overwhelmingly favours greater spending on the NHS, even when higher taxes are spelt out. Intriguingly, the Labour Party's Commission on Social Justice rejected the idea of an earmarked 'health tax' on the grounds that it would soften the constraint on NHS spending too much, with increased health care not necessarily the most effective way of improving population health.

At the edges, the war of attrition between the Treasury and health spenders will continue and, as it does so – depending on the complexion of the government – some further regular non-catastrophic items may follow 'teeth 'n specs' which have now largely left the public sector for most of the population.

Much the same can be said for education, second to health in the public agenda, but recently above it for politicians. The changing labour market has made education and skills attainment of more and more importance, and the UK remains behind many of its competitors, alarmingly so on some measures. One way or another we shall provide more pre-school and more education for 16–18-year-olds. Given that in the long run teachers' salaries will eventually have to keep up with rising pay elsewhere it is hard to see school and pre-school spending falling as a share of GDP, even though the size of the school-age population is forecast to fall.

But if education and health spending are higher up the political agenda and are protected – as they have been in comparative terms in recent years – what of social security? Will accommodating rising demands for them leave room for social security to maintain or increase its share of GDP as the pressures of ageing or suggestions for improvements imply?

There is nothing in the numbers discussed above which rules this out, but it is hard to find many politicians who would support this route, and it is perhaps in this area where the complexion of government will make the greatest difference. Is there therefore a plausible second route where, in this respect at least, public welfare spending could be cut, despite the upward pressures?

Proposals – mainly associated with the right-wing think-tanks – to achieve this have two main elements: first, increased use of means-testing to confine public provision to those with below average incomes only, in some formulations using such 'targeting' to *increase* resources at the bottom, at the cost of those higher up; and second, encouraging private insurance and other mechanisms as ways of meeting 'welfare' needs for those with high and average incomes.

It is hard to see that this kind of strategy would succeed in *increasing* resources reaching the bottom of the income distribution. First, without compensation, switching from social insurance or tax-funded social security is clearly highly regressive. Under tax-funded welfare, payments into the system are made in proportion to income, while under private insurance premiums they necessarily have to be in proportion to *risk* – any insurer who did not set premiums according to risk would quickly go out of business. Even if risks of unemployment and sickness were equal across the population, such a switch would mean higher costs for the poor, but lower costs for the rich. In reality this is exacerbated by the way in which such risks are actually greater for those with low incomes.

Second, trying to establish a system of compensation or protection for those with below-average incomes would imply an *increase* in the use of means-testing within social security, exacerbating the problems for both incentives and perceived fairness for those just above any income cut-offs already seen in the poverty, unemployment or savings traps, adding to the pressures towards fraud and the general disrepute of the system as a whole. The experience of the 1980s also suggests that although increased means-testing may save public spending in the short term, some of these savings prove illusory in the long run.

Third, withdrawing 'universal' benefits is unlikely to leave the tax constraint unaffected. People's willingness to pay tax is related at least in part to what they get out of the system. If those with average and higher incomes have to pay privately towards costs which were formerly tax-financed, one would expect acceptable tax levels to fall – the resources which are supposed to be freed up for the poor in this approach might simply melt away.

In fact, it could even be worse if private provision turns out to be less efficient or more expensive than collective provision – as the example of US health care suggests it is in some cases.[3] In this case the tax constraint might be tightened *more* than the spending demands on government – it could lose much more of its income than of its responsibilities, making the net fiscal position worse rather than better.

The problems of using private insurance as an escape route leave us still with the irresistible force of slowly but inexorably rising welfare demands meeting the possibly immovable political object of the resources available to meet them.

However, there may be an alternative way out which, whatever one thinks of its *a priori* merits, may be what actually happens. Parts of this can be seen in some of Frank Field's proposals for social security reform but also in other areas of debate on social policy. These ideas have three elements in common:

- provision is carried out in some way at arms-length from government, and spending is outside the public budget;
- payment is compulsory and probably income-related, but is not part of general taxation; and
- payment comes from identifiable beneficiaries and is earmarked in some way for them.

Examples of this kind of approach would include:

- ideas such as those of Frank Field or the recent Retirement Income Inquiry for compulsory second-tier pensions, which would increase the minimum amounts those in work would be expected to contribute to occupational pensions or to mutual organisations of some kind (Field, 1995, 1996; Anson, 1996);
- controversial but increasingly widely supported proposals for substantial parts of the cost of maintenance – and even tuition – for students in higher education to be funded by a form of loan, repayment of which would be made as a percentage of income

---

3. See Burchardt and Hills (1997) for an examination of the scale of problems of this kind in three areas where private insurance has been taking a greater role in the UK than hitherto: mortgage payment protection, permanent health insurance and long-term care insurance.

administered alongside the national insurance system, with faster repayments by those with high earnings and slow repayments by those with low subsequent earnings (Glennerster *et al*, 1995);

- compulsory payments into some form of national long-term care insurance, either taking the form of a direct addition to social insurance or an income-related payment through a 'National Care Insurance Scheme' to organisations at arms-length from government as recommended by the Joseph Rowntree Foundation's recent *Inquiry into the Costs of Continuing Care* (Joseph Rowntree Foundation, 1996).

Closely related are other developments like the transfers made under the provisions of the Child Support Act, which are also compulsory but are not taxation, and other forms of 'legal welfare' in Le Grand's (1996) terminology.

There are two main strands of objection to this kind of outcome. First, economic purists point out the potential inefficiencies of dividing what are in effect publicly determined resources between a plethora of different 'kitties', the relative buoyancies of which may not reflect their overall priority (see, for instance, Wilkinson, 1994). Second, political purists may be quick to describe such devices as simply 'smoke and mirrors' disguising an increase in effective taxation and hidden public spending.

There is something to be said for both objections. However, form may actually matter – some of these 'arms-length' institutions with clearly labelled revenue sources may in fact be more efficient forms of provision than traditional public provision financed by general revenues. They may also turn out to be the only way in which the scissors of demands and revenues can be closed without unnecessary pain.

REFERENCES

Anson, Sir J (chair) (1996) *Pensions: 2000 and beyond*, Retirement Income Inquiry.

Barclay, Sir P (1995) *Inquiry into Income and Wealth, Volume 1: Report*, Joseph Rowntree Foundation.

Brook, L, Hall, J and Preston, I (1996) 'Public spending and taxation' in Jowell, R et al (eds) *British Social Attitudes: the 13th report*, Dartmouth.

Burchardt, T and Hills, J (1997) *Pushing the Boundaries: Private welfare insurance and social security*, JRF.

Castle, B and Townsend, P (1996) *We CAN Afford the Welfare State*,

Security in retirement for everyone.

Commission on Social Justice (1994) *Social Justice: Strategies for renewal*, Vintage Books.

Department of Social Security (1996) *Social Security Departmental Report*, Cm 3213, HMSO.

Dilnot, A, Disney, R, Johnson, P and Whitehouse, E (1994) *Pensions Policy in the UK: An economic analysis*, Institute for Fiscal Studies.

Falkingham, J and Hills, J (eds) (1995) *The Dynamic of Welfare: The welfare state and the life cycle*, Prentice Hall/Harvester Wheatsheaf.

Field, F (1995) *Making Welfare Work: Reconstructing welfare for the millennium*, Institute of Community Studies.

Field, F (1996) *How to Pay for the Future: Building a stakeholders' welfare*, Institute of Community Studies.

Giles, C, Johnson, P, McCrae, J and Taylor, J (1996) *Living with the State: The incomes and work incentives of tenants in the social rented sector*, IFS.

Glennerster, H, Falkingham, J and Barr, N (1995) 'Education funding, equity and the life cycle' in Falkingham, J and Hills, J (1995).

Government Actuary (1995) *National Insurance Fund Long Term Financial Estimates* (Third Quinquennial Review) HC (1994-95) 160, HMSO.

Green, A (1996) 'Aspects of the changing geography of income and wealth' in Hill, J (1996b).

Gregg, P and Wadsworth, J (1996) 'More work in fewer households?' in Hills, J (1996b).

Hancock, R and Weir, P (1994) *More Ends than Means: A guide to pensioners' incomes in Great Britain during the 1980s*, Age Concern Institute of Gerontology.

Heath, A, Jowell, R and Curtice, J (eds) (1994) *Labour's Last Chance? The 1992 Election and Beyond*, Dartmouth.

Hills, J (1993) *The Future of Welfare: A guide to the debate*, Joseph Rowntree Foundation.

Hills, J (1995) 'Funding the Welfare State', *Oxford Review of Economic Policy*, Vol. 11, No.3.

Hills, J (1996a) 'Tax policy: are there still options', in Halpern, D *et al* (eds) *Options for Britain*, Dartmouth.

Hills, J (ed) (1996b) *New Inequalities: The changing distribution of income and wealth in the UK*, Cambridge University Press.

HM Treasury (1996) *Public Expenditure: Statistical Analyses 1996-97*, Cm 3201, HMSO.

Joseph Rowntree Foundation (1996) *Meeting the Costs of Continuing Care: Report and recommendations*, JRF.

Labour Party (1996) *Getting Welfare to Work: A new vision for social security*, The Labour Party.

Le Grand, J (1996) 'New visions of welfare' in Sasson, H and Diamond, D (eds) *LSE on Social Science*, LSE Books.

Lipsey, D (1994) 'Do we really want more public spending?' in Jowell, R *et al* (eds) *British Social Attitudes: The 11th Report*, Dartmouth.

Mulgan, G and Murray, R (1993) *Reconnecting Taxation*, DEMOS.

Nuttall, S *et al* (1995) 'Financing long-term care in Great Britain', *Journal of the Institute of Actuaries*, Vol. 121, No. 1.

OECD (1995) 'Effects of ageing populations on government budgets' in *Economic Outlook*, June, OECD, Paris.

Office of Population Censuses and Surveys (1993) *National Population Projections 1991-based*, Series PP 2, no.18. HMSO.

Oppenheim, C and Harker, L (1996) *Poverty: the facts* (third edition), CPAG Ltd.

Philo, C (ed) (1995) *Off the Map: The social geography of poverty in the UK*, CPAG Ltd.

Townsend, P and Walker, A (1995) *The Future of Pensions: Revitalising National Insurance*, Fabian Society.

Wilkinson, M (1994) 'Paying for public spending: is there a role for earmarked taxes?', *Fiscal Studies*, Vol 15, No 4.

16 New paths for social security
Lisa Harker

Most commentators agree that the social security system is in need of reform. But there is less consensus as to what kind of reform is needed. Debates in and outside the political arena have tended to focus on single issues or have been weighed down by the difficulties of reconciling contradictory goals. In recent years much focus has been placed on the affordability of social security and the means by which the growth in the social security bill can be stemmed. Less attention has been paid to other considerations.

As Carey Oppenheim notes in Chapter 2, there has been a dramatic growth in poverty and income inequality over the last two decades. Between 1979 and 1993/94 the number of individuals living in poverty rose from one in ten to one in four and the risk of poverty tripled among families with children (DSS, 1996a). The social security system has not only failed to prevent this decline in living standards but has actually exacerbated the growth in poverty and inequality. The uncoupling of the uprating of benefits with rises in earnings (or prices if higher) has widened the gap between the incomes of the rich and poor (Hills, 1995) and restrictions in benefit paid to certain groups and the shift towards means-testing has pushed more and more people into poverty (see Chapters 5 and 6).

As we approach a new millennium, the answers to the problems of poverty and inequality are not the same as they were when the modern social security system was established. Society in the late twentieth century is very different: family and working patterns have been transformed, the age profile of the population has altered and new kinds of insecurity have emerged which threaten the lifestyle of a growing proportion of the population (Hutton, 1995). Concern about expenditure on social security go hand in hand with questions about the legitimacy of the welfare state. The challenge we face is how to ensure a secure future for all in a diverse and uncertain world.

FAMILY STRUCTURES

To date the British social security system has responded to changing family patterns in *ad hoc* ways. The modern social security system was founded on a specific model of the family: married couples were to be treated as a single unit, with men as breadwinners and married women as housewives and carers (Beveridge, 1942). Today 'the family' is an increasingly elusive concept. The term now refers to a kaleidoscope of living patterns, due to the increase in cohabitation, separation, divorce, remarriage and lone parenthood (see Chapter 7).

The social security system has only partially recognised the fundamental changes to family structures. There has been a reluctance on the part of government to validate non-traditional relationships (such as cohabiting and gay couples) by treating them identically to traditional families. Yet at the same time some 'non-traditional' forms of relationships have been recognised in social security in order to reduce the advantages they might enjoy over married couples. The *ad hoc* response to changing family structures has resulted in anomalies in the way different living circumstances are recognised within the system (Harker, 1996).

Concern about social security and family structure has focused on how benefits might encourage 'non traditional' living arrangements. While it is certainly the case that social security can influence behaviour – such as whether or not to take up paid work – it is not clear to what extent decisions about family lifestyle are affected by social security payments. Despite claims that the availability of benefits has been responsible for family break-up (Murray, 1984; Morgan, 1995), research suggests that many factors influence decisions about parenthood and living arrangements (Whiteford and Bradshaw, 1994). Indeed, it seems unlikely that the diversification of family structures can be attributed to social security entitlement, particularly when entitlements are arguably meagre.

In order to meet modern needs, the social security system must respond to the needs of different family types and their lifestyles.

While there have been some moves away from the assumption that married women are dependent on their husbands for income, the social security system has yet to match the tax system in terms of independent assessment and the dependency of women on men continues to be reinforced by the way in which the means-tested benefits system makes it uneconomic for a partner of a low paid or unemployed person to take work.

WORKING PATTERNS

There have been equally profound changes in working patterns over the last two decades. Part-time work is now growing at a faster rate than full-time employment and what has been termed 'atypical' working (such as self-employed, temporary work and zero-hour contracts) is no longer atypical at all.

The shake-up in the nature of work has been matched by the emergence of a generation of non-workers. Since the 1970s unemployment levels have increased dramatically (see Chapter 12). Although the official unemployment rate has recently started to fall, it remains almost twice as high as the number in April 1979, when there were 1,089,100 unemployed people, a rate of 4.1 per cent (DE, 1995; DfEE, 1996).

Men make up an increasing proportion of those without work (DfEE, 1996). New forms of working have largely been taken up by women, although men are increasingly having to take part-time and 'atypical' work. The growth in employment in the next century is predicted to be almost entirely among women, which will reduce the gap between male and female labour-force activity rates.

The changing distribution of work has had a profound effect on family income. By 1990 twice as many households were out of work than in 1975, yet the proportion of fully employed households was 10 per cent greater than in 1975. The growth in low-paid employment has made it increasingly difficult for families, particularly those with children, to manage on one income, prompting the decline of the 'breadwinner' model.

The risk of insecurity has increased especially, but not only, for those with non-traditional working patterns. Social security has, in John Blackwell's words, 'not been designed for those in intermittent unemployment or in part-time jobs' (Blackwell, 1994). National insurance contributions are dependent on having earnings over a minimum level and the payment of adequate contributions and so, consequently, many 'atypical' workers fail to qualify. The tightening of national insurance eligibility criteria, described in Chapter 6, has compounded their exclusion. The increasing instability of employment has meant that fewer workers are able to build up the required contributions, excluding millions of low paid workers – many of whom are women – from access to benefits. Furthermore, the national insurance system is entirely based on a limited concept of work-related risks – it does not, for example, fully recognise the impact that caring has on the interruption or cessation of earnings.

COST

The cost of social provision is rightly of concern to policy makers. Much has been said and written about the rate at which social security spending has grown. Certainly there has been a significant increase in the social security budget since 1979 – from 23 per cent of government expenditure to 31 per cent in 1996. As a share of GDP, expenditure on social security has increased from 9 per cent in 1979 to almost 13 per cent in 1996 (Field, 1996a).

However, as Oppenheim has argued in *The Welfare State: putting the record straight* (1994), a reduction in spending on social security should not be the driving force for reform. Expenditure on social security is largely a reflection of problems or policies made outside the system, such as high unemployment, lack of affordable high quality childcare and deregulation of the housing market. Moreover, as Hills argues in Chapter 15, the welfare state *is* affordable and solutions to reducing spending lie principally outside the social security system.

Nevertheless, the changing nature of the population, its working patterns and family structures, pose new challenges for the affordability of welfare. The ageing of the population together with the changing nature of work and growth in unemployment has altered the so-called 'dependency ratio' – the balance between those who are in work and paying social security contributions and those who are claiming social security. The full-employment model on which the modern social security system was founded is no longer appropriate for the insecure labour market of today and, without reform, cannot guarantee sufficient income for its members.

CONSENSUS ON WELFARE REFORM

One of the crises facing the welfare state in the 1990s is said to be the apparent lack of consensus on the desirability of welfare (Alcock, 1996), although, as John Hills (Chapter 15) and Peter Townsend (Chapter 17) point out, the general public support spending on the welfare state. Certainly doubts about the role of the state in welfare lie at the heart of proposals which have emerged from the political Right. This is underpinned by a belief that state welfare provision removes choice and control from individuals. There may also be a wider disquiet among some of those whose contributions support those who rely on social security but who see little of current relevance in the system for themselves. In this sense, the legitimacy of the collective nature of social security is being brought into question. The solution, the New Right argues, lies in community-based welfare support rather than a state welfare system.

In contrast, thinking on welfare reform by the Left has been less radical and has continued to promote the principles of state collectivism, thereby supporting the beliefs on which Beveridge's welfare state was founded. This commitment to state provision has been unfairly interpreted by some as a unwillingness to accept any element of individual responsibility (Green, 1996) or an unwillingness to acknowledge changes in family and work patterns. An emerging theme of the Centre Left's thinking on welfare – typified by the work of Frank Field MP – is a careful emphasis on personal responsibility and the social security system's perverse encouragement of self interest (Field 1995, 1996a, 1996b). This is an emerging theme in New Labour polices. Deacon (1996) has noted, for example, that, in outlining his vision of a stakeholder society, Tony Blair has spoken of the need to eliminate the 'social evil of welfare dependency amongst able-bodied people'. In this sense some sort of consensus between New Right and the Centre Left on the undesirability of state welfare may be emerging, although thinking on the Left is as yet underdeveloped.

AN OUT-OF-DATE BENEFIT SYSTEM

- 'Untraditional' families treated differently by different parts of the social security system.
- Women's dependency on men continues to be reinforced.
- The national insurance system does not provide support for a growing number of 'atypical' workers or non-workers who are carers.

NEW PATHS FOR SOCIAL SECURITY

Social security ought to have many roles: to protect people from poverty, and relieve its impact; to redistribute resources from rich to poor, from those without children to those with children, from men to women, and over an individual's lifetime; and to maximise opportunities for self support by increasing access to the labour market and reducing poverty traps. In delivering support, the social security system should be transparent to claimants, administrators and tax payers and should not be socially divisive, stigmatising or of hindrance to families in their chosen living arrangements. It is against such criteria that any reform of social security should be judged (Harker, 1996).

Current debates are striking by their general lack of vision as to the future of social security. While various options have been proposed by academics, policy-makers and others, most proposals have offered isolated policy options rather than an overall social security model. Here, various full or partial models are considered. A snap-shot assessment does injustice to some of the thinking behind the models and a more thorough analysis is certainly necessary. Nevertheless, it is helpful to take a systematic approach to considering possible ways forward.

CHANGE DRIVEN BY DESIRE TO CUT COSTS

The fundamental issue is how the objective of a declining share of public spending in GDP, or even a stable one, can be squared with maintaining the provision of these front line services at a level and standard which the public expects or needs. These are choices which no political party has really faced up to. (Institute for Fiscal Studies/ Goldman Sachs, Press release on *The Green Budget*, 9 October 1996.)

Government policy towards social security since the late 1980s has been driven by a desire to reduce expenditure and, as discussed in Chapter 6, has led to restricted entitlement. At the same time greater emphasis has been placed on reducing fraud within the system with a view to making benefit savings. Cost-driven reform fails to address the main problem of benefit recipients, namely poverty, and instead actually causes further hardship. While expenditure is necessarily a consideration policy makers must pay attention to, it cannot be the driving force for change without seriously undermining the first aim of any social security system: to meet need.

A FOCUS ON DELIVERY

Driven by a desire for a reduction in expenditure on social security, increasing attention has been paid to improving efficiency in the delivery of benefits. There is no doubt that improvements are necessary: with between £2.2 and £3.5 billion worth of means-tested benefits going unclaimed in 1994/95 (DSS, 1996b), and evidence of millions of pounds worth of errors in benefits payments each year (Committee of Public Accounts, 1996), ensuring the accurate payment of benefits is vital if the intended goals of social security are to be met. A challenge for social security as we enter a new millennium is ensuring that the increasing use of information technology helps rather than hinders the meeting of these goals.

All too often, however, so-called 'efficiency improvements' to social security, such as those discussed earlier by Howard, hide real cuts in provision and support. The Conservative Government's Change Programme, launched in 1996, aimed to improve efficiency in the delivery of social security and reduce administrative costs by 25 per cent over three years. Changes introduced under the Change Programme up to now have met the latter but not the former aim. The abolition of the Benefits Agency Helpline and closure of some local benefit offices, for example, certainly reduced expenditure but at a cost to the efficiency of the social security system and the living standards of thousands of individuals. Once more this drive for reform undermines the goals of social security to reduce poverty and inequality.

PRIVATISATION

Another reform prompted by cost-cutting aims was the proposal to privatise social security, either in the delivery of state benefits – such as the administration of child benefit payments by the private sector – or through the provision of actual schemes. The opportunities for some individuals to take out private insurance already exists in relation to pensions, sickness benefits and, to a more limited extent, to cover other contingencies such as unemployment. Further privatisation would increase the role of private insurance and possibly largely replace state provision of certain benefits.

It is unlikely that private administration or provision of benefits would ever replace the state social security system entirely. The administration of complex benefits is unlikely to be attractive to the private sector and their complexity could not be compromised without jeopardising their effectiveness in meeting needs. It is hard to imagine how those benefits which are less complex – such as child benefit, where 2 per cent of expenditure goes towards administration – could be delivered more effectively by the private sector. The cost of administration is connected to the complexity of the benefit concerned, not the administrative system itself.

In terms of the private provision of benefits, it is unlikely that the private sector would wish to cover all risks or be prepared to take on the non-insurance elements of the current system – both means-tested benefits and non-contributory benefits. Research already indicates that those living on low incomes or in insecure employment are unlikely to be adequately covered by any private insurance scheme (NACAB, 1995; Howard and Thompson, 1995). A private insurance model for social security is therefore unlikely to meet the goal of protecting against the risk of poverty for all and would favour some individuals over others, for example, those distinguished on the basis of their working patterns. The most vulnerable, and at greatest risk, would be the group most likely to lose out.

A SYSTEM RELIANT ON MEANS-TESTING

In 1992, the UK had a higher proportion of means-tested family benefits than any other country in the European Union (Scheiwe, 1994). Expenditure on means-tested benefits has increased by almost 300 per cent since 1979 – ten times more than the increased expenditure on insurance benefits (Field, 1996a). The rapid growth in means-testing, as outlined by Piachaud in Chapter 5, has been promoted as enabling a better 'targeting' of resources. In the context of concern about the growth in social security expenditure, there initially appears to be some logic in restricting payments to those who need them most. But such apparent logic is based on two flawed assumptions. First, for reasons discussed earlier, a reduction in expenditure on social security should not be the driving force for reform. Secondly, means-tested benefits do not ensure that those most in need of support actually receive it. The principal problem with means-tests is unavoidable: assessing entitlement on the basis of means (and therefore reducing entitlement when means increase) traps individuals in poverty by making low-paid employment unattractive and further discourages them from saving or increasing their income. In addition, means-tested benefits have a lower take-up than non-means-tested benefits and are costly to administer.

Field (1995) has criticised the over-reliance of social security policy on means-testing but places greater emphasis on the behavioural response to the incentives and disincentives created by means-tested benefits. He charges the Government with *naivety* in not anticipating individuals' responses to perverse incentives and argues that endemic dishonesty is destabilising the social security system. While this raises important issues about social security and behaviour, Field's radical proposals for reform – the expansion of a more inclusive social insurance system – are in danger of being overshadowed by the ferocity of his language about behaviour and character, in the same way that the work of commentators on the Right have dealt with such concerns at the expense of all else (Murray, 1984; Mead, 1992).

Few argue that means-tested benefits will ever be entirely eliminated from the British social security system; it is likely that some form of residual welfare will always be needed in order to provide a safety net for those who, for whatever reason, are not adequately covered by insurance provision. Proposals to make the income support system more proactive in helping individuals into work may benefit claimants but only if accompanied by employment creation policies. Nevertheless, no system reliant on means-testing will escape the problems inherent in such forms of assessment: low take-up, disincentives to work and save, and complex and expensive administration. Means-tested benefits cannot prevent poverty.

TAX/BENEFIT INTEGRATION

Various types of tax/benefit integration have been proposed, including basic income, social dividend, participation income and negative income tax. While there are important differences (Parker, 1995), the central premise of each proposal is the same: to provide an income guarantee that is not conditional on not working by giving a tax deduction to all those with incomes above a certain level and a cash credit with low/no incomes. For ease of commentary, a basic income is considered here.

By providing security of income for all citizens, a scheme such as a basic income would play an important poverty prevention role if set at a high enough level. Most commentators recognise, however, that a basic income scheme would have to start at a low rate if it is to be economically feasible. Other than cost, the main opposition to such a scheme is its potential impact on work incentives. Although a basic income would lower the risks of taking precarious or 'atypical' employment, it would discourage some from working at all. In addition, the practical difficulties of integrating the procedures of different government agencies – with different timetables, traditions and types of clients – would be considerable and costly.

There are some clear arguments in favour of tax/benefit integration. Parker and Sutherland (1991) have shown that a basic income would redistribute in favour of families with children and that the gains for those on the lowest incomes would be significant. There would be some redistribution of resources from rich to poor and from men to women (Parker, 1991). Nevertheless, the practical problems, concerns about cost and the impact on work incentives appear to be significant barriers to reform along these lines.

THE FUTURE OF SOCIAL INSURANCE

The social, economic and demographic changes that have occurred since the 1940s makes Beveridge's model of social security – one which places emphasis on insurance benefits over means-tested assistance and based on a 'breadwinner' model – outdated. Given the modern labour market, the growth in female employment and the increase in two-earner families, a move back to Beveridge is not feasible.

Nevertheless in the insecure 1990s the insurance principle itself still has enormous potential. The limitations of the national insurance system is that it fails to provide cover for a sufficient proportion of the population. A modified Beveridge model could extend insurance-based benefits to more individuals than are currently included (see Harker, 1996; Townsend and Walker, 1995). Entitlement to social insurance could be broadened to cover more diverse working patterns and acknowledge a wider range of activities which prevent individuals from taking paid work. This could be achieved by replacing the individual contribution record with an alternative contingency test or by extending contribution credits. Field (1995) has promoted the idea for social insurance provision of this sort; his proposals include an unemployment insurance benefit to which those who, for example, take work for a short period and become unemployed again are entitled.

Another advantage to insurance benefits over means-tested benefits is that they are based on individual rather than household entitlement.

Given the outdated notion of dependency of women on men which is still inherent in much of the social security system, greater moves towards more individual autonomy in the assessment and payment of benefits are needed. While individualisation of benefits cannot counteract some of the inequalities outside the social security system it is a useful mechanism by which to be as neutral as possible with regard to family structure. By assessing each individual's needs separately, the system would aim to prevent and relieve poverty when an individual's circumstances indicated a high risk of impoverishment.

A more inclusive social insurance system would have the potential to be highly redistributive, work disincentives would be reduced and the system could be simpler than the current one through reduced reliance on means-testing. How far this model would go towards preventing poverty would depend on the extent of the coverage of social insurance benefits. Adequate cover would be costly and this would have to be met either by increased national insurance contributions or direct taxation, which throws some doubt on its political viability.

A COMPREHENSIVE APPROACH

Social security does not, and cannot, work in a vacuum. The way in which social security policy interacts with labour market, employment and other social policies is critical in determining its effectiveness in reducing poverty and inequality. While new paths for social security have been considered here, it is important to emphasise that a more comprehensive approach is ultimately necessary.

In *A Secure Future?* (Harker, 1996) I outlined the 'Family and Work' model, a set of policies based in and beyond the social security system which principally aim to offer security to all families with children. While not entirely a comprehensive model in its focus of entitlement, there is much to suggest that families with children are in need of particular attention given the rapid increase in family poverty since 1979.

The model is based on the premise that parents need support both to meet the costs of having children and in order to maintain the family income through paid work. It consists of social insurance benefits payable on an individual basis, a flat-rate child benefit payment paid to all families regardless of their circumstances and a supplementary payment for support with childcare or childrearing costs. The model aims to prevent poverty through financial support to all family types regardless of employment status and give parents a genuine choice as to whether they work or not, while at the same time offering a guarantee of support in recognition of the costs of having children.

Prevention of poverty among families with children is the motivation behind the 'Family and Work' model and income would be redistributed from families without children to families with children. The biggest barrier to introducing such a model is its cost, which would be significant – particularly if benefit levels were set at an adequate level. Tax rates needed to fund such as system are likely to be significant. Perhaps this is why no country has fully implemented such a model, although the welfare systems of Denmark and Sweden come close.

CONCLUSION

The future paths for social security are, as yet, unclear. But what is assured is that the social security system cannot remain as it is or return to what it was. Here it has only been possible to consider briefly some of the possible ways forward. The potential for providing security for all appears to lie with a modern social insurance system, the details of which need yet more consideration. The needs of particular groups, such as families with children, must be carefully examined.

No reform can be achieved in a short space of time – the changes that have occurred in the 50 or so years since the Beveridge report cannot be addressed in one parliament. However, policy reform could begin immediately, led by an overarching vision of what we want the social security system to provide. In a world of increasing change, the search for security is ever more pressing.

REFERENCES

Alcock, P (1996) 'Welfare and self interest', in Field, F, *Stakeholder Welfare*, Institute of Economic Affairs.
Beveridge, W (1942) *Social Insurance and Allied Services*, Cmnd 6404, HMSO.
Blackwell, J (1994) 'Changing work patterns and their implications for social protection' in Baldwin, S and Falkingham, J (eds) *Social Security and Social Change*, Harvester/Wheatsheaf.

Committee of Public Accounts (1996) *Department of Social Security Appropriation Accounts, 1994-95, Class XIII Vote 1 Errors in Income Support, Fraud and Security*, House of Commons, HMSO.

Deacon, A (1996) 'Welfare and character', in Field, F, *Stakeholder Welfare*, Institute of Economic Affairs.

DE (1995) *Employment Gazette, Historical Supplement No 1, April*, HMSO.

DfEE (1996) *Labour Market Trends, August*, Col 104, No 8, Office of National Statistics.

DSS (1996a) *Households below Average Income Statistics 1993/94, a statistical analysis*.

DSS (1996b) *Income Related Benefits: Estimates of take-up in 1994/95*.

Field, F (1995) *Making Welfare Work*, Institute of Community Studies.

Field, F (1996a) *Stakeholder Welfare*, Institute of Economic Affairs, Choices in Welfare Series No.32.

Field, F (1996b) *How to pay for the future*, Institute of Community Studies.

Green, D (1996) 'Welfare and civil society' in Field, F, *Stakeholder Welfare*, Institute of Economic Affairs.

Gregg P and Wadsworth J (1996) 'More work in fewer households?' in Hills, J (ed) *New Inequalities: the changing distribution of income and wealth in the United Kingdom*, Cambridge University Press.

Harker, L (1996) *A Secure Future? Social security and the family in a changing world*, CPAG Ltd.

Hills, J (1995) *Inquiry into Income and Wealth*, Joseph Rowntree Foundation.

Howard, M and Thompson, P (1995) *There may be trouble ahead*, Disability Alliance and the Disablement Income Group.

Hutton, W (1995) *The State We're In*, Jonathan Cape.

Mead, L (1992) 'The new politics of the new poverty', *Public Interest*, Vol 103, p109.

Morgan, P (1995) *Farewell to the Family? Public policy and family breakdown in Britain and the USA*, Institute of Economic Affairs, Choices in Welfare Series, No 21.

Murray, C (1984) *Losing Ground: American social policy 1950-1980*, Basic Books, New York.

NACAB (1995) *Security at Risk: CAB evidence on payment protection insurance for public policy*.

Oppenhiem, C (1994) *The Welfare State: putting the record straight*, CPAG.

Parker, H (1991) *Citizen's Income and Women*, BIRG Discussion Paper No 1.

Parker, H and Sutherland, H (1991) *Child Tax Allowances? A comparison of child benefit, child tax reliefs, and basic income as instruments of family policy*, STICERD.

Parker, H (1995) *Taxes, Benefits and Family Life: the seven deadly traps*, Institute for Economic Affairs.

Scheiwe, K (1994) 'Who is supported? Social security for families with children between family law and social security regulations in Belgium, Germany and the United Kingdom', *International Social Security Review,* 3-4, pp45-67, International Social Security Association, Geneva.

Townsend, P and Walker, A (1995) *The Future of Pensions: revitalising national insurance,* Fabian Society.

Whiteford, P and Bradshaw, J (1994) 'Benefits and incentives for lone parents: a comparative study', *International Social Security Review,* 3-4, pp69-89, International Social Security Association, Geneva.

17 Redistribution: the strategic alternative to privatisation
Peter Townsend

This chapter puts the case for *redistribution* (including the redistribution of original earnings and wealth, the redistribution of access to employment and the fairer distribution of the terms of trade) as the 'big' idea necessary to British and global politics. The driving idea of the 1980s and 1990s – *privatisation* – has had its day, and its ideological rather than rational implementation has made things a lot worse.

The key structural problem for Britain at the end of the 20th Century is *social polarisation*. The previous chapters in this book provide ample testimony. But it is not just Britain's problem. The divide is deepening between First and Third Worlds and between rich and poor in many of the countries in each of these regions (Townsend, 1993, 1996; Townsend and Donkor, 1996). The problem is therefore a lot different from what it was 50, or even 20, years ago. Europeans have done most to detail the insidious process and defend decent standards of welfare. But alarm in the United States, for example, is now growing. J K Galbraith's prescient *The Age of Contentment* (1992) was brushed aside, but support for such ideas in the late 1990s is coming from unexpected quarters. In his presidential address to the Population Association of America the demographer Douglas S Massey (1996) said,

> In the twenty-first century the advantages and disadvantages of one's class position will be compounded and reinforced through ecological mechanisms made possible by the geographic concentration of affluence and poverty, creating a deeply divided and increasingly violent social world.

What are the remedies? There has to be a strategic mix of remedies, with estimated effects being properly calculated. This condition is not anywhere taken seriously. Consequently the prospect of greatly improving matters in Britain or internationally seems to be slipping further and further into the distance, with little hope in the coming years of the trend being halted or even slowed down. One example is the European Programme to Combat Poverty (see Chapter 4). The first programme (1975–80) was ambitious, and produced a huge number of country reports, but was disappointingly inconclusive. The second (1986–89) offered little in the way of consolidation or even a meaningful research programme. The third (1990–94) led to the formulation of more exact cross-national indicators but retreated from a tentative measure of poverty into a 'varied vocabulary of disadvantage' (Room, 1996) and into the provision and scrutiny of a very small number of local projects across Europe. Even the identification of policies which could be calculated to reduce or increase the extent of poverty remained unclear. And the fourth programme? It has been vetoed.

REASONS FOR POVERTY GROWTH

Why is the problem getting worse so quickly in many rich and poor countries? Growing poverty is being fostered remorselessly from a number of directions. In pursuit of competitive prices and larger profits the market is pressing for cuts in wages, performance related (low) pay, downsizing, cuts in the costs of contributing directly and indirectly to public services or of meeting workers' rights and, if all else fails, redeployment to low-paid sectors overseas. Because of company mergers and the extraordinary growth of multi-national corporations and of the international financial system, encouraged by the edicts of monetarism, the muscle to reinforce these trends has grown disconcertingly. Corporations with larger budgets than many countries can acquire legal and political as well as buying and selling power.

Around the world, strong governments have aided and abetted these trends, while weak governments, especially of Third World countries, have not been able to resist them. Whether in conformity with the theories of structural adjustment or of liberalisation, of Reaganism or of Thatcherism, many have undertaken measures to deregulate and privatise and, as a direct consequence, have created more unemployment, cut public spending and public services and greatly weakened progressive systems of taxation. Economically growth is being driven in the interests of a declining proportion of the population. Socially the class system has become deeper, and more heavily scored.

There have been a few preliminary attempts to disentangle the effects of different measures (in the US for example by Perlman, 1992, and in the UK by Hills, 1995) but it is difficult to be precise about the exact contribution by different factors to the overall result. That kind of work simply has yet to be done.

But it is reasonably clear from a range of work that while the precise effect cannot be calculated the principal causal elements are:

- *deregulation* (in Britain, for example, by the abolition of Wages Councils and certain employment rights);
- *privatisation* (especially of free or heavily subsidised public services),
- *disemployment* (more scope to make redundancies, reduce obligations to disabled workers, 'retire' people prematurely before the age of 60 or 65 and issue temporary contracts without entitlement to benefits or without employer contributions to benefits);
- *reduction in public spending* (for example, public housing, and sickness and unemployment benefits);
- *restructured taxes* – from progressive to regressive, and from direct to indirect (cutting wealth taxes and rates of income tax, extending VAT on necessities, easing taxes on employers, removing the Treasury's contribution and increasing the lower paid employee's contribution to national insurance); and
- *centralising political control* of the entire structure (restricting local authority and trade union resources and powers, and appointing a huge number of quangos).

Each of these elements could be set out and discussed in detail. To achieve a less impoverished, integrated or economically productive society there would be ingredients which we could identify as blatantly harmful, harmless or even mildly beneficial. No one would expect accounts – or stock-taking – of complex strategies, anymore than complex inventories, to be uniformly balanced. It is the *direction* of the whole strategy – whether it is increasing or reducing social polarisation – and what are the principal causal elements which have to be changed which are at issue.

At the end of the 1992 Government's parliamentary term it is ironic, as well as tragic, that the measures being reinforced are the very policies which have already widened living standards dramatically in Britain in the last 18 years. They have been reiterated in an extreme form by the Conservative Party in the run-up to the 1997 election. The basic flat-rate retirement pension is to be privatised – though only for those reaching working age after the year 2000. The state earnings related pension scheme is to be abolished. Social services are to be largely privatised. London Transport is to be privatised. The top rate of income tax is to be brought down to 20 per cent. There are to be no restrictions on top earnings. Depending on how they are implemented these measures will have lesser and greater effects on the distribution of living standards. But on the evidence of recent history in Britain – and incidentally in countries where the same measures have been adopted – living standards will continue to widen. When will it end?

THE ALTERNATIVE STRATEGY: REDISTRIBUTION

There is an alternative strategy which can alter the trend and, while it can of course take different forms, is the only convincing alternative available to achieve success. It can be expressed in a single word: 'redistribution'. It is the only idea which, when fully developed, can begin to deal with the disastrous British, and world, phenomenon of social polarisation. The term is liable to be misinterpreted or restricted to suit the convenience of particular regimes. Therefore it has to explained carefully.

'Redistribution' does not denote a common social situation – like poverty, social exclusion, social injustice, homelessness or a divided society – which invites concern. The problem is implicit in the form of action which the idea suggests. Neither does it denote a strategy – like privatisation, liberalisation or deregulation – which cannot in principle or on all the evidence be calculated to do much about the problem. In past and current usage it *does* denote the direction of the structural change which must be engineered to address social polarisation and related concerns.

In the past 'redistribution' has been widely used to describe intervention by government to correct the unequal distribution of earned income through the institutions of taxation but also the benefit systems and public services of the welfare state. But this is a narrow interpretation. The meaning of 'redistribution' must be widened to include less unequal constructions of earnings and of shares in the value of goods and services produced for import and export or for home consumption.

All too easily the operational definition of precious principles and concepts can be demeaned politically, professionally and administratively so that they pose less of a threat to established interests. Radical social aims can be frustrated.

An effort to break free from this stranglehold has to be made. Thus, it is not enough for research to deal only with the minimum benefits and services available to the poor. It will have to deal with the entire structure of wage and wealth disparities, including those which govern top earnings, bonuses and wealth accumulation and the corresponding structure of social relations. The exposition of conditions which affect any segment of the population cannot be successfully marshalled without some recognition of the social hierarchy as a whole to which that segment belongs, and the factors which affect that membership. As the authors and readers of this book will know, hundreds, if not thousands, of research reports dealing with the bottom end of the distribution but only a tiny handful dealing with the top end have been issued during the 1990s. Yet the form and depth of the entire social hierarchy is conditioned by the decisions made and the conventions reasserted at the top end of the hierarchy: as the reported behaviour of the 'top cats' of the privatised utilities in Britain in the mid-1990s testifies.

'Redistribution' should properly include redistribution of gross or original earnings, which would lead to more informed recognition of the contributions made to overall production and services by many people in the lower ranks of earnings. At least the reasons for the dispersion of earnings would have to come under public scrutiny. The limited range of wage studies of the 1980s and 1990s does not seem to represent even minimal justification for current wage differentials or the rapidly changing wages hierarchy of recent years in both big companies and small businesses, as well as in some parts of the public sector.

We need to transform the nature of our strategic thinking. What are other examples? Giving effect to equality of opportunity makes no sense if the structure of existing inequalities – especially for newly born children and those entering schools in different areas, but also for others across the age spectrum – and the forces determining inequality of outcome are not addressed. Greater equality of opportunity will not do much unless the distribution of earnings and wealth becomes much more equal at the same time. Limited objectives will not be achieved unless a process of give and take in the whole structure takes place. Again, a minimum wage makes no sense unless it is linked to a minimum income for those unable to work and unless it is also linked to the moderation of the whole unequal structure of earnings and the management of that structure. The good intentions of measures which are expressed and developed without reference to their structural context, or the forces which are shaping that context, can be frustrated by knock-on reactions elsewhere. The strategic perspective has to be unitary – and if it is unitary 'redistribution' can become the big driving idea.

THE NEED TO UNIFY OBJECTIVES: LINKING ACTION ON POVERTY AND SOCIAL EXCLUSION

All of this implies giving greater attention to the means of combating and compensating discrimination against unpaid work, particularly the work of women, and against those seeking entry or re-entry to paid work. And this illustrates the possibilities of linking an attack on both social exclusion and poverty through better-devised national and cross-national programmes as well as through future international and scientific research.

When, during the 1970s, increasing attention began to be given to 'social exclusion' as a principal criterion of poverty I failed to appreciate some of the positive arguments. 'Poverty' seemed to me to be the critical concept on which to build scientific analysis of those structural changes in world society which produced unnecessarily severe social and economic problems. Money and the market, through capitalism, had made the distribution of income, and of resources supplementary to income, like wealth, and goods and services in kind, the key determinant of everyday standards of living. Lack of sufficient income, and resources supplementary to income, had effects, like premature death and different forms of material and social deprivation, which were as socially destructive as they were economically inefficient. External criteria had to be used in pinpointing the level of resources ordinarily required in a society for households and individuals to meet both material and social needs, and the value of having social *deprivation* as a principal general criterion was that it seemed to include conditions brought about by exclusion.

Discrimination and exclusion seemed to be important ideas but secondary because they were effects rather than causes or, at best, by-products of the engines of market-manufactured class.

Along with many others in the United States and Europe, I believed that the attention given to 'social exclusion' was a diversion from important issues or a whim to please the French because they stood at the heart of the creation of the European Union. I was wrong: mainly because the term helps us to pay more attention not just to the denial of rights but also to the external creation and control of need. Unlike Anglo-Americans, the French have continued to be strongly attached to the values of solidarity and citizenship. Social relationships were more highly prized. By contrast, Anglo-American individualism has allowed human needs to be interpreted as wholly self-induced.

Yet the term is relatively new, even if it has been gaining ground fast. *The Blackwell Dictionary of Twentieth Century Social Thought*, for example, contains nothing about social exclusion. It was published as late as 1993 and 12 of the contributors to the encyclopaedia were from France. Then there are problems of usage. I had been one of those social scientists who had found historical treatments of poverty unsatisfactory. Policies to eradicate the phenomenon depend not just on demonstrable effect but upon demonstrable meaning and measurement. Resources to satisfy hunger, and the individual need for shelter, clothing and bodily warmth, was an insufficient – and derogatory – interpretation of the human condition. Resources to satisfy basic needs was better but still an insufficient reflection of what was required to fulfil the needs of individuals who were social animals and of the communities and populations of which they were contributing and not only dependent members.

'Social exclusion' directs attention to the marginalised and excluded and to the potential instruments of their exclusion. But at the same time as the term has penetrated scientific and political thought doubts have accumulated about its operational use. Specific and practical measures to meet or diminish social exclusion have been hard to formulate. Two conclusions might be drawn from a variety of different studies in the mid-1990s (Gaudier, 1995; Rodgers *et al*, 1995; Paugam, 1996; Guidicini *et al*, 1996; Friedmann, 1996; Gore and Figueiredo, 1996; Jordan, 1996; Abrahamson, forthcoming).

One conclusion is that the idea deserves an independent life as an instrument of the formulation of civil and political rights, the treatment of immigrants and asylum seekers, and access of residents and non-residents to the infrastructure of civil institutions. The second conclusion is to absorb valuably into the definition, measurement and analysis of poverty the external forces bringing about that condition and the continuing denial of the means of access to the resources needed to overcome the problem. As a result more attention can be paid to the power relations of the structural hierarchy of incomes and other resources in the difficult job of unravelling the causes and specifying a programme of action. In operational terms it means enlarging the number of indicators necessary to measure 'social deprivation' which, along with 'material deprivation, are the major criteria for determining the exact 'poverty line' of income – including cash incomes and the value of other resources equivalent to income.

REDISTRIBUTION: PLANNING

What, therefore, would a redistributive strategy which embodies an anti-poverty programme look like? The Government would have to set up a comprehensive structural programme which would also be cross-departmental – which, on the basis of historical precedents, or lack of them, would represent an act of faith. Moreover, models from the recent past are not encouraging. The Borrie Commission, with its strong Centrist rather than Labourist representation, called attention to the growth of inequalities but did not proceed to outline an integrated strategy which in its various parts could be demonstrated to deal with them. The report raised suspicions that the widening inequalities engineered by monetarist policies were being accepted rather than convincingly opposed. Small value seemed to be being placed on the need for redistributive structural change, including international as well as national social control of multi-national companies.

The Dahrendorf Commission's report on Wealth Creation and Social Cohesion was a hastily constructed and extraordinarily uneven treatment of the problem, and was short and scrappy. Other, more restricted, attempts to model the future have been even more unsatisfactory. For example, the Anson Committee's report on the future of pensions favoured privatisation and the committee seemed to be unaware of the international evidence showing privatisation to be an instrument of increasing inequality. In the new jargon of 'targeting' and 'safety nets' it anticipated an even bigger role for means tests without even quoting the contrary studies.

This has left a vacuum in planning. The papers prepared for Labour's policy forum in May 1996 were preliminary skirmishes rather than practical illustrations of the visionary strategies required to deal with the problem. They were strongly criticised at the time for being vague and evasive. The two statements from the Shadow Cabinet team in July: Getting Welfare to Work: A New Vision for Social Security, and Security in Retirement, were also over-cautious and left glaring gaps. Too many of the monetarist themes of the 1980s – low public spending, withdrawal from progressive taxation, and private funding instead of collective pay-as-you-go – seemed to be being picked up instead of being challenged. It was difficult to see, strategically or practically, how growing inequality and poverty could be halted and reversed.

But if these public statements failed to square up to the immense scale of the structural problem the Conservative Government's record is much worse. The Conservative Government has ignored and dismissed the problem. It has financed virtually no scientific research into modern forms of poverty, the relationships between crime and poverty, premature mortality or disability and poverty, or social cohesion and poverty. In the mid-1990s Peter Lilley, the Secretary of State for Social Security, repudiated the existence of poverty in Britain while at the same time signing up to international agreements in which not only was the concept taken seriously – whether by the United States, the European Union or the international agencies – but was acknowledged to exist in poor and rich countries alike. Thus a programme to reduce poverty was the principal agreement of 117 countries at the 1995 World Summit on Social Development. Britain signed that agreement. Yet Peter Lilley refused to fulfil a pledge to prepare a national plan during 1996 to eliminate 'absolute' and reduce 'overall' poverty. This has prompted 150 organisations, including Church Action Against Poverty, ATD Fourth World, Christian Aid, Oxfam, the Child Poverty Action Group, Barnardos, the Low Pay . Unit and Save the Children, to set up a national coalition and campaign for early national action.

There is also strong public support for an integrated and ambitious programme. In 1996 I was a member of Channel Four's Poverty Commission. It took evidence in different parts of the country and collected a wide range of reports. This was an all-Party Commission, selected to represent the whole political and professional spectrum. With Right-wing support it went a lot further than New Labour's

1996 proposals. It advocated redistribution, especially in the public sector: by better taxation, putting a limitation on high earnings as well as raising low earnings, investing more heavily in public housing, further education and public transport, strengthening social insurance, creating more credit unions and, most important of all, more jobs (Channel 4, 1996, especially pp27-29). In paving the way for such a programme, the Commission called for common acceptance that the problem existed, and that its eradication was in the best interests of the future prosperity of all.

A large number of opinion surveys over the last two decades demonstrate the readiness of the public to increase spending on social services and social security, with a majority accepting higher taxes to achieve that purpose.

INTERNATIONAL AND TECHNICAL CONDITIONS FOR A PLAN OF CAMPAIGN

'Monitoring' needs to be more effective. The growing severity of poverty has to be tracked year by year, and trends explained stage by stage. In the past the contribution to the scale of the problem of each of the social security 'reforms', the reductions in personal income taxation, and the programmes of deregulation and privatisation, have not been assessed. Unless this can be remedied the application of grand theory will be worthless.

This contemporary and historical neglect matters because if scientific and statistical documentation can be routinised it would show what would have to be done to halt the slide into poverty. It would also put the timidity of some existing proposals from Labour into stark proportion.

There has to be a restructuring of the institutions of power, if the new policies are to work. Greater control of arrogant elites – in the multinational companies generally and not only in the boards of the privatised utilities, among the new managers of the NHS and the banks, Ministers and the Permanent Secretaries who serve them – and strengthening of the powers of working people, grassroots organisations, public services and democratically elected local authorities as a counterweight, gets too little scrutiny in Britain.

One irony is that sweeping forms of privatisation have brought such major problems (see Chapter 13) that stronger methods of regulating private utilities and services have had to be introduced.

On the one hand, public administration has been scorned and derided. On the other, it has had to be readmitted by the back door.

The argument for a better-balanced 'mixed economy' of private and public sectors has grown immeasureably in the 1990s. The signs are to be found everywhere: in public outrage at the excesses of privatised companies and services, in the pusillanimous powers of regulators, and, perhaps most significantly, in the splits developing among the international agencies – as between the IMF and the World Bank – and the more defensive and even critical stance over privatisation of a number of them. A more substantial role for public ownership and public services has not just to be contemplated, but deliberately created.

AN ILLUSTRATION OF REDISTIBUTION

The job to be done is illustrated in the ferment over 'the Welfare State'. Increasingly there is a two-track approach, especially in Europe. Some countries are going down the privatisation road, or feel they are obliged to do so. Others have been putting up an effective resistance, and, on the available evidence, have been achieving better results in terms of patterns of social stability and the spread of living standards. This is the model found in countries like the Netherlands and Sweden, or even Japan, where more constructive and relevant ideas about the future of welfare are being developed and where employment rates, incidentally, are high. In these three countries the ratio of the incomes of the richest 20 per cent to the poorest 20 per cent is, according to the UNDP, 4:5, 4:6 and 4:3, compared with between 9:6 and 18:3 in Singapore, Australia and Chile, and 9:6 in the UK.

One of the key issues is private funding of pensions, or care of disabled and older people, versus public pay-as-you-go. On the evidence from these two groups of countries as well as from well-argued comparisons (for example, Hills, 1995) the public alternative is the best. If we compare private funding, where individuals build up entitlement to benefit during their lifetimes, and collective pay-as-you-go, where the youngest two generations successively pay the pensions of the oldest two generations through social insurance contributions, the second has long-term as well as short-term advantages for the vast majority of the population.

A report on Comparative Experiences of Privatisation, from the

UN Conference on Trade and Development (1995), had been started from a perspective favourable to privatisation but went on to concede all kinds of problems. After the privatisation of pensions in Chile in the 1980s, 4.1 million workers (86 per cent of the total labour force) were 'affiliated' to the new system by 1991. However, it turned out that only 2.5 million of these were contributors. Nearly half the workers in the country (48 per cent) had no access to secure pensions, because of 'loss of jobs, lack of incentives, late payment by employers of the employee contributions collected by them and a high proportion of independent, informal workers, together with a high incidence of poverty'. There were many contributors 'with acquired benefits less than the guaranteed minimum'. High marketing costs made the commissions 'more expensive than they need to be'. Administration was costly and there was no evidence that the total volume of investment in savings had increased.

The UN report recognised that similar problems applied around the world. It concluded that private pension schemes should now be expected to play a smaller role than believed in the 1980s and that there should be a mixed system of public and private schemes, with public insurance or pay-as-you-go as the bedrock, providing pensions of some 30 to 40 per cent of previous earnings in retirement.

This would not be a bad preliminary objective of an incoming Labour Government: aiming, say, to raise the basic pension for a single person to at least 20 per cent of average earnings, with the state earnings related pension scheme or a closely similar scheme quickly providing another 10-20 per cent. There is of course an argument for going much further. But this would be a responsible safeguard for the population. Pensions are central to the entire future of the Welfare State because the livelihood of the whole population – young contributors and also current beneficiaries – is at stake. Their collective savings are a basis for national investment and for additional private savings. An adequate basic pension for all can be provided only in a public scheme. It is administratively cheaper and simpler than its private counterparts, the value is more predictable and secure, and it is economically and socially desirable.

The Conservatives have declared that they will, if elected, reinforce private pension schemes at the expense of the state alternatives. This will indeed cut future public spending, but only because the value of the pensions received by future generations of low-paid and middle-paid workers with variable work records will be much lower – partly to meet unnecessarily high and wasteful costs of administration and private subsidies, and partly because many will be unable to become members of viable schemes because of their low pay, moves between jobs and irregular employment. In the mid-1990s the Conservative Government has raised far more from national insurance contributors than they have paid out in benefits – to subsidise private schemes and feather-bed the rich. By the year 2000 the excess is due to become £5 billion and more a year. By making the contributory system more principled Labour can easily accommodate increased costs for those on low incomes. Most employed and self-employed people would be likely to gain from a modernised social insurance system, and women in particular would be better off than under either the current or the proposed Conservative scheme.

A CHANGE OF DIRECTION

If this key decision is taken many other problems contributing to the excessive rates of poverty in Britain can be similarly resolved. 'Redistribution' within a modernised welfare state could allow statutory income rights for citizens, limits on high earnings as well as a minimum wage, reduction of means tests, reduction of wasteful tax allowances, and fair taxation of the rich to finance better public services and create more jobs, especially for the young. Child benefit and disability allowances, can be strengthened and even a 'participation' income introduced for those who take on caring responsibilities for children and the elderly and disabled. All this is easily within the means of an incoming administration. If interpreted imaginatively 'redistribution' can take account of the rearrangement of responsibilities or activities as well as resources over the lifetime of the individual and between generations (Walker, 1996).

There has to be a concerted change of direction. Statements from the Labour leadership have not yet fulfilled the hopes of millions of people. But there are good signs of the acceptance of some of the redistributive principles on which a major new strategy might be based. The Shadow Chancellor, Gordon Brown, has made repeated references to a fairer tax system. On 20 January 1997 he said, 'A fair tax system also means a commitment to the progressive principle – that the tax burden must be based on a willingness to pay.'

The Labour leader, Tony Blair, has also called attention repeatedly to the need to halt the social decline of the last two decades. In a speech on 24 January 1997 on 'The 21st Century Welfare State' he acknowledged that 'poverty, insecurity and inequality have increased on an unprecedented scale' with the clear implication that this must be reversed, and said 'It is our task to create a genuine "one nation" society'. The planned cuts in class sizes, the windfall tax and the pledges to get hundreds of thousands into training and into work represent a beginning. Each of these examples illustrate the acceptance of the need for a strategy of redistribution. The critical questions are how far and how fast?

The initial costs will have to be modest. In the first year one per cent of total personal disposable income, or £5 billion, could cover a renewed link between earnings and the basic retirement pension, restoration of unemployment benefit for 16–18-year-olds, improvement of universal child benefit, more rented public housing to reduce the numbers of homeless and first steps to include better child care and provision for older people and disabled people. Progress in reducing overall poverty and halting the 'growing divide' will need to be demonstrated.

The cost would be lower than that proposed by the Conservatives in seeking to subsidise private pensions. An incoming administration could reduce over-indulgent tax allowances by, say, 5 per cent (£2 billion) and by freeing part of the excess of national insurance income over outgoings engineered by Peter Lilley (say, £3 billion). There would be no need to review income tax in that first year. The proposed 10 pence starting rate and other adjustments would have to play their part in a principled long-term plan to reorganise the tax system as a whole during the five years of the next Parliament. Personal income taxation and wealth taxation, as well as limits on high earnings, 'top-hat' pensions and other features of national waste will have their place. What could be done is documented in good work by social scientists (for example Hills, 1988; Atkinson, 1989).

Through the principle of redistribution a long-term, affordable and familiar, indeed popular, strategy of social change can be put into effect. This would include broadly based and not oppressively conditional social security – which would be of interest to people with middle and high incomes and not only the low paid. It would include measures to restore the best principles as well as practices of public service, in rented housing, health, education and environment. And therefore it would help to create large-scale additional employment.

REFERENCES

Abrahamson, P (1997, forthcoming) 'Combatting poverty and social exclusion in Europe,' in Beck W, Van der Maesen L and Walker A, *The Social Quality of Europe*, Kluwer Law International, Netherlands.

Atkinson, A B (1989) *Poverty and Social Security*, Harvester Wheatsheaf.

Channel 4 (1996) *The Great, the Good and the Dispossessed*, The Report of the Channel 4 Commission on Poverty, Channel 4 Television.

Friedmann, J (1996) 'Rethinking poverty: empowerment and citizen rights,' *International Social Science Journal*, No 148, pp161-72.

Galbraith, J K (1992) *The Culture of Contentment*, Houghton Miflin, Boston and New York.

Gaudier, M (1995) *Poverty, Inequality, Exclusion: New Approach to Theory and Practice*, International Institute for Labour Studies, ILO, Geneva.

Gore, C (1996) 'Social Exclusion and the Design of Anti-Poverty Strategy in Developing Countries,' International Institute for Labour Studies, Policy Forum on Social Exclusion, New York, 22-24 May, 1996, publication forthcoming.

Gore, C and Figueiredo, J B (1996) *Social Exclusion and Anti-Poverty Strategies*, International Institute for Labour Studies, in conjunction with UNDP, IILS, Geneva.

Guidicini, P, Pieretti, G and Bergamaschi, M (1996) *Extreme Urban Poverties in Europe: contradictions and perverse effects in welfare policies*, FrancoAngeli, Milan.

Hills, J (1988) *Changing Tax: how the tax system works and how to change it*, CPAG.

Hills, J (1995) *Income and Wealth*, Vol 2, York, Joseph Rowntree Foundation.

Jordan, B (1996) *A Theory of Poverty and Social Exclusion*, Cambridge, Polity Press.

Massey, D S (1996) 'The age of extremes: concentrated afflence and poverty in the twenty-first century', *Demography*, Vol 33, No 4, pp395-412.

Nolan, B and Whelan, C T (1996) *Resources, Deprivation and Poverty*, Oxford, Clarendon Press.

Paugam, S (ed) (1996) *L'Exclusion: L'Etat des Savoirs*, Editions la Decouverte, Paris.

Perlman, S (1992) 'Keynes and anti-poverty policy,' *Review of Social Economy*, XLIX, No.p 3.

Rodgers, G, Gore, C and Figueirido, J B (eds) (1995) *Social Exclusion: Rhetoric, Reality, Responses*, Internatiomal Institute for Labour Studies, ILO, Geneva.

Room, G (1990) *'New Poverty' in the European Community*, Macmillan.

Room, G (ed) (1996) *Beyond the Threshold: the measurement and analysis of social exclusion*, the Policy Press.

Townsend, P (1993) *The International Analysis of Poverty*, Harvester

Wheatsceaf.

Townsend, P (1996) *A Poor Future: can we counter growing poverty in Britain and across the world?* Lemos and Crane.

Townsend, P with Donkor K. (1996) *Global Restructuring and Social Policy: the need to establish an international welfare state,* Policy Press.

UNCTAD (1995) *Comparative Experiences with Privatisation: policy insights and lessons learned,* UN, New York and Geneva.

Walker, A (ed) (1996) *The New Generational Contract,* UCL Press.

18 Conclusion: prioritise poverty now
Carol Walker and Alan Walker

This is the fourth volume, produced by CPAG, to evaluate the impact of Conservative government policies on the poor (Bull and Wilding, 1983; Walker and Walker, 1987; Becker, 1991). Each has been published shortly before a general election with the aim of encouraging the political parties and the media to ensure that issues relating to the most vulnerable groups in society are firmly at the centre of the election debate. Each volume has contributed to the public debate by examining the trends in poverty and inequality in Britain and the part paid by key social policies in addressing the needs of the poor. Each has also put forward a plan for future action and sought to encourage future governments to put the needs of poor people at the centre of the political agenda. Such critical assessment is not party political. It follows in the tradition of evaluating the impact of government policies in relation to the poor which began with earlier Labour governments (Field, 1978; Townsend and Bosanquet, 1972; Bosanquet and Townsend, 1980) – work that should be required reading for all Shadow Cabinet members!

If there is a single message that needs to be taken from the contributions to this volume it is, sadly, the same one that was made by previous assessments of the 1979/83, 1983/87 and 1987/92 Conservative governments, the poor are *still waiting* for the increasing prosperity, so long promised, to trickle down as far as them. Now though, we can say with certainty, based on extensive empirical evidence covering 18 years, that it will not happen unless a future government is prepared to divert resources their way; in other words, to give priority to the abolition of poverty and to carry out a redistribution of resources from rich to poor.

The requirement to continue putting the needs of poor people at the centre of the political debate is more, rather than less, essential in 1997 than it has been even in the past. As Robin Cook has pointed out: 'The poor may be many times more than top tax-payers – but they get a tenth of the public attention'.

POVERTY OF POLITICS

Poverty persists and is growing, but it is at the bottom of the political agenda. In 1993/94:

- one-quarter of the population were living in poverty (defined as 50 per cent of average earnings); nearly three times the number as in 1979;
- nearly one-third of all children were living in poverty compared to 10 per cent in 1979.

Thus, a significant minority of British people are unable to share in the growing prosperity of the country as a whole. As both Carey Oppenheim (Chapter 2) and Tim Lang (Chapter 14) show, poor families have to go without basic commodities, adequate heating, clothing and even an adequate and nutritious diet. And yet, at each election since 1979, the Conservatives have claimed the precious mantle of the 'Party of the Family'.

Moreover, Britain stands out internationally in having experienced the largest percentage increase in income inequality between 1967 and 1992 and the biggest increase in child poverty – both of which have risen by more than 30 per cent (Dennehy *et al*, 1997). This compares with other European countries, such as France and Spain, that have seen no increases in child poverty and some, such as Belgium, the Netherlands and Germany, that have seen only small increases. Some 4.2 million people under 16 years old live in poverty in Britain and, for some, poverty kills: *they run four times the risk of dying before they reach the age of 20 than their more affluent counterparts.*

In recent years the Conservative Government has made some concessions to accepting that poverty (though not necessarily called by that name) exists. As Carey Oppenheim points out, the obfuscation of official statistics on income distribution began to clear in the second half of the 1980s, and, as Michaela Benzeval (Chapter 11) shows, the Government came round to accepting the existence of 'variations' if not 'inequalities' in health. 'Big deal' would be an understandable response from families living in poverty. They might ask why it is that child poverty has not risen in France and Spain when it has soared in Britain?

Despite signing up to a programme to reduce poverty at the 1995 World Summit on Social Development, Peter Lilley, as Secretary of State for Social Security, reported that Britain would not be drawing up a national poverty eradication plan as agreed because, he claimed:

> the recommendations ... principally relate to the needs of under-developed countries, which need to harness their economies to achieve basic goals such as the provision of clean water and adequate food supplies. The UK (already has) the infrastructure and social protection systems to prevent poverty and maintain living standards.

In addition, the Conservative Government has endeavoured to diffuse the argument about the growing number of people living on incomes below half average incomes (as based on the HBAI), by suggesting that the position of many people at the bottom of the earnings distribution is not a permanent one because circumstances, and therefore financial status, change. However, as was shown in Section One, any movement which occurs tends to be within very narrow limits: from unemployment to low paid work and back again; or up and down the bottom half of the income distribution. It is very difficult for people to move out of poverty, they just become more or less poor. They remain economically insecure even though the severity of this insecurity may rise or fall slightly.

SOCIAL POLARISATION AND INEQUALITY

Inequality has grown excessively since the late 1970s. As Section Two illustrates, inequalities in education, housing, health, employment and income and wealth are now wider than at any time since the war. Government policies have done nothing to redress the less favourable economic position of either women or people from minority ethnic communities. In some critical respects the situation has deteriorated as a direct result of government policies.

- The earnings divide: the gap between the high and low paid is now wider than ever before.
- There is a growing divide between households with work and

those with no work. It is becoming harder for people to move from unemployment into employment.

- There is a growing tax divide: the increasingly regressive nature of fiscal policy, and in particular the switch from direct to indirect taxes, hits the poor hardest.

- Women continue to be over-represented in lower paid jobs and more dependent on a less and less generous social security system, as well as being affected more by cuts in welfare provision.

- The 'race' divide means that people from Black and minority ethnic communities are more likely to be unemployed, low paid and discriminated against than white people. The savage clampdown on assistance given to refugees and asylum-seekers impacts on these groups in particular.

- Recent education policy has led to increasing polarisation between schools; and a growing divide between the educational experiences of children attending schools in poor compared to affluent areas.

- Growing economic inequalities have been accompanied by widening health inequalities resulting in, 'unnecessary death, disease and disability (which) is both an economic loss and a social injustice' (Chapter 11).

LOOKING TO THE FUTURE

In Chapter 17, Peter Townsend presents a radical alternative to the failed policies of the past to tackle the growing epidemic of poverty and social polarisation. Redistribution has been out of fashion in the political debate in recent years, as Ruth Lister pointed out in her conclusion to *The Growing Divide* (Lister, 1987). A process of 'inverse distribution' has taken place instead (Becker and Bennett, 1991) with the rich being made richer and the comfortable even more so. This increasing social polarisation can only be stopped by redistribution.

While not everything can be achieved overnight, Townsend suggests that important steps can be taken to reverse the negative pattern of the past, and shows how countries which have retained redistribution as a tenet of their welfare policy, as opposed to going along the alternative British path of privatising welfare, have been able to sustain successful economies. The Conservative Government sees further privatisation as the best way of meeting welfare needs in the future. The Labour Party is arguing for a fairer taxation system and has recognised the existence of poverty and inequality, however, the policy pronouncements it has made so far are relatively modest. And the Shadow Chancellor's commitment to retaining the previous government's tax and spending plans seriously limits the scope for action.

John Hills discusses the cleft-stick within which policy-makers now find themselves: the opposing pressures of increased demand and needs for welfare services versus political, and more arguably, economic pressures to contain spending and reduce direct taxation. However, as he points out, some of the arguments maintaining that the welfare state is in crisis, for example with respect to the ageing of the population, have been grossly exaggerated. As John Hills has demonstrated elsewhere, over the next 50 years, on current policies, population ageing and pension maturation create *no* long-term crisis in the funding of social security, in fact, its cost will fall relative to GDP. However, this is partly due to the decreasing relative value of pensions and other benefits. But there is another way:

> Alternatively, benefit relativities could be maintained but the cost of public welfare spending would rise as a share of GDP, and with it taxation in some form. The scale of such a rise, building up over the next 40-50 years, is clearly perfectly feasible, and would not take welfare spending above what is already the average elsewhere in Europe relative to GDP. However, it is equally clearly incompatible with political aspirations for lower taxes. (Hills, 1995).

Although both the Conservative and Labour Parties have committed themselves to low (direct) taxation strategies, Hills questions whether the British public is as keen on tax cuts as is commonly suggested. As well as showing that over 60 per cent of respondents support higher taxes in return for higher spending on services, the latest *British Social Attitudes Survey* revealed that:

> Particular spending programmes were more likely to get a higher priority when they were seen as both personally and nationally beneficial – further confirmation that public support for the main pillars of the welfare state derives from a combination of self-interest and some notion of the public good. (Jowell *et al*, 1996)

The survey also revealed a 'fair degree of support from the better off for core government spending programmes'. The British public, therefore, still retains a strong allegiance to the welfare state and, in particular, to public provision for health and education. Within social security spending, state pensions are named as being first or second priority for extra public spending by over two-thirds of respondents. Though only 25 per cent ranked the needs of the unemployed as high, on average 70 per cent agreed with the statement that: 'Unemployment should be a higher priority than inflation', and 52 per cent agreed with the statement that 'government should redistribute income from the better off to the less well off' (Jowell *et al*, 1996).

Unfortunately the Government has decided not to appeal to these instincts of fairness and justice on the part of the British public and has, instead, sought to emphasise opposite, base ones. The Labour Opposition has followed the Government's lead too readily and, as a consequence, the political debate has often been reduced to the lowest common denominator. It is surely an indictment of government priorities that, on the one hand, Benefit Advice Lines have been scrapped for being 'the luxury end' of benefits delivery, even though each year millions of people are missing out on benefits to which they are entitled, while, on the other, 'Beat-a-Cheat' lines asking people to inform on their workmates and neighbours are advertised widely. While benefit fraud is an important and wholly legitimate target, the methods used are inappropriate and insulting to the honest people who make up the majority of claimants. It is sad too that the Labour Opposition chose one of its few Supply Days in Parliament to discuss benefit fraud, not benefit poverty. At times the two main political parties seem to be competing with each other to see who is the toughest on fraud. To paraphrase, it is about time each was 'tough on benefit fraud, and *tough on the causes of benefit fraud*' (see Cook, 1989). The pendulum has swung too far. What is needed is an effective and efficient benefits system that prevents fraud, not a campaign to hound claimants on the basis of an anonymous telephone 'tip-off'. In a recent television programme on the 'Beat-a-Cheat' line, one woman was visited six times on the basis of anonymous allegations – and each time shown to be a legitimate claimant.

Lisa Harker and Marilyn Howard demonstrate that, far from preventing people from falling into poverty, the social security system actually exacerbates the problem. The value of benefits has fallen; more groups of people are being excluded from its protection, either permanently or temporarily. Reliance on means-tested benefits has increased, despite the 'discredited' past of this type of payment (Deacon and Bradshaw, 1983). Harker sets out an agenda for a new, more positive social security system which reflects the changed nature of British society and the changing labour market, such as more diverse 'non-traditional' family structures; changing working patterns, where there is now more part-time work and other forms of 'atypical' work; the insecurity of the labour market, and greater experience of intermittent work.

The social security system has been the subject of almost constant review and reform for over 20 years. However, the changes have been concerned less with meeting the needs of its recipients than simplifying administration and cutting the budget (Walker, 1993). Savings in social security should not be made by cutting the level and scope of benefits, leading to further individual misery and hardship. The answer lies in *preventing* people becoming dependent on social security. Similarly the high profile being given to welfare-to-work schemes – which are often misleadingly portrayed as a panacea but they can mean just transfering people from out-of-work welfare to in-work welfare – implies, yet again, that the fault lies with the claimant, who is apparently happy to sit back and be kept by the state.

No future government can ignore the cost of the social security system, which now accounts for over one third of all public spending. However, as Lisa Harker argues, this expenditure is not the fault of those reliant on benefits, it is caused by problems and policies outside the system and their control. It is an ironic contradiction, for example, that whenever the level of unemployment is high, govern-ments concentrate on establishing punitive regimes to force unem-ployed people off benefit rather than creating the conditions in which the missing jobs can flourish; it happened in the 1930s and again in the 1980s and 1990s (Deacon, 1976; Murray, 1995).

Reform of the social security system which focuses only on the reduction of spending exacerbates the problem of poverty, and causes hardship for those who, because of their status, already feel marginalised from the rest of society. It is time to stop making the poor pay for their poverty; poverty is the responsibility of everyone in Britain. The size of social security spending is not the primary problem, it is merely a symptom of failures elsewhere in society and the economy in particular.

PRIORITISING POVERTY

The evidence amassed in this volume stands as a huge indictment of the disastrous record of four Conservative governments towards Britain's most vulnerable and insecure citizens. As if that were not enough, however, the evidence shows that it was not a matter of indifference. The Government's own strategy of inequality has been at the heart of the growth of poverty and social exclusion over the last two decades. For the Prime Minister to suggest, as he did to the Conservative Central Council in Bath on 15 March 1997, that his ambition for a fifth Conservative term was to ensure that the 'have-nots' can join the 'haves' is simply astonishing.

The Government's strategy of inequality has not worked – if it was intended to make everybody better-off by unleashing wave of entrepreneurial activity. Cynics may argue that it was only ever intended to fill the pockets of the already rich and, in fact, it has done so. But the effects of the policies – on direct taxation, social security, employment, health and so on – reverberate throughout society: in the social fracture, polarisation and manifold social exclusion, as well as in the adverse fiscal consequences of increased indirect taxes and government borrowing. They finally fall most heavily on the poor whose benefits have been cut and whose prospects of achieving even some minimum level of economic security have been undermined.

Of course, this disastrous record of four Conservative governments also represents a challenge to the Labour Opposition. The report, *Unemployment and the Future of Work*, produced by the UK's Christian Churches, emphasises the nature of this challenge:

> In the general election campaign, the political parties are competing
> for votes by promising lower taxation. When so many are living in
> poverty and unemployment, it is wrong to give priority to the claims
> of those who are already well off (*The Observer*, 16 March 1997).

We agree. In fact, combating poverty and social exclusion should *not* be a party political matter, but a moral one. As Dr Johnson said: 'A decent provision for the poor is the true test of civilisation.'

The Conservative Government's record speaks for itself. What of the Labour opposition? The Shadow Chancellor, Gordon Brown, in his John Smith Memorial Lecture, argued that Labour must restore equality to its proper place in the trinity of socialist values (alongside liberty and community) and he has been emphatic in saying that

Labour means business when it comes to tackling poverty and inequality in Britain (*New Statesman*, 20 September 1996). This is good news for the poor and socially excluded. But we hope that he has learnt the lessons from previous periods of Labour government and, especially, the need for planned redistribution. Establishing a national poverty reduction target, backed by an annual poverty report (Atkinson, 1996), would be clear proof that a Labour government meant business.

We sincerely hope that whoever has responsibility for preparing the assessment of the next government's record on behalf of CPAG will be able to report some good news, rather than the depressing catalogue of increasing poverty and social exclusion, growing social divisions, individual misery, premature death and the massive waste of human potential documented in this volume. Four Conservative governments have left Britain divided; the British people should make a substantial reduction in poverty and social exclusion the acid test of the next government.

REFERENCES

Atkinson, A B (1996) 'Drawing the Line', *Guardian*, 6 November, p9.

Becker, S (1991) *Windows of Opportunity: public policy and the poor*, CPAG.

Becker, S and Bennett, F.(1991) 'Conclusions: a new agenda', in Becker, S (1991) *Windows of Opportunity: public policy and the poor*, CPAG.

Bosanquet, N and Townsend, P (eds) (1980) *Labour and Equality: a Fabian study of Labour in power, 1974-79*, Heinemann.

Bull, D and Wilding, P (eds) (1983) *Thatcherism and the Poor*, CPAG.

Cook, D (1989) *Rich Law, Poor Law: different responses to tax and supplementary benefit fraud*, OUP.

Deacon, A (1976) *In Search of the Scrounger*, Bell.

Deacon, A. and Bradshaw, J (1983) *Reserved for the Poor*, Basil Blackwell and Matin Robertson.

Dennehy, A, Smith, L and Harker, P (1997) *Not To Be Ignored: young people, poverty and health*, CPAG.

Field, F (1978) *Children Worse Off Under Labour?*, CPAG.

Hills, J (1995) 'Funding the welfare state', *Oxford Review of Economic Policy*, vol 11, No 3, pp27-43.

Jowell, R, Curtice, J, Park, A, Brook, L and Thomson K (eds) (1996) *British Social Attitudes: the 13th report*, 1996/97 edition, SCPR.

Lister, R (1987) 'Conclusion II: there is an alternative' in Walker, A and Walker C (eds), *The Growing Divide:a social audit 1979-87*, CPAG.

Murray, I (1995) *Desperately Seeking … A Job, A critical guide to the 1966 jobseekers allowance*, Unemployment Unit.

Townsend, P and Bosanquet, N (eds) (1972) *Labour and Inequality*, Fabian Society.

Walker, A and Walker, C (eds) (1987) *The Growing Divide:a social audit 1979-87*, CPAG.

Walker, C (1993) *Managing Poverty: the limits of social assistance*, Routledge.

The Conservatives' diary
Policies affecting poor families: June 1979 – August 1996

*Fran Bennett**

1979

June: Budget: income tax cuts benefit highest paid most; tax cuts outweighed by increase in VAT for those on average earnings or below; prescription charges rise from 20p to 45p and some dental charges rise; 50p increase in one parent benefit but no increase in child benefit.

September: Regulations: unemployment benefit to be paid fortnightly, except for those on short-time working or who choose to be paid weekly.

November: Previous year's shortfall in uprating of short-term benefits not made good. Pensions and other long-term benefits not fully protected against increase in VAT.

1980

February: Price of school meals raised from 30p to 35p. 1,050 extra DHSS staff for anti-fraud work.

March: Budget: child benefit to be increased by 75p in November (but £1.20 increase required to restore April 1979 value); instead, improvements in one parent benefit and family income supplement; lower rate band of tax abolished.

April: Prescription charges rise to 70p and dental charges up; charge of £2 for sight test (except for

---

* *Entries from June 1979 – July 1991 are slightly edited and shortened versions of those included in:*

    'Mrs Thatcher's Diary' by Ann Stanyer in *Thatcherism and the Poor* (edited by David Bull and Paul Wilding, CPAG, 1983)

    'Mrs Thatcher's Diary' by Huw Edwards in *The Growing Divide* (edited by Alan Walker and Carol Walker, CPAG, 1987)

    The Conservatives' Diary' by Jill Vincent in *Windows of Opportunity: Public policy and the poor* (edited by Saul Becker, CPAG, 1991)

The latest entries, for August 1991 to August 1996, draw heavily on 'Main Events', published in each edition of *Poverty* (CPAG). As with previous entries, the main focus is on income and social security issues.

under-16s). Council house rents up on average by 21 per cent. National insurance contributions up by 0.25 per cent.

July: Social Security Act 1980: provides for breaking of link between earnings and benefits uprating and for changes to supplementary benefit system. Social Security (No 2) Act 1980: provides for abolition of earnings-related supplement, 5 per cent 'abatement' (reduction) of short-term national insurance benefits and invalidity benefit and cuts in strikers' and various other benefits (*see* November 1980 and January 1982). Education (No 2) Act: local education authorities (LEAs) no longer required to provide nursery education, or school meals (other than for children in families on supplementary benefit or family income supplement); LEAs can now charge and provide what they wish.

November: Social Security Act 1980: Supplementary Benefit Commission abolished, with some functions replaced by Social Security Advisory Committee. New supplementary benefit scheme comes in (*see* July 1980). National insurance and supplementary benefit rates aligned, reducing supplementary pensions by 40p pw. Claimants lose two weeks of increase due to uprating being two weeks later than normal. Pensions and other long-term benefit increases linked to estimates of price rises only; consequently lower than if still related to earnings. Short-term and invalidity benefits

increased by 5 per cent less than forecast of price rises (*see* July 1980). Changes made in method of uprating national insurance child dependency additions, resulting in cuts in real value in this and subsequent years. Family income supplement and mobility allowance raised by more than inflation.

December: Prescription charges up to £1. School-leavers denied supplementary benefit until end of school holidays after they leave.

1981

March: Budget: personal tax allowances frozen, but child benefit increased in line with inflation. Social Security Act 1981: intention to claw back in November 1 per cent overpaid in 1980 because of overestimate of inflation.

April: Social Security Contributions Act 1981: provides for increase in range of low earnings over which national insurance contributions paid and a reduction in Treasury supplement to National Insurance Fund, thus requiring higher increase in contribution rates. Council house rents up on average by 45 per cent. National insurance contributions up by 1 per cent.

July: Extension of long-term rate of supplementary benefit for men 60 or over if unemployed for a year or more and stop registering for work. Government commitment to maintain child benefit at November 1980 value, subject to economic and other circumstances. Poverty figures to be published biennially rather than annually.

September: Education Act 1980: assisted places scheme comes in, with more generous help for assisted pupils with school meals, uniform grants and travel to school.

November: 1 per cent clawback on benefit increases; shortfall in benefit uprating – 2 per cent lower than inflation, except mobility allowance raised by more than rate of inflation.

December: Shortfall to be made good only for certain long-term benefits.

1982

January: Social Security (No 2) Act 1980: earnings-related supplement to unemployment, sickness, widows' and maternity benefits starts to be phased out.

March: Budget: 2 per cent shortfall to be made good for all benefits; child benefit to be increased in line with inflation, but personal tax allowances by more; no statement on status of 5 per cent abatement when unemployment benefit brought into tax (*see* July 1982); mobility allowance to be tax-free. New mothers to receive child benefit monthly; existing recipients and limited group of new recipients (eg, lone parents) can opt to continue weekly payment.

April: Prescription charges rise to £1.30; glasses up from £8.30 to £15 per lens; charges for routine dental treatment from £9 to £13 maximum. Council house rents up by average 19 per cent. National insurance contributions up by 1 per cent.

June: Government announces lone mothers claiming one parent benefit not to be asked about their sex lives. Self-certification of short-term sickness introduced.

July: Unemployment benefit taxable; attempts by Conservative backbenchers to make good 5 per cent abatement fail. National insurance contribution conditions for maternity grant abolished (though 26-week residence rule).

October: End of compulsory registration at job centres and consequent changes in method of counting unemployed people and in 'availability for work' test.

November: Social Security and Housing Benefits Act 1982: housing benefit payable to some council tenants on supplementary benefit (*see* also April 1983). Supplementary benefit uprated on basis of Retail Price Index minus housing element, ie, at 0.5 per cent less than other benefits. Increase in supplementary benefit capital limit to £2,500. Government to claw back this year's overestimate of inflation rate from benefits.

December: Postal claims introduced for unemployed supplementary benefit claimants.

1983

March: Child benefit increased by 11 per cent – making good previous cut; tax allowances increased by 14 per cent.

April: Industrial injury benefit abolished. Social Security and Housing Benefit Act 1982: statutory sick pay introduced: first eight weeks of sick pay responsibility of employers – low rates for low-paid; no additions for dependants; taxable and subject to national insurance contributions. Prescription charges up to £1.40. National insurance contributions up by 0.25 per cent. Housing benefit payable instead of rent rebates and allowances for all tenants, and instead of rate rebates for tenants and owner-occupiers (*see* also November 1982). Widespread chaos results from implementation of housing benefit. Thousands of tenants receive no benefit or wrong amount due to computer or administrative error. SHAC reports 2.5m tenants worse off as a result of scheme. Regulations published allowing married women to claim national insurance dependency additions.

July: Prime Minister refuses to give assurance that unemployment benefit will be increased in line with inflation like other national insurance benefits.

August: Department of Employment steps up drive against alleged fraud with establishment of Regional Benefit Investigation Teams.

October: DHSS *Low Income Families* Tables show rising tide of poverty in Great Britain.

November: Autumn statement: housing programme cut by £465m in 1984/85, housing benefit by £230m; 5 per cent abatement of unemployment benefit, but not other benefits, made good; statutory sick pay does not compensate for 5 per cent abatement of sickness benefit; benefits now uprated on historical method, not predicted inflation: increase 2 per cent less than under old method. Invalidity trap abolished. Review of pensions announced.

December: Announcement of abolition of 'normal household duties test' and replacement of non-contributory invalidity pension (NCIP) and housewives' NCIP by severe disablement allowance.

1984

January: Conservative backbench revolt forces government to modify proposed housing benefit cut to £185m.

February: DHSS orders major drive in 59 areas into alleged social security abuse: unemployment review officers question 18–25-year-olds about why they left jobs; Social Security Policy Inspectorate interviews young people not joining Youth Training Scheme (YTS). White Paper outlines huge reduction in spending on school meals from £414m in 1983/84 to £257m in 1984/85;

Hertfordshire County Council first local authority to abolish school meals for all children except those statutorily entitled to them. Review of housing benefit announced. Government refuses UK support to UN International Year for the Homeless.

March: Further increase in prescription charges to £1.60. Budget: tax allowances raised by 12 per cent. Child benefit increases no longer announced as part of Budget.

April: Government announces 'most comprehensive review of social security system for 40 years'. Estimated 2.5m people worse off following housing benefit cuts.

May: Review of maternity benefits announced.

June: November benefit upratings announced, together with cuts of over £100m. Government admits almost 2m disabled and elderly people face benefit cuts of 50p to £1. Child benefit increased by less than increase in personal tax allowances.

September: DHSS announces six-month freeze on amounts of supplementary benefit paid to people in board and lodgings and in private or voluntary residential homes.

October: Departmental enquiry announced into local government finance, including 'whether local democratic accountability could be improved by reducing rate rebates so that poor people would feel full cost of council spending'. Most married women excluded from Community Programme by new regulation requiring participants or their spouses to be on unemployment benefit or supplementary benefit.

November: Autumn statement: substantial restrictions on supplementary benefit for those in lodgings and private residential and nursing homes; proposed increase in housing benefit children's needs allowance cancelled; 5 per cent abatement in invalidity pension made good but invalidity pensioners no longer to receive both earnings-related component and age-related invalidity allowance. Public expenditure on housing cut by £65m for 1985/86 (although Treasury had planned £650m cut).

1985

February: Postal claiming to be available to all supplementary benefit claimants by end of May.

March: Budget: real increase in tax thresholds and restructuring of national insurance contributions announced; new regulations result in housing benefit cuts of up to £5.47 pw for 110,000 tenants in high rent areas. DHSS announces regulations forcing unemployed 16-25-year-olds in board and lodgings to move every two, four or eight weeks according to area, or face big cuts in benefit.

April: 25 per cent increase in dental

charges: dentists claim patients not exempt from charges would pay most of cost of their treatment for the first time. Abolition of pensions 'half-test' rule for married women announced.

May: Green Paper proposes means-testing home improvement grants. Schools Inspectorate reports spending cuts on school buildings adversely affecting quality of education.

June: Green Paper on review of social security published. 35p cut in child benefit announced as part of benefit uprating; 850,000 families with a young unemployed, disabled or pensioner relative living at home to have reduction in housing benefit.

July: Employment Secretary announces plans to remove all young people under 21 from wages council regulations, and confine councils to setting only a single minimum rate and overtime rate for those 21 and over. Proposals to allow employers to opt out of statutory sick pay published in consultative document. YTS extended to 2 years for 500,000 young people. Enquiry into British housing, chaired by Duke of Edinburgh, recommends abolition of mortgage interest tax relief.

August: High Court finds government restrictions on board and lodgings payments unlawful.

September: Government appeals against High Court decision – defeated in Court of Appeal.

October: New, temporary regulations to curb board and lodgings supplementary benefit payments also declared unlawful, by House of Commons Statutory Instruments Committee; regulations subsequently withdrawn.

November: Environment Secretary announces £185m cut in capital spending on housing.

December: White Paper on Social Security published, with certain changes from Green Paper, including proposal to modify not abolish state earnings-related pension scheme.

1986

January: Social Security Bill introduced into Commons. Secretary of State for Scotland announces replacement of domestic rates with community charge (poll tax) on all adult residents.

February: Rent controls for new tenants to be phased out after election. Cuts in legal aid announced, particularly hurting low-income families with children.

March: Budget: basic rate of income tax reduced to 29 per cent and personal allowances raised in line with inflation. Green Paper on Reform of Personal Taxation proposes transferable allowances for married couples.

April: European Court finds UK in breach of EEC law on sex discrimination by refusing to pay invalid care allowance to married and cohabiting women. Statutory sick pay extended from eight to 28 weeks.

May: White Paper *Building Businesses ... Not Barriers* proposes removing or reducing a number of rights for employees.

June: Review of student grants, including possibility of introducing loans, announced.

July: Social Security Act 1986 and Wages Act 1986 receive Royal Assent. DHSS *Low Income Families Tables* released as Parliament begins summer recess. Restart scheme for long-term unemployed launched, including compulsory interviews – individuals failing to attend interviews, or refusing 'available work', risk having benefit suspended for up to 13 weeks (from October).

August: Cuts in supplementary benefit single payments introduced. Revised exceptionally severe weather payments scheme announced for some supplementary benefit claimants. Official figures show annual number of families accepted as homeless is 94,000.

October: Changes in industrial injuries scheme implemented; voluntary unemployment penalty extended from 6 to 13 weeks and reduced rates of short-term national insurance benefits abolished. Benefits to be increased by 2 per cent in April 1987. 35p cut in child benefit made in 1985 will not be made good. Housing benefit expenditure to be reduced by £68m:

average loss of 47p pw for pensioners and 56p for other claimants. Tightening up of procedures announced for assessing availability for work of newly unemployed.

November: Autumn statement: statutory sick pay to be cut by £18.5m pa; housing spending to increase by 14 per cent – for repairs to existing properties, not new building.

1987

January: Trigger temperature for exceptionally severe weather payments to be increased in response to 'severest weather for 40 years'. Supplementary benefit claimants under pension age to receive only half mortgage interest for first 4 months on benefit; further freeze on board and lodging supplementary benefit payments announced.

March: Further increase in prescription charges announced: 12-fold cash increase of 1,100 per cent since 1979. Budget: basic rate of tax cut by 2p; personal allowances increased in line with inflation; Chancellor widely criticised for failing to help unemployed people and low-paid. Health Education Council's Report, *The Health Divide*, shows social inequalities in health widening in the 1980s.

April: Abolition of £25 maternity grant for all mothers: women on family income supplement and supplementary benefit can apply to newly-established (non-discretionary) social fund; statutory maternity pay paid by employers replaces maternity benefit; abolition of death grant and replacement by help from (non-discretionary) social fund for those on family income supplement, housing benefit or supplementary benefit.

May: Announcement that income support will include compensation for average amount claimants are expected to pay towards rates.

June: Conservatives win third term. Queen's speech confirms 16–17-year-olds who refuse YTS place will lose right to benefit and that poll tax will be introduced in England and Wales, a year after its introduction in Scotland (*see* January 1986).

July: Government says poll tax will be phased in over 4 years, beginning in April 1990 at a target figure of £100 per adult. From April 1988 everyone liable for rates will pay at least 20 per cent. Regulations under Social Security Act 1986 published, to come in in April 1988.

September: Government publishes plans to revive private sector in rented housing, to widen choice for tenants and restrict role of local government.

October: Participation in Community Programme schemes limited to people unemployed for 12 months or more. Benefit uprating announcement: child benefit to be frozen, social fund budget to be about £200m. Figures for new income support rates for April 1988 reveal cuts of 50p per adult. Plans announced for 300 extra fraud investigators.

November: From April 1988, period people are disqualified from unemployment benefit if voluntarily unemployed to be doubled to six months, saving £37m in a full year. Abolition of free dental check-ups and eye tests announced.

December: Error in past inflation measure detected: some claimants compensated.

1988

February: White Paper signals demise of Community Programme, to be replaced by schemes which pay benefit plus a small top-up. Further measures announced to counter benefit fraud and to tighten up 'availability for work' testing.

March: Budget: reduces top tax rate from 60 to 40 per cent and basic tax rate to 25 per cent; 'independent' taxation to be introduced – married man's tax allowance to be replaced by married couple's allowance (paid to man in first instance). Local Government Finance Bill brings in poll tax – Conservative backbench MPs reduce government's majority to 25 over a proposed 'ability to pay' system, and to 63 for Bill itself.

April: Prescription charges up by 20p to £2.60. Social Security Act 1986, heralded as most fundamental reform since Beveridge, comes fully into force: income support replaces supplementary benefit, family credit replaces family income supplement, social fund replaces single and urgent needs payments. After controversy, capital limit raised from £6,000 to £8,000 for housing benefit. Employees can choose between occupational pension schemes, SERPS and personal pension schemes. Government calculates that 35 per cent of supplementary benefit claimants will lose, 46 per cent will gain, rest will stay the same; others calculate far higher proportions of losers. Government announces that poll tax rebates will be extended to over a million more as taper is reduced from 20 per cent (under rate rebates) to 15 per cent under poll tax rebates.

May: Government publishes first edition of new statistical series, *Households Below Average Income* (*HBAI*), for 1981, 1983 and 1985, with final edition of *Low Income Families* (*LIF*) for same years. *LIF* Tables show 9.3 million people living on or below supplementary benefit level in 1985. *HBAI* Tables show rise in real income after housing costs of 8.4 per cent for bottom tenth of population, in comparison with 4.8 per cent for average (*see* April 1990). National Audit Office report criticises service in local DHSS offices, especially time taken to clear claims and accuracy.

July: DHSS split into Department of Social Security (DSS) and Department of Health (DH).

September: Employment Training (ET) scheme starts, giving 600,000

people per year average of 6 months' training on 'benefit plus' (*see* February 1988). 16-17-year-olds can no longer claim income support if required to be available for work, except where 'severe hardship'. Draft guidelines on charges for school activities published. Government announces it is to abolish Training Commission. First in series of OPCS reports on disability shows over 6 million disabled adults.

October: New, more restrictive, conditions for contributory benefits, which cut 40,000 people from unemployment count. SHAC and Shelter say homelessness has doubled in 11 years since Housing (Homeless Persons) Act.

November: Second OPCS disability report shows disabled adults have to spend extra £6.10 per week on average. New cold weather payments scheme implemented. White Paper proposes that student grants be frozen and supplemented with loans from 1990/91; full-time students will no longer be eligible for income support, unemployment benefit or housing benefit (*see* July 1990).

1989

January: Review of NHS sets out key changes, including self-governing status, new funding systems for health authorities and own budgets for GPs.

February: Local Government and Housing Bill sets out further measures to remove housing provision from local authorities and to control their housing finance.

March: Budget: changes to national insurance contributions (*see* October). 16-17-year-olds living independently to get higher income support; housing benefit increased for all 16-17-year-olds. Payments to young people leaving care to be disregarded for benefit purposes. Government announces establishment of Training and Enterprise Councils to coordinate local training, to be run by business.

April: Child benefit frozen for second year running; average of 50p extra per child added to child rates of income support. Social fund budget frozen for second year. Housing benefit transitional protection (after 1988 cuts) reduced. Prescriptions up 20p to £2.80; payment for sight tests introduced. Introduction of poll tax in Scotland. Changes to benefits for board and lodging claimants and abolition of time limits (*see* March 1985).

May: Plans announced to introduce agency status for majority of social security operations. Secretary of State John Moore's speech, 'The end of the line for poverty', argues that absolute poverty no longer exists, that relative poverty is no more than inequality and that academics and others are really just attacking capitalism.

June: 50-plus Jobstart launched: over 50s to get £20 a week in part-time jobs of 10 hours a week or more and paying less than £2.57 an hour.

July: Social fund officers warned they are overspending budgets and must cut back.

August: Leaked DSS document shows poll tax debts to be deducted direct from benefits.

October: Additional premiums for very elderly and disabled people on income support. Institute for Fiscal Studies report that new government 'poverty statistics' removed 1m people from the poorest group. 'Actively seeking work' replaces 'availability for work' for unemployment benefit claimants, imposing stricter eligibility test. Abolition of earnings rule for pensioners. Employees' national insurance contributions 2 per cent of earnings up to lower earnings limit and 9 per cent above.

November: All 16-17-year-olds to be interviewed about their claim for income support. £250m extra help announced for homeless people over two years.

December: Regulations exclude unemployment benefit claims from people earning over lower earnings limit.

1990

January: Social Security Bill gives pension proposals, and disability benefit measures, including abolition of earnings-related invalidity benefit. Prime Minister launches drive to make fathers pay maintenance for their children. National Insurance Fund will be £1.7bn in deficit in 1990/91, due mainly to contribution refunds to people contracting out of state earnings-related pension scheme. Government announces proposals on disability benefits.

February: High Court judgment that guidance on local social fund budgets is defective. Report shows 40 per cent fall in prescriptions dispensed due to price rises. Fewer than 1 per cent of unemployed claimants interviewed under Restart are placed in jobs.

March: Budget: capital limits for poll tax rebates and housing benefit to be doubled; government forced to backdate for Scotland. Workplace nurseries no longer taxed as benefit in kind for employees. Social fund budget increased by £10m (from loan repayments). Government announces extra £50m for poll tax transitional relief scheme. Independent Living Fund, set up to help disabled people, runs out of money (but is later saved). Government says average poll tax will be £363; about 10m people will get rebates. Measures announced to enforce maintenance payments.

April: Child benefit frozen for third year running. Prescription charges up to £3.05. Poll tax introduced in England and Wales. Capital limits for means-tested benefits raised. Independent taxation implemented. Rules tightened for unemployed people on benefit. Major mistakes

revealed in government 'poverty figures': poorest 10 per cent had only half average income growth in 1982-85 (*see* May 1988). Virtual freeze in social fund budget.

May: Social Services Committee says government statistics on low incomes are unsatisfactory and misleading; its report shows 12.2m people on or below income support level in 1987.

June: Government announces plans to deduct maintenance direct from wages before liable parents default.

July: HBAI statistics show income after housing costs of poorest 10 per cent went up only 0.1 per cent between 1979 and 1987, compared with 23 per cent for average. Social Security Bill denies housing benefit to students.

August: Record levels of mortgage arrears and house repossessions reported. *British Medical Journal* shows health gap between rich and poor widened in last ten years. National Audit Office report shows doubling in numbers of homeless people since 1987.

September: Government issues new directions and guidance for social fund, to reassert control of local office budgets.

October: £10 premium for carers on income support. Disregard for lone parents on housing benefit increased. White Paper on child support published (*see* July 1991).

November: Criminal Justice Bill

contains plans to deduct fines direct from benefit. John Major is new Prime Minister, promoting vision of 'classless society'. Disability Benefits Bill proposes new disability living allowance and disability working allowance.

December: Severe disablement allowance age-related additions introduced. Restart courses compulsory for some long-term unemployed (40 per cent cut in benefit for refusal). Government promises 1,000 beds in London for homeless people.

1991

January: New Select Committee on Social Security established.

February: Job-start programme (top-up of low wages for long-term unemployed taking jobs) to be scrapped. Cold weather payments increased from £5 to £6 per week and rule on seven consecutive days' freeze temporarily waived. National Audit Office report on social fund criticises inconsistency in decisions, and indebtedness for claimants with multiple loans. Court of Appeal rules Secretary of State within his rights in depriving around 400,000 people of severe disability premium.

March: Budget: £140 deduction from poll tax bills to be financed by rise in VAT from 15 to 17.5 per cent; child benefit to be increased from October by another £1 for first/only child (to £9.25) and for others by 25p (to £7.50), and to be index-linked from April 1992, with claimants on income support and family credit getting identical increases; freeze on married couple's allowance, one parent benefit and lone parents' additional tax allowance. Extra £55m announced to help unemployed.

April: Uprating: most non-means-tested benefits up by 10.9 per cent and means-tested benefits by 8.1 per cent. Child benefit £1 pw higher for first or eldest child, but frozen at £7.25 for others. One parent benefit frozen. Major reforms of NHS introduced: self-governing trusts, purchaser/provider split, internal markets. New Benefits Agency and Contributions Agency launched. Income support and housing benefit for people in residential care and nursing homes paid under similar rules to those for people in own homes. Prescription charges up to £3.40. *Breadline Britain* survey shows over 11 million living in poverty (defined as lacking three or more necessities). Council tax plans announced, with 100 per cent rebates to be reintroduced: likely implementation 1993/94.

May: Successor body to Independent Living Fund to be created in 1993. Social Security Committee report shows 2 per cent rise in incomes of poorest tenth between 1979 and 1988, compared to 33.5 per cent for average; between 1979 and 1988 numbers below half average income grew to 11.8 million – from 9.4 per cent of population to 21.6 per cent; proportion of children in households below half average income doubled, to 1 in 4. White Paper proposes training credits for all 16-17-year-olds leaving full-time education.

June: Consultation paper on legal aid published. Cold weather payments to be changed: can be paid on forecast of 7-day freeze; and no application necessary. Benefits Enquiry Line launched for people with disabilities. Royal Assent for Act to introduce disability living allowance and disability working allowance in April 1992 (*see* November 1990).

July: Citizen's Charter launched, promising better standards in public services and rights to redress. Child Support Act receives Royal Assent, setting stage for new system of child maintenance and establishment of Child Support Agency (*see* October 1990). Minor concessions in severe hardship payments for 16- and 17-year-olds announced.

August: Social fund budget increased by £10m for grants and £30m for loans. Implementation of regulations to cut back on arrears of unclaimed benefit.

October: Employment Action (temporary work scheme for unemployed, paying benefit plus £10 per week) is launched. Children Act 1989 comes into force – but fears expressed over inadequate resources. Uprating statement: most non-means-tested benefits to go up

by 4.1 per cent in April, and means-tested benefits by 7 per cent (lower rise than anticipated, due to revision of index).

November: Council Tax Bill published, exempting some students from paying. Payment of income support for mortgage interest direct to lenders announced, for those with arrears. Regulations on severe disability premium (in income support) limit number who can get it. Only one in 100 claimants given compulsory Restart interview get jobs.

December: Government opts out of 'social chapter' in European negotiations at Maastricht, but ratifies UN Convention on Rights of the Child. Changes to *Households Below Average Income* announced, including annual publication of *HBAI* and benefits take-up figures. Poll tax concession for some school-leavers announced. Mortgage 'rescue' scheme announced for homeowners in difficulty: income support for mortgage interest to be paid direct to lenders; and some owners to get housing benefit as housing association tenants.

1992

January: *Economic Trends* shows trend towards greater equality in wealth now reversed. *Social Trends* shows share of total income going to richest fifth of households has grown since 1979 'at each stage of tax/benefit system', and share of poorest has shrunk. Lowest-paid tenth of manual workers now earn lower percentage of average than in 1886. Government announces poll tax debts can be pursued for 6 years. Benefits Agency launches Customer Charter. Over 74,000 families in England and Wales got court repossession orders in 1991 (35 per cent increase on 1990). Further £6.2m announced for social fund.

February: DSS spending plans show growth of over 3 per cent per year in real terms over next three years. Long-term unemployment increases by biggest monthly rise (to 747,000) since records started nearly a decade ago.

March: Budget: new 20p tax on first £2,000 of income; married couple's allowance frozen. Election date announced and party manifestos published.

April: Prescriptions go up to £3.75 per item. Benefits uprating; plus change in definition of 'full-time' work from 24 to 16 hours per week for income support and family credit. Conservatives win election with reduced majority; Peter Lilley is Secretary of State for Social Security. Disability living allowance and disability working allowance are introduced.

May: Unemployment at 9.5 per cent, with sharp rise in south. Government announces 'capping' of local authority budgets. Payment of income support for mortgage interest direct to lenders starts (*see* December 1991).

June: Mortgage rescue scheme has little impact (*see* December 1991). Water disconnections almost trebled in past year, to over 21,000. Unemployment highest for nearly five years. Pilot schemes to set up 'one-stop' benefit offices announced.

July: Dentists vote not to accept any new NHS patients; dental charges cut. White Paper, *The Health of the Nation*, published, with emphasis on prevention but not on poverty. Government-commissioned research shows social fund fails to meet many needs or help most needy. Report says gap between deprived inner city areas and others unchanged over last 15 years; City Challenge winners, competing for government funds for inner city, are announced. *Households Below Average Income* for 1979-1988/89 shows income of bottom tenth after housing costs fell in real terms by 6 per cent (compared with average increase of 30 per cent). Cabinet agrees new method to control public spending.

September: Regulations laid to deduct unpaid fines from benefit from October. Survey of social impact of water metering shows hardship for minority. *House Conditions Survey* for 1991 shows one in 20 properties in England and Wales unfit for human habitation.

October: Pensioners on income support get £2 per week extra (£3 for couples). Unemployment rises to over 10 per cent. European Community maternity directive agreed. Asylum and Immigration Appeals Bill puts strict time limits on asylum appeals. Survey shows rural England 'in decay' due to closure of local services.

November: Autumn statement: cuts in legal aid planned; Employment Action and Employment Training for unemployed to be merged. Uprating statement: most benefits to go up with inflation in April; controls to be tightened on invalidity benefit and on fraud; hardship payments for childless unemployed not 'actively seeking work' to be removed (some exemptions conceded later). Long-term unemployment up to 956,000 (one in three). Independent Living Fund closes to new applicants (*see* April 1993).

December: After school child care initiative launched by Government. Labour Party sets up Commission on Social Justice to review employment, tax and benefits policy.

1993

January: *Low Income Families* statistics, published by Social Security Committee, show 11.3m on or below income support level in 1989. Government agrees to small changes in new maternity pay deal (forced on UK by EU); National Audit Office report shows errors in nearly one in three statutory maternity pay/ statutory sick pay cases. House repossessions started to fall in 1992.

February: Government announces long-term review of public spend-

ing, with social security as top target; DSS spending plans show social security running £3.7bn ahead of forecasts of a year ago. Unadjusted unemployment tops 3 million; long-term unemployed above 1 million (first time in five years). Limit on income support for mortgage interest announced: £150,000, reducing to £125,000.

March: Budget: extension of 20p tax band; VAT to be imposed on fuel – proposals for compensation for poorest are vague. Increase of 1 per cent in national insurance contributions, and reduction of some tax reliefs, over 2 years. Social fund budget for 1993/94 is £44m higher. Number of homeless in bed and breakfast starts to fall. Reports claim nearly 100,000 16- and 17-year-olds have no visible source of income, and two out of three youth trainees leave with no qualifications. Jobplan workshops (week-long courses for long-term unemployed) are launched, with refusal resulting in loss of benefit.

April: Prescription charges go up by 50p to £4.25. New community care system, and new child support scheme, are implemented. Council tax is introduced, with lower bills for 2 out of 3 households. Benefits uprating. Some measures to help unemployed into work announced. Over-30s get 1 per cent rebate for personal pensions. Two new funds set up to replace Independent Living Fund, to help severely disabled.

May: New compensation arrangements for benefit delays announced. Report details administrative chaos of introduction of disability living allowance.

June: Households Below Average Income figures show fall in real income for poorest tenth after housing costs of 14 per cent (compared to a rise of 36 per cent for average, and 62 per cent for top tenth) between 1979 and 1990/91.

July: Government announces inquiry into 'apparent discrimination' against couples with children in allocation of council homes. DSS report claims social security budget will be unsustainable in future years if not cut.

August: Wages Councils (fixing pay levels for the low-paid) abolished.

October: Plans announced to end priority to statutorily homeless in council housing. Government is considering identity cards for claimants, after report claims £5bn a year is lost through benefit fraud (*see* May 1996).

November: First 'unified' Budget brings together tax and spending; 2 years' plans announced. Personal tax allowances frozen and married couple's allowance reduced; national insurance contributions to be increased by 1 per cent. Plans announced for compensation in benefits for VAT on fuel.

December: Social security plans include replacing sickness and invalidity benefit with incapacity

benefit, and unemployment benefit and income support for unemployed with job seekers' allowance (lower for under-25s, and non-means-tested for only six months). Fraud Board set up to focus more effort on benefit fraud. Government plans to phase in equalising of retirement age at 65 for men and women between 2010 and 2020.

1994

January: Unemployment drops below 10 per cent; many jobs created are part-time. European Commission figures show UK became one of European Union's poorest countries in 1980s.

February: Child support formula changed, to give phasing-in period for absent parents facing higher payments and higher margin above income support level.

March: UK found in breach of European law on qualifying period for part-timers' employment rights; and has to improve maternity pay (*see* October 1994) to meet Pregnancy Directive.

April: VAT on fuel introduced at 8 per cent. Prescription charges rise to £4.75. Tax changes leave thousands worse off. Benefits uprating.

May: Court ruling that European employment protection rules apply to transfer of public sector contracts. Civil Rights Bill for disabled people talked out in Commons, with government help. Prime Minister calls for tough action against 'offensive' beggars.

June: Government figures show recession has narrowed north-south divide. Some 76,000 teenagers have no job or training scheme place, or income support. Reports reveal big rise in numbers on low incomes since 1961, and larger gap between highest and lowest paid than at any time this century. UN report finds many children in richest nations, including UK, now have poorer quality of life than those in 'developing' countries.

July: Tony Blair elected Labour leader. *Households Below Average Income* shows numbers with income below half the average rose from 5 million in 1979 to 13.9 million in 1991/92.

August: New 'habitual residence test' introduced for claims for income support, housing benefit and council tax benefit, to combat 'benefit tourism'.

September: Child Support Agency's chief executive resigns. Report shows poorest tenth of households experienced lower inflation rate than official figure in recent years.

October: 'Back-to-work' bonuses proposed, giving part-time workers credits of £1,000 to cash in on move to full-time work. Child care costs up to £40 per week can be offset against earnings for in-work means-tested benefits. Commission on Social Justice sets out proposals to reform tax and benefits. Maternity changes introduced (*see* March 1994).

November: Budget: proposal to increase VAT on fuel to 17.5 per cent (*see* December 1994). Announcements made about an extension of housing benefit and council tax benefit for 4 weeks for those unemployed for 6 months or more on taking up a job, incentives for employers to employ the long-term unemployed and faster administration of family credit claims (from April 1996). Pilot project for in-work benefit help to couples and single people without children is also announced (to start from October 1996).

December: Benefit uprating revised, due to government U-turn on VAT on fuel (which remains at 8 per cent). Child Support Agency announces plans to suspend action indefinitely on cases where the parent with care was on income support before April 1993.

1995

January: Child Support White Paper proposes capping maintenance payments, taking into account some travel and housing costs in child support calculation, and introducing cash bonuses for parents with care taking up paid work. Homeless charities claim 17,000 people live in bed and breakfast in London – more than 6 times official figure. Report of UN Committee on the Rights of the Child on UK's implementation of UN Convention condemns the level of child poverty in the UK.

February: Joseph Rowntree Foundation Inquiry into Income and Wealth launches its report, documenting growing inequalities between rich and poor and calling for action. Eurostat figures show UK in 1992 as fifth poorest country in European Union. Proposals announced to cut maximum hours which unemployed students over 19 can study before losing benefit from 21 to 16 hours a week.

March: UN Summit on Social Development takes place in Copenhagen; governments commit themselves to drawing up plans to eradicate poverty. Social Security Committee publishes *Low Income Families* figures, showing 24 per cent of population, and 29 per cent of children, living on or below income support level in 1992.

April: Benefits uprating. Incapacity benefit replaces sickness/invalidity benefit, with the introduction of a new 'all work' test; estimates suggest up to 220,000 people may lose benefit. Child support changes include new allowances in the formula, and a cap on current maintenance payments of 30 per cent of normal net income (*see* January 1995).

May: Six-month delay in full introduction of jobseeker's allowance announced. Consultation paper on legal aid proposes limiting the budget through cash-limited block grants. Reports show significant movement in and out of poorest tenth, and an increase in the expenditure of the poorest tenth in real terms between 1979 and 1992.

June: *Households Below Average Income* for 1979–1992/93 shows that income fell by 17 per cent in real terms after housing costs for the poorest tenth (compared with an average increase of 38 per cent); these figures were later revised to 18 and 37 per cent.

July: Government pilot scheme for nursery vouchers for parents of 4-year-olds announced (*see* February 1996). More home visits will be made to claimants as part of anti-fraud action. European Court of Justice backs claimant in test case arguing that cost of child care should be taken into account when calculating family credit. Unemployment at highest level since end of 1992. Repossessions rose in last six months, for first time in four years. Family credit and disability working allowance claimants can get an extra £10/week if they are working 30 hours/week or more.

August: By 1992/93, 30 per cent of people were living in households getting at least one means-tested benefit.

September: Cabinet meeting discusses shake-up to curb welfare spending.

October: Proposals announced to

restrict benefits for people seeking asylum in the UK. Government extends free prescriptions to men aged 60-64, after European Court of Justice rules their exclusion is discriminatory. Income support for mortgage interest drastically reduced; claimants are expected to take out mortgage insurance cover instead.

November: Budget: one parent benefit and lone parent premium to be frozen from April 1996; housing benefit to be restricted for people under 25. Labour Party's scheme for unemployed under-25-year-olds would include benefit cut for refusing job or full-time education. Minimum child support payments by absent parents to be more than doubled.

December: New social fund guidance restricts payments for certain maternity and funeral related payments (under non-discretionary social fund).

1996

January: International Year for the Eradication of Poverty is launched. Housing benefit regulations introduced, limiting benefit to a local reference rate. DSS says over half a million people claimed £1.4bn benefit fraudulently in 1995.

February: New benefit rules remove entitlement for many asylum seekers and other persons from abroad. Plans announced for 'Change Programme', heralding 25 per cent

cut in the cost of administering benefits over next 3 years, including a review of the legal basis of decision-making and appeals.

April: Benefits uprating: most benefits up in line with inflation, but one parent benefit and lone parent premium frozen. Amount of child care expenses disregarded in in-work means-tested benefits increased (*see* October 1994). Labour Party announces plans to review payment of child benefit for 16- to 18-year-olds as part of a review of funding of higher education and training. Departures from child support formula, for absent parents to take account of special factors and for parents with care to ask for a reassessment of maintenance payments, are piloted in some areas (*see* January 1995). Series of anti-fraud drives in major urban areas started by the Benefits Agency.

May: 'Smart card' launched, to replace benefit payment books and combat benefit fraud. Unemployment fell to its lowest level for five years.

June: After defeat in Court of Appeal over withdrawal of benefits for asylum seekers, Government plans legislation to reinstate original intention. Regulations laid to increase benefit penalty for parents with care refusing to cooperate with Child Support Agency without 'good cause', and in the longer term to subsume one parent benefit into child benefit and lone parent premium into the family premium.

July: Inter-departmental review of housing benefit for those in supported accommodation announced. Benefits Agency freephone advice line is scrapped. Administration of child benefit to be transferred to the private sector. Government plans announced to delay age-related increases in means-tested benefits for children until the September following their birthday, and to abolish increased rate for 18-year-olds.

August: Telephone 'hotline' to report benefit fraud is launched. Consultation paper is published on national child care strategy.